Race and the Incidence
of Environmental Hazards

Race and the Incidence of Environmental Hazards

A Time for Discourse

EDITED BY

Bunyan Bryant and Paul Mohai

School of Natural Resources and Environment
University of Michigan, Ann Arbor

Westview Press

BOULDER • SAN FRANCISCO • OXFORD

Published in 1992 in the United States of America by Westview Press, Inc., 5500 Central Avenue, Boulder, Colorado 80301-2877, and in the United Kingdom by Westview Press, 36 Lonsdale Road, Summertown, Oxford OX2 7EW

Library of Congress Cataloging-in-Publication Data
Race and the incidence of environmental hazards : a time for discourse
     /edited by Bunyan Bryant and Paul Mohai.
          p.   cm.
     ISBN 0-8133-8513-X
     1. Environmental health—United States.   2. Minorities—United
States—Health and hygiene.   I. Bryant, Bunyan I.   II. Mohai, Paul.
RA566.3.R33   1992
363.72'87008'693—dc20   92-26064
                                                                             CIP

Printed and bound in the United States of America

The paper used in this publication meets the requirements
of the American National Standard for Permanence of Paper
for Printed Library Materials Z39.48-1984.

10   9   8   7   6   5

Contents

Acknowledgments

We wish to express our thanks to the following individuals for their help and support of the Conference on Race and the Incidence of Environmental Hazards: James E. Crowfoot, former Dean of the School of Natural Resources; Charles D. Moody, Vice Provost for Minority Affairs; James S. Jackson, former Associate Dean, Horace H. Rackham School of Graduate Studies; William C. Kelly, Vice President for Research; and Linda S. Wilson, former Vice President for Research—all of the University of Michigan.

For editorial assistance, we acknowledge Miriam E. Zweizig, Elise P. McLaughlin, and Terry Calhoun. And for their assistance during the Conference, we thank Stephanie Cronen, Angela Nagel, and Patrick Francis. Also, special thanks to Kathy Hall and Shelley Shock for their help and support.

Thanks and appreciation also go to Christalee Bryant, Jean Carlberg, and Caroline Mohai.

Bunyan Bryant
Paul Mohai

1

Introduction

Bunyan Bryant and Paul Mohai

For the last fifteen years or so, the civil rights movement has faltered as government and corporate America have reordered their priorities and as civil rights leaders have struggled in vain to bring currency to a movement that has lost its momentum. Both the death of prominent civil rights leaders and the benign neglect of policy makers have blunted the edge of the civil rights movement, even though the conditions that spawned this movement are, in many instances, worse now than they were three decades ago. Today we have more segregated schools, housing patterns, homeless people, and the economic gap between blacks and whites has increased significantly. However, a resurgence of that movement may be taking place as minority and oppressed communities across the nation begin to

Bunyan Bryant is an Associate Professor in the School of Natural Resources at the University of Michigan, Ann Arbor, and did post-doctoral work at the University of Manchester in England on Town and Country Planning. His current research interests include developing case studies on corporate, agency, and community responses to hazardous waste sites. Professor Bryant has recently written a book called: Environmental Advocacy: Concepts, Issues and Dilemmas, *and a manual called:* Social and Environmental Change: A Manual for Advocacy and Organizing. *In addition to teaching courses on social change and presenting papers at professional conferences, Professor Bryant is a consultant to a number of nonprofit environmental organizations across the country.*

Paul Mohai is Assistant Professor in the School of Natural Resources at the University of Michigan. Professor Mohai has been studying environmental attitudes and the environmental movement in America for a number of years. He has also studied the factors influencing government decision making, including the role of public participation as well as the factors contributing to citizen involvement. His most recent research involves analyses of blacks' concerns about environmental quality issues and the incidence of environmental hazards in low income and minority communities. Dr. Mohai has published the findings of his work in a variety of journals, including Social Science Quarterly, Natural Resources Journal, Journal of Forestry, Society & Natural Resources, *and* Environmental Law.

Both Drs. Bryant and Mohai were co-organizers of the University of Michigan Conference on Race and the Incidence of Environmental Hazards held January 1990 in Ann Arbor, Michigan. They were also co-principal investigators of the University of Michigan's 1990 Detroit Area Study, which investigated the extent of awareness and concerns of minorities about environmental hazards in their neighborhoods.

redefine their struggle in terms of a safe and clean environment being a basic right for all, regardless of race or color. Each day minorities are becoming more aware of the millions of inner city children who are being exposed to lead poisoning, causing irreversible mental retardation and impaired growth. Pregnant farmworkers exposed to pesticide sprays are prone to birth deformity as they eke out a living from the land. Prenatal exposure to dangerous chemicals in the high tech industries contributes to numerous birth defects and premature births. Uranium contaminated Navajo land and water are believed to contribute to the high incidence of organ cancer in Navajo teenagers—seventeen times the national average.

We became involved with issues of environmental equity after becoming acutely aware that minority communities were disproportionately exposed to environmental hazards, more so than affluent white communities, and by the struggle that was being waged in minority and low-income communities across the country. One of the first highly visible struggles took place in Warren County, North Carolina, where both blacks and whites strategically placed their bodies in front of trucks to prevent them from carrying soil laced with PCBs to a landfill located in a predominantly black area. As a result of this struggle, Walter Fauntroy, participant in the struggle in Warren County and a congressional delegate from Washington, DC, requested that the General Accounting Office do a study. This study reported that three of the four largest commercial landfills in the South are located in communities of color. In 1987, while attending a meeting at the Federation of Southern Cooperatives in Sumter County, Alabama, Bryant had an opportunity to visit one of these landfills, the largest in the nation—not too far from the Federation. This facility receives hazardous waste from 48 states and 3 foreign countries. Sumter County is approximately 70 percent black and one of the poorest counties in the nation. The landfill has been the site of much controversy regarding its safety in both the black and the white communities. Even though both blacks and whites attempted to organize against the facility, it was difficult to do so because the landfill offered higher paying jobs compared to other places within the county, donated money to civic and church organizations, and paid about half the county's tax revenues. Those "hooked on toxics" fought any effort to destroy their jobs at the landfill; these were the best paying jobs they ever had, giving them a chance to improve their living condition. It was on this trip that Wendell Paris, a community activist, gave Bryant a copy of the newly issued 1987 United Church of Christ "Report on Race and Toxic Wastes in the United States." The report stated that among a variety of indicators race was the best predictor of the location of hazardous waste facilities in the U.S. We were deeply moved by both the United States General Accounting Office and the United Church of Christ Reports and by the scholarly writings of Robert Bullard and Beverly Wright.

For a number of years Mohai has been studying environmental attitudes and the factors prompting people to take political action on environmental issues. Although studies exist which have examined the relationship of socioeconomic status with environmental concern and activism, few have examined the environmental orientation and actions of people of color. In spite of the general lack of evidence, the conventional wisdom has been that people of color are not concerned about environmental quality issues. In the course of searching for background information which might lead to some hypotheses about the environmental concerns and actions of people of color Mohai was referred by Bryant to the U.S. General Accounting Office and the United Church of Christ reports. The evidence in these reports appeared stunning and compelling and suggested that people of color have a greater stake in the environment than their white counterparts. This evidence raised serious doubts about the conventional wisdom regarding the lack of concern of minorities about environmental quality issues (see Mohai, 1990) and also motivated an extensive search for other evidence of the relationship of toxics and race (see Mohai and Bryant, 1992, in this volume). Over a dozen such studies covering a two decade period were found. These studies overwhelmingly corroborated the evidence of the General Accounting Office and the United Church of Christ reports and intensified our concerns about the issues surrounding environmental equity. Our mutual interest and desire for a further exploration of these issues eventually led us to convene a retrieval/dissemination Conference on Race and the Incidence of Environmental Hazards held at the University of Michigan School of Natural Resources in Ann Arbor, where we asked scholars and activists working in this area to present their latest findings, discuss their ideas and, together, search for solutions.

Nine of twelve scholar-activists who presented papers at the Michigan Conference were people of color. Robert Bullard, Associate Professor of Sociology at the University of California at Riverside, Beverly Wright, Associate Professor of Sociology at Wake Forest University, and Charles Lee, Director of Special Projects on Toxic Justice of the Commission for Racial Justice of the United Church of Christ, were key in helping us identify conference participants. This was the first time that a retrieval/dissemination conference was held in the country where the majority of presenters of scholarly papers on race and the incidence of environmental hazards were people of color, a major step forward in getting such scholars to focus their attention, as a group, upon this issue. Before the Conference, race and the incidence of environmental hazards was seldom an issue—the disproportionate impact of environmental pollutants on minority communities was not recognized by policy makers or the white community. Today that is no longer true. Policy makers at high levels of the Environmental Protection Agency, for instance, are engaged in shaping and implementing policies related to environmental equity. The Conference helped to give national visibility to the debate on environmental equity, thus increasing the awareness of other government agencies and lay people alike. And while scholars had worked on various aspects of this issue, the Conference proved to be a vehicle where scholar-activists could come together to share their latest findings in an integrated whole, and to take steps to disseminate information about this important issue.

Two presentations were made concurrently, followed by two critiques from panel members before questions from the audience. The scholars and activists not only presented original papers, but several times throughout the Conference small core groups of participant observers (representatives from federal and state agencies such as the U.S. Environmental Protection Agency, the Agency for Toxic Substances and Disease Registry, the Governor's Office of the State of Michigan, the Michigan Department of Minority Health, the Michigan Department of Natural Resources, and others) along with presenters, met daily for an hour and a half each time to share information, and to focus on strategies for change and follow-up.

These small core group discussions proved to be intense and informative, and added much to the overall success of the Conference. During the final plenary session, each core group presented strategies for change and follow-up they had generated over the last several days; it was felt that we could ill afford not to follow-up on strategies that had been generated in the core groups. In fact some core groups called for an international conference on environmental equity for the following year, but most felt that a much larger national environmental conference, involving mainly community activists should be organized. The Michigan Conference led to four separate workshops on "Environmental Racism," which were a part of a large number of workshops, panels, movies and videos celebrating Martin Luther King Day activities at the University of Michigan in January of 1991. In October of 1991, under the leadership of the United Church of Christ Commission for Racial Justice, the First People of Color Environmental Leadership Summit was organized. Dr. Benjamin Chavis, Executive Director of the United Church of Christ Commission for Racial Justice, Ms. Gail Small, Esq., Executive Director of Native Action, the Honorable Toney Anaya, former Governor of the State of New Mexico, and Dr. Sygnman Rhee, President-Elect of the National Council of Churches were co-chairs. More discussion about the Summit is given in the concluding chapter.

Another such follow-up strategy of the Michigan Conference was a meeting with key government officials. A subgroup of conferees stayed behind and drafted a memo requesting a meeting with Louis W. Sullivan, Secretary, United States Department of Health and Human Services, William K. Reilly, Administrator, United States Environmental Protection Agency, and Michael R. Deland, Chairman, Council on Environmental Quality, with carbon copies sent to all governors, various state legislators, and the Congressional Black Caucus. In this memo we proposed to discuss the agencies' involvement in:

1. Undertaking research geared towards understanding environmental risks faced by minority and low income communities;
2. Initiating projects to enhance risk communication targeted to minority and low-income population groups;

3. Requiring, on a demonstration basis, that racial and socioeconomic equity consideration be included in Regulatory Impact Assessments;
4. Ensuring that a racial and socioeconomic dimension is overlaid on present and future geographic studies of environmental risk;
5. Enhancing the ability of Historically Black Colleges and Universities (HBCUs) and other minority institutions to participate in and contribute to the development of environmental equity;
6. Appointing special assistants for environmental equity at decision-making levels within these agencies; and
7. Developing a policy statement on environmental equity.

We met with William Reilly and an assistant of Michael Deland, on September 13, 1990. Because of scheduling problems we were unable to meet with Louis Sullivan. Of all the people we met with in Washington, including Congressman John Lewis, and staff members of Congressmen John Conyers and Ron Delums, the Council on Environmental Quality was least familiar with this issue. By the time we arrived in Washington, Administrator Reilly had already sent a memo to his 12,000 EPA employees recognizing Black History Month and stating more specifically the inherent value of having a multi-cultural workforce reflective of American society to help ensure an equitable environmental policy. He also put together an internal work group to work on issues raised at the Michigan Conference. And, on April 9, 1990, at the National Minority Environmental Career Conference at Howard University, he stated:

> [P]articipants in the January 1990 University of Michigan Conference on Race and [the Incidence of] Environmental Hazards conducted an intensive review of environmental risk from a socio-economic perspective. This review pointed out significantly disproportionate health impacts on minorities due to higher rates of exposure to pollution.

To our knowledge, this was the first public recognition by the EPA that environmental hazards disproportionately impact people of color and the first time an Administrator of the EPA had agreed to meet with any group of primarily people of color to discuss environmental equity issues. It is also the first time that an EPA Administrator put together an internal workgroup to focus directly on these issues. This workgroup has now been working on a report on the disproportionate impact of environmental hazards upon communities of color for almost two years. While Administrator Reilly has made important strides in recognizing the disproportionate impact of environmental hazards on people of color, and has directed the agency to address this issue, the proof of the pudding will be not in the discourse or in the report itself but in tangible and productive outcomes.

It is abundantly clear that new political winds are beginning to blow across the country, altering the environmental movement, as people of color take up their struggle under the environmental banner as an alternative way of giving recognition to their unsung history of fighting for justice and clean, safe neighborhoods. Confronted with massive exposure to hazardous waste, threatened by freeways, urban decay, or by huge urban development—surrounded by concrete streets, buildings, parking lots, and playgrounds, cutting them off from wilderness areas— people of color have positioned their struggle for economic and social justice squarely in the front seat of the environmental movement. People of color are beginning to realize that issues of environmental degradation, economics, power, politics, and racism are intricately interwoven and cannot be separated. Will people of color be able to redefine the traditional environmental movement to include issues of social justice? Is a decent paying and safe job a basic right or a privilege? With respect to the former question, environmentalists have long been remiss for not observing the urban environment as one that needs attention. As a consequence, they are viewed with suspicion by people of color, particularly as national environmental organizations try to fashion an urban agenda in the 1990s. To champion old growth forests or the protection of the snail darter or the habitat of spotted owls without championing clean safe urban environments or improved habitats of the homeless, does not bode well for future relations between environmentalists and people of color, and with the poor. It is not that forming positive relations with people of color and the indigent are impossible, but environmental organizations will have to earn their respect by being deeply committed to working with people of color to improve their biophysical environment, by responding to their quest for social justice. This relationship can never move off first base unless the urban agenda is dealt with in a fundamental way.

Is a clean safe environment a civil right? Communities of color across the land are beginning to feel they have the same right to clean, air, water, and an unpolluted land base as are more affluent suburbanites. They are questioning why their communities are used as receptacles for toxic and hazardous waste and polluting industries. They are in some cases downright angry that their communities are being poisoned so that others may live in affluence and in clean-safe biophysical environments. People of color also believe that decent and safe jobs are a civil right. Too often, mayors of cities are caught in the dilemma of having to choose between building commercial incinerators or landfills in order to woo industrial jobs for people who need them and environmentalists who claim pollutants from incinerators, landfills, and industries are not worth the price of long-term health effects. Although decent paying jobs in polluting industries may be an alternative to crime and delinquency, long-term health effects from polluted environs may mitigate against short-term economic gain. Even now the impoverished condition of communities of color and low-income people correlates with their health status.

An analysis of the statistical health chart may be interpreted to mean that the true meaning of the trickle down theory is not money or wealth but environmental stressors, giving rise to multiple health problems, and an abbreviated life expectancy. Those who are most vulnerable to environmental insults are among the millions in this country that are the least able to afford health insurance. Environmental health risks are inextricably linked to political economy of place, where "political and economic power are key factors which influence the spatial distribution of residential amenities and disamenities" (Bullard and Wright, 1987). Because of their impoverished condition, people of color can ill afford to move to the suburbs where cleaner air, water and neighborhoods abound.

People of color have grown distrustful of government agencies which try to find new and old ways of disposing environmental hazards in their communities; opposition to siting of hazardous waste facilities is now pervasive in communities across the country. Will compensation for mitigating public opposition to hazardous waste facility siting be enough? Even though it is appealing that multiple parties would benefit from negotiated facility siting, some will benefit more than others. Those that benefit the least are usually in close proximity to hazardous waste facilities and therefore are beginning to show the most public resistance; they are being asked to bear high personal costs (in the form of risk) while benefits of the facility accrue to often times more affluent and larger outside populations (Portney 1985). While O'Hare (1977) argues that economic incentives could be offered to local residents so that perceived benefits would eventually outweigh the perceived risks, the problem is that there is no way of calculating risks that are beyond the immediate perception. For example, although risks may not be a major problem now, fifteen years later, when local community groups begin to experience various health effects, negotiated economic benefits may not nearly be enough to compensate them for long-term and life-threatening illnesses.

It is ironic that Martin Luther King gave his life to improve the quality of life of the garbage workers in Memphis, Tennessee. Little did we know that garbage disposal would be the new frontier of the civil rights movement in communities of color around the country. People of color have taken their stand against hazardous landfills and the building of commercial hazardous waste facilities and polluting industries in their neighborhoods. They have taken a stand against those who would use their neighborhoods as waste disposal sites to potentially worsen their living and health conditions. More recently the Gulf Coast Tenants Organization has spearheaded a struggle against polluting chemical industries that are impacting people of color along a 144 mile stretch between New Orleans and Baton Rouge, Louisana. The Southwest Network for Environmental and Economic Justice has organized themselves to fight for an improved quality of life of people in the region. There are untold numbers of grassroots organizations that are beginning to use environmental concepts to advance the struggle for justice. Certainly more community groups will organize themselves to engage in multiple resistance against large corporate polluters which create more waste for disposal. This struggle by community groups across the country will intensify until social and environmental justice has been served.

In the second chapter of this volume Lee brings us up to date since the United Church of Christ report was published by describing a number of communities which are engaged in multiple resistance to the siting of hazardous landfills in their neighborhoods and attempts by both civil rights and environmental organizations to work together. Both Historically Black Colleges and Universities and the federal government are beginning to address the need to include more minorities in teaching and learning about environmental issues and professional careers in this area. In the third chapter, Taylor states that minorities are also concerned about environmental issues; she gives an historical account of the environmental movement, showing how it must change in order to attract minorities, suggesting that minorities will become involved if such groups deal with issues of survival and basic needs. She states that "to diversify environmental organizations, one would have to radically restructure the agenda, change hiring practices and staff assignments, redistribute resources and redistribute the costs and benefits of environmental policies."

In Chapter 4, Davis demonstrates that the Congressional Black Caucus has the highest average support of conservation issues than any other group in Congress. In Chapter 5, Gelobter discusses how environmental pollution is regressively distributed and how "government may serve to aggravate the already regressive and discriminatory distribution of pollution that('s) face(d) by minorities." In Chapter 6, Bullard states that blacks are beginning to asks questions such as: "Are the costs borne by the black community imposed to spare the larger community? Can environmental inequities (resulting from industrial facility siting decisions) be compensated? What are acceptable risks?" In Chapters 7, 8 and 9, West, Fly, Larkin, and Marans, and Wright, speak to the issue of health. West, et al., found that while whites fish primarily for recreation in the Detroit River blacks fish for both recreation and food, exposing themselves to municipal and industrial contaminants. In her chapter, Wright discusses the disproportionately numerous health problems of minorities, resulting from hazards they face in the work place.

In Chapter 10, White not only explores the dangers of pollutants to health and how minority communities are used for repositories because of a "least cost option," he documents the impact of environmental stressors from the Rollins incinerator on a middle class black community in Alsen, Louisana. Chapters 11-12 are case studies. Bailey and Faupel explore the political, economic, and racial dynamics of Sumter County, Alabama, which is 70 percent black and contains the nation's largest landfill. Robinson gives us a glimpse of the multiple and long-term problems of uranium mining experienced by Navajos living near the Rio Puerco of western New Mexico, as well as actions taken by them to protect themselves and their children from the long-term effects of such mining. In Chapter 13, Mohai and Bryant[1] review 15 studies which have examined the distribution of environmental hazards by income and race. Along with results from the 1990 Detroit Area Study, they find that racial biases in the distribution of environmental hazards are not a function of poverty alone. Both Perfecto and Mpanya make the international connection in Chapters 14 and 15. Perfecto illuminates the transfer of toxics banned in this country to the Third World—only to return to us in our food supply. Mpanya clearly speaks to the issue of dumping of hazardous waste in African countries. What follows is an attempt to examine some critical social and environmental issues related to minorities. We hope the framework and the specific topics we laid out here will continue to be useful for future discourse.

Notes
1. Although this chapter was not written until after the Conference, we thought that it was important to include it.

2

Toxic Waste and Race in the United States

Charles Lee

I have been asked to write on the "situation regarding hazardous wastes and race since the United Church of Christ study." In so doing, I must necessarily touch upon the interrelationships between many sectors of society as they relate to this subject, including government, academia, grassroots communities, and the environmental and civil rights movements. Moreover, I must necessarily provide information on the background and events leading up to the study as well as the factors motivating it. This charge is broad in nature and I attempt to present both our perspectives on the study's place in issues of environment and race as well as its specific impact on these issues.

The study referred to in my charge is "Toxic Wastes and Race in the United States: A National Report on the Racial and Socio-Economic Characteristics of Communities Surrounding Hazardous Waste Sites." This study, published by the United Church of Christ Commission for Racial Justice and released at the National Press Club in Washington, D.C. on April 15, 1987, is the first comprehensive national study of the demographic patterns associated with the location of hazardous waste sites. At that time, Dr. Benjamin F. Chavis, Jr., Executive Director of the United Church of Christ Commission for Racial Justice, coined the phrase "environmental racism."

In response to the Commission for Racial Justice report, Dr. Linda Rae Murray, former Director of Occupational and Environmental Medicine at Meharry Medical College, said the report was the "first time anyone has looked at the placement of toxic dumps nationally. It proves that issues of race and class are most important determinants of where hazardous waste facilities are placed" (1987). Dr. Victor W. Sidel, former President of the American Public Health Association, called it "an extremely important contribution to the discussion both of toxic wastes and of selective health risks to minority communities" (1987). Rep. John Conyers (D-MI) called the report "a powerful indictment of those who argue that poor health

---

Charles Lee is the Director of Research for the Commission for Racial Justice for the United Church of Christ. One of the most publicized works of the Commission is its report, "Toxic Waste and Race in the United States: A National Report on the Racial and Social-Economic Characteristics of Communities with Hazardous Waste Sites."

and other problems in black, Hispanic and minority communities are self-inflicted" (1987).

The *Atlanta Constitution* editorialized that "the United Church of Christ Commission for Racial Justice put an end last week to speculation that white America has been dumping its garbage in Black America's backyard.... [T]hat puts an extra burden of responsibility on public health and environmental inspectors to spot potential problems before they become health hazards. Where to look? The Commission report points the way" (Editorial, 1987).

Before proceeding, I must caution the readers of this article regarding the perspective of the author of this article. As the individual who directed this study and authored this report, I am necessarily not in the best position to critique it. Nor is the United Church of Christ Commission for Racial Justice a disinterested party; we clearly see ourselves as an advocacy organization on issues of "environmental racism."

In addition, I want to emphasize that this paper only gives a partial review of the developments since the publication of "Toxic Wastes and Race in the United States." There is a need to do an in depth study of this subject, something which has begun to take place. In addition, theoretical models for analyzing such developments also need to be developed.

Background

We do, however, bring a unique perspective as a national organization which has done pioneering work in the area of environment and race. It should come as no surprise that the United Church of Christ Commission for Racial Justice study is, rather than the starting point, a culmination of nearly five years of work in this area. A brief description of this background will help to answer an often asked set of questions, i.e.; "Why is a civil rights organization like the United Church of Christ Commission for Racial Justice working around issues of the environment?" and "What does race have to do with environment?"

The Commission for Racial Justice is the national civil rights agency of the United Church of Christ, a 1.7 million member Protestant denomination which has its roots among the Congregationalist forefathers of this nation. Long active in social advocacy causes such as the Abolitionist Movement, the United Church of Christ, along with its predecessor denominations, has always been proud of its outspoken social witness. The Commission for Racial Justice was formed during the 1960s, at the height of the civil rights movement, and at the present time, remains the only national denominational entity solely devoted to racial justice advocacy. This history alone merits an entire discussion, one which by itself would be quite lengthy and is not central to this essay. We allude to it, however, to provide background for the institutional basis for our work in environment and race.

In 1982, residents of predominantly African American, Warren County, North Carolina approached the Rev. Leon White, then director of the Commission's North Carolina/Virginia Field Office, regarding the proposed siting of a poly-chlorinated biphenyl (PCB) landfill. For nearly four years, the residents had been protesting the State of North Carolina's plan to take soil laden with PCBs which had been illegally dumped along 210 miles of highway, for disposal in a landfill near Afton, North Carolina.

Although White had no background in environmental issues, he was a veteran of the civil rights struggles in the South and quickly saw the potential for applying these lessons to this struggle. White catalyzed a series of events which culminated in a campaign of non-violent civil disobedience to block the PCB trucks. Over five hundred arrests took place, including White, Chavis, Dr. Joseph Lowery of the Southern Christian Leadership Conference, and Congressman Walter E. Fauntroy (D-DC). For the first time since the late sixties, African American and white activists in the deep South joined together in protest. White and others were responsible for what some describe as a "merger of the environmental and civil rights movements." Clearly, without this intervention, Warren County could easily have remained another passing incident rather than evolving into the significant event that it has become.

As dramatic as they were, the events in Warren County were unsuccessful in preventing the unwanted landfill from being sited. If one were to use that criterion as a measure of the grassroots community's opposition, one would have to conclude that the community's efforts amounted to little. The struggle was significant, however, in many other different ways.

First, it prevented the state from making the Warren County site anything other than a non-active PCB landfill. Although the State of North Carolina used the PCB crisis to publicly rationalize the landfill's siting, there were documents which clearly stated the state's intentions to use it for other hazardous wastes. Second, it caused the State of North Carolina to reexamine its entire perspective on the siting issue, beginning with Governor James Hunt's declaration of a two year moratorium on hazardous waste landfill siting.

Finally, it focused national attention on this issue and generated further investigation of the relationship between pollution and minority communities. Subsequent to his arrest, Fauntroy requested a study on the racial demographics of hazardous waste sites. This report, produced by the U.S. General Accounting Office (GAO), found three out of the four landfills in the Southeast to be located in predominantly poor and African American communities. Although it examined only four off-site landfills in the U.S. Environmental Protection Agency's Region IV, the GAO study was unique as one of the only studies to date on the relationship between race and toxics (U. S. General Accounting Office, 1983). Moreover, it was a predecessor to "Toxic Wastes and Race in the United States":

The GAO study, while important, was limited by its regional scope. It was not designed to examine the relationship between the location of hazardous waste facilities throughout the United States and the racial and socio-economic characteristics of persons residing near them. Nor, prior to our current report, had there been a study to ascertain whether the GAO finding was indicative of any national patterns (United Church of Christ Commission for Racial Justice, 1987: 3).

This statement aptly describes the void in research around pollution problems in minority communities when the Commission for Racial Justice first came across this issue. Due to the lack of research focused on environmental problems confronting racial minority communities, we needed to do first hand investigation. Our initial work consisted primarily of traveling across the country and conducting locally based, educational, organizational and mobilizational efforts in African American, Hispanic and Native American communities impacted by environmental problems, many of which have led to ongoing work by participants. Besides this fact-finding, we wanted to highlight the most prominent examples of this problem, some of which included the following:

1. The nation's largest hazardous waste landfill, receiving toxic materials from 45 states and several foreign countries, is located in predominantly African American and poor Sumter County, in the heart of the Alabama Black Belt (Gunter and Williams, 1984);

2. The predominantly African American and Hispanic Southside of Chicago, Illinois has the greatest concentration of hazardous waste sites in the nation (Nelson, 1987);

3. In Houston, Texas, six of the eight municipal incinerators and all five of the municipal landfills are located in predominantly African American neighborhoods. One of the two remaining incinerators is located in a predominantly Hispanic neighborhood (Bullard, 1984: 95);

4. African American residents of a West Dallas neighborhood whose children suffered irreversible brain damage from exposure to lead from a nearby smelter won a $20 million out of court settlement (Bullard, 1987a: 12);

5. Pesticide exposure among predominantly Hispanic farm workers causes more than 300,000 pesticide-related illnesses each year. A large percentage of farm workers are women of childbearing age and children. This may be directly related to the emergence of childhood cancer clusters in McFarland and Delano, California (Wasserstrom and Wiles, 1985);

6. Navajo Indians were used as the primary workforce for the mining of uranium ore, leading to alarming lung cancer mortality rates. In addition, the Navajo community in Shiprock, New Mexico, where 1,100 tons of radioactive sands and nearly 100 tons of radioactive waste water flooded the Rio Puerco River, is one of numerous Native American communities near uranium mills and nuclear facilities (Shuey, 1984: 42);

7. Three executives in Illinois were convicted of murder in the death of a Polish immigrant worker from cyanide poisoning. This plant employed mostly Hispanic and Polish immigrants who spoke and read little English. The skull and crossbones warning labels were erased from the cyanide drums (Asher, 1984; Greenhouse, 1985);

8. Fraying asbestos was discovered in the housing projects of Chicago. Asbestos, a ticking time bomb which causes crippling lung diseases and cancer, is an especially serious problem in substandard housing common to most of the nation's inner cities (Allen, 1986); and

9. Puerto Rico is one of the most heavily polluted regions of the world. For example, Puerto Rico's underground aquifers have been contaminated by massive discharges from pharmaceutical companies, oil refineries and petrochemical plants. La Ciudad Christiana, a small community near Humacao, is the only community in North America which has been relocated due to mercury poisoning (Puerto Rico Industrial Mission, 1986).

Although we began to uncover numerous instances of racial minority communities impacted by environmental pollution, there was no research comprehensive enough to counter the claim that the above stated cases were merely exceptions and not the rule. This pointed to the clear need for new research.

We believed that much of the work of the Commission for Racial Justice consisted of helping to "continually define and redefine" the various forms of racial injustice in the context of rapid and ever-changing political, social, economic conditions. Chavis reiterated this concept in his preface to "Toxic Wastes and Race in the United States."

We realize that involvement in this type of research is a departure from our traditional protest methodology. However, if we are to advance our struggle in the future, it will depend largely on the availability of timely and reliable information (United Church of Christ Commission for Racial Justice, 1987).

Summary of Findings

The findings of the Commission for Racial Justice's research was compiled in the report, "Toxic Wastes and Race in the United States." The racial composition of a community was found to be the single variable best able to explain the existence or non-existence of commercial hazardous waste facilities in a given community area. Minorities, mostly African and Hispanic Americans, are strikingly overrepresented in communities with such facilities. Communities with a single hazardous waste facility were found to have twice the percentage of minorities as communities without such a facility (24 percent vs. 12 percent). Communities with two or more facilities have more than three times the minority representation than communities without any such sites (38 percent vs. 12 percent). Although, as expected, communities with hazardous waste sites generally proved to have lower socio-economic status, the economic status of residents was not as good a predictor of a facility's existence as race itself.

The study found that more than fifteen million African Americans and eight million Hispanic Americans lived in communities with one or more hazardous waste sites. The locations of uncontrolled toxic waste sites also display a disproportionate impact on racial minority communities. The study has conclusively shown that African Americans in particular are overrepresented in the populations of metropolitan areas with the largest number of uncontrolled toxic waste sites. Although African Americans comprise 11.7 percent of the general population, the percentage of African Americans is markedly higher in those six cities that top the hazardous waste list:

TABLE 1   Six Cities Which Lead the Hazardous Waste List

Cities	No. of Sites	Percent African Americans
Memphis, TN	173	43.3
St. Louis, MO	160	27.5
Houston, TX	152	23.6
Cleveland, OH	106	23.7
Chicago, IL	103	37.2
Atlanta, GA	94	46.1

The study further shows that three of the five largest commercial hazardous waste landfills in the United States, accounting for approximately 40 percent of the total commercial landfill capacity, are located in overwhelmingly African or Hispanic American communities. The largest of these, the site at Emelle, Alabama, accounts for one quarter of this total capacity (United Church of Christ Commission for Racial Justice, 1987).

In discussing a context for examining toxic wastes and race, we identified three key issues:

1. A major obstacle to engendering much needed awareness and action around environmental concerns within racial minority communities is lack of information. As a whole, community activists have found the acquisition of information to be a difficult task. One recent survey found that nearly "nine out of every ten groups (88 percent) perceived obstacles to obtaining information" (Freudenberg, 1984a). The information necessary tends to be highly technical or legal in nature. Moreover, institutional resistance to providing information is likely to be greater for groups such as racial minorities;

2.   The hazardous waste issue, as well as other environmental problems, has become very much linked to the state of the economy in a given community. These communities have been, and continue to be, beset by poverty, unemployment and problems related to poor housing, education, and health. These communities cannot afford the luxury of being primarily concerned about the state of their environment when confronted by a plethora of pressing problems related to their day-to-day survival. Within this context, racial minority communities become particularly vulnerable to those who advocate the siting of a hazardous facility as an avenue for employment and economic development. Thus, proposals that economic incentives be offered to mitigate local opposition to the establishment of new hazardous facilities raise disturbing social policy questions; and

3.   Consideration of the racial and socio-economic status of a community when dealing with hazardous wastes is critical from a public health perspective. Many reports, such as the Report of the Secretary's Task Force on Black and Minority Health, have documented the lower health status of minority populations (U. S. Department of Health and Human Services, 1985). This status needs to be considered when priorities are set for cleanup of hazardous waste sites. Furthermore, consideration of existing health status needs to be incorporated into the decision-making process for location of new facilities. Lacking this, there is the risk of compounding serious preexisting health problems in these communities.

The report concludes with 25 specific recommendations, geared toward federal, state and municipal governments, churches and community organizations, academic institutions, philanthropies and others. It should be noted that this study focused upon hazardous waste sites. This was not meant, however, to imply that hazardous wastes are necessarily a more widespread or dangerous environmental problem than others. The primary reason for looking at hazardous waste sites was the existence of nationally comprehensive data, i.e., the Comprehensive Environmental Response, Compensation and Liability Act Information System (CERCLIS) and national directories on commercial facilities. Many other problems in minority communities, such as air pollution, workplace exposure, pesticides, lead poisoning, asbestos, municipal waste and others, are either equally or more serious.

Grassroots and Political Activism

The most significant and long-lasting set of developments during the past several years has been the increasing activism of minority communities. Since the Warren County incident, there has been a remarkable upsurge in minority communities taking up the struggle around environmental concerns. This upsurge can be measured in terms of the number and the diversity of communities involved, their geographic distribution, their varied racial and ethnic backgrounds, and the different kinds of environmental problems addressed. However, grassroots and political activism can also be measured in terms of the maturity, level of organization and the strategic perspectives of many organizers involved in this issue. As some of the following examples show, many of the communities working to combat environmental threats have developed highly sophisticated organizing strategies.

In 1987, residents of Los Angeles, California successfully blocked the construction of a garbage incinerator, the Los Angeles City Energy Recovery Project (LANCER), in a predominantly African American inner-city neighborhood. This resulted from a five-year struggle which involved the repeated mobilization of hundreds of residents for demonstrations and hearings. Their struggle was complicated by the fact that Los Angeles' mayor, Tom Bradley, and other elected officials were African American. During this process, local activists used tactics such as making public the waiver of Los Angeles' South Africa Divestiture Ordinance. This was done to accommodate Ogden-Martin, the facility's private operator, which had yet to sever its commercial ties in South Africa. A University of California/Los Angeles study concluded that the incinerator's environmental impact report and other key documents contained serious inconsistencies. Even though he had already committed $12 million towards LANCER, Bradley asked the city council to withdraw the project (Russell, 1989).

In Robeson County, North Carolina, a predominantly African and Native American area, the Center for Community Action spearheaded a campaign encompassing four counties along the Lumbee River in Southeast North Carolina to resist the siting of two facilities. The first facility, a commercial low-level radioactive waste incinerator, was rejected by the state after a concerted campaign which involved demonstrations of approximately 4,000 people. The second involved a regional chemical waste treatment plant. In 1988, the state legislature passed a water quality bill much more stringent than the national bill and would have derailed this facility. However, the EPA has sought to void North Carolina's statute (National Council of Churches, 1987/1988).

In Albuquerque, New Mexico, as the result of a workshop conducted in December, 1984, by the United Church of Christ Commission for Racial Justice, the Southwest Organizing Committee (SWOC) began to focus on the environmental problems of the area. SWOC employed a strategy which linked voter registration with education around environmental problems. This strategy was combined with action campaigns in specific neighborhoods. For example, the Albuquerque area has especially serious problems with groundwater contamination. SWOC conducted water testing sessions in local communities and was successful in getting new water lines laid in certain neighborhoods. It also conducted city-wide environmental tours, for the purposes of educating residents as well as holding accountability sessions for political candidates and elected officials. This project had the support of the National Council of Churches, which joined SWOC in holding an "Interdenominational Hearing on Toxics in Minority Communities" in September, 1989 (Southwest Organizing Committee, 1989).

In Louisiana, a bi-racial coalition of community, environmental and labor groups joined together to focus attention on the environmental problems associated with a corridor between Baton Rouge and New Orleans. The coalition, called the Louisiana Toxics Project, is composed of the Gulf Coast Tenants Association, the Delta Chapter of the Sierra Club, the Louisiana Environmental Action Network and the Oil, Chemical and Atomic Workers Union. It started when a group of tenants attended a national environmentalist meeting early in 1988 in Atlanta, Georgia and realized that they could do something about the poisoning of their communities. In November, 1988, the coalition conducted an eighty-mile, ten-day march along the Mississippi River between Baton Rouge and New Orleans. According to Pat Bryant, the project's director, "the myth that African Americans are not interested in protecting the earth has been proven a lie in Louisiana" (Southern Organizing Committee for Economic and Social Justice, 1989: 3).

The United Farm Workers Union (UFW), after the 1985 finding of aldicarb-contaminated watermelon from California, began to focus upon pesticide problems affecting farmworkers (United Farm Workers Union, 1985). This led to their "Wrath of Grapes" national boycott. This boycott was meant to focus national attention on the plight of migrant farmworkers and demanded the banning of five pesticides (United Farm Workers Union, 1986). One tactic used to further this boycott was a month long fast by Cesar Chavez. Chavez's fast was carried on by others, including the Rev. Jesse Jackson and Dr. Benjamin Chavis. By the beginning of 1989, the boycott had caused a serious decline in grape sales in the New York metropolitan area, the single largest table grape marketing area in the nation. Along with a national boycott, the UFW worked in conjunction with the National Farm Worker Ministry, a church-based support group, to work with childhood cancer victims in the San Joaquin Valley (Hoagland, 1987).

These are but a few of the emerging and ongoing grassroots communities active around environmental issues. They reflect the significant growth in public awareness of toxic pollution in racial minority communities. While the Commission for Racial Justice report may have played a part in engendering this awareness, the upsurge in minority-based community activism generally has its own dynamics and reflects the overdue recognition of a social reality, i.e., the disparate distribution of environmental contaminants in their communities.

The report, however, did provide, for the first time, a nationally comprehensive study that gives credence to those who want to focus on these issues, either for overall public policy development or for grassroots activists addressing specific problems in racial minority communities. Because of this report and others, "sufficient evidence of the impact of toxics in racial and ethnic communities has come to the fore to silence anyone who would argue that there is no connection between pollution and race" (Lee, 1987a).

No example serves to illustrate this better than the following article regarding the successful campaign of residents of Hancock County, Georgia, spearheaded by Cynthia Smith, to prevent the siting of an incinerator in their county:

> They talked about the 'blackness' of the issue, quoting from the United Church of Christ's study on toxic wastes and race to the residents of this 78% black county. When Hancock residents started coming together to oppose the facility in September 1987, they called themselves Citizens Against Hazardous Wastes in Hancock County. Prayer vigils, rallies, public meetings, and lots of door-to-door talking with folks paid off in generating a unified base of support and a strong voice. CAHW used that voice to successfully block the facility. They spoke of racism, planned to sue the county for several instances of barring residents from a public meeting, and considered recalling their county commissioners from office (Stults, 1988: 3).

Although other communities in the South do not seem to be fundamentally different from Hancock County, few of them which confront environmental issues for the first time are likely to have the stunning success of Hancock County. Many of the issues which were raised in "Toxic Wastes and Race in the United States," particularly those related to economics and the hazardous waste issue, present major obstacles.

For example, the proponents of the LANCER project approached Gilbert Lindsay, an African American city councilman who represented the district surrounding the proposed plant, and offered a $10 million community development fund to finance improvements in a community center, to be named after his wife (Russell, 1989: 26). Another example involves a plan to rehabitate the Love Canal, New York, area. A bill was envisioned that would allow the construction of low income housing in the area. Among the persons most willing to relocate in such an area of questionable safety would be African Americans in a neighboring housing project, whose situation had never been addressed throughout the many years of controversy over the Love Canal landfill.

The interrelated issues of economics, politics and the lack of community environmental consciousness have exerted a powerful influence in Sumter County, Alabama, site of the nation's largest hazardous waste landfill. Originally a smaller landfill owned in part by the son-in-law of former Governor George Wallace, the facility was purchased and expanded by Chemical Waste Management, Inc. Throughout this process, Sumter County residents were not aware of the site's real purpose. For example, one commonly held belief was that the plant was involved in the production of fertilizer, a logical use of the dolomite chalk formation (otherwise known as Selma chalk) upon which the area rests. If anything, the facility provided much needed employment for this highly depressed area. Not until workers began to complain about working conditions and health problems did the truth about the facility begin to emerge.

The landfill, through a surcharge on each barrel of waste transported to the site, also provides revenues to the area, particularly the school system. This has been labeled by local activist, John Zieppert, as "blood money". However, the area does suffer from a low tax base and lack of economic development. At the same time, the Alabama Black Belt remains a particularly contentious battleground for African American political rights. One example of these continuing struggles during recent years is the persecution of African American leadership for alleged voting fraud. Indeed, such issues have taken precedence over environmental problems, which correctly or incorrectly, are viewed as luxury concerns.

In many ways, Sumter County is illustrative of the dichotomy between traditional civil rights and environmental agendas. Traditional civil rights organizations have focused on traditional issues such as employment, housing, education, economic development and political participation to the exclusion of environmental concerns. Moreover, there exists a historical enmity between these two movements. Since its inception, the environmental movement has in the main viewed problems in racial minority communities as an unwelcome stepchild. For example, during Earth Day activities in 1970 at San Jose College, organizers bought a brand new cadillac and buried it. The Black Student Union demonstrated in protest, contending that such money could have been better spent on the problems of the inner cities. Several years later, the membership of the National Sierra Club was polled on the question of whether it should increase involvement in urban poor and minorities. The proposal was rejected three to one (Freudenberg, 1984b: 212-213). In 1984, Ronald Taylor, in *U.S. News and World Report,* asked in an article by the same name, "Do environmentalists care about the poor?" For these and other reasons, traditional civil rights organizations have long viewed "environmentalism" with distrust and hostility.

On the other hand, the civil rights movement has also been faulted for its lack of concern over environmental issues. In a recent commentary, Paul Ruffins, Executive Director of Black Network News, said that despite the growing evidence of minority exposure to toxins,

> such organizations as the NAACP and the Urban League—exquisitely sensitive to threats to minorities in areas such as education, housing, jobs, AIDS and drugs, have almost completely ignored environmental hazards. For example, the program for a recent Urban League Conference offered more than 20 forums, from child care to the lack of minority teachers. Not one was dedicated to environmental issues (Ruffins, 1989).

Much has been made of the perception that environmentalists and minority-based organizations, whose support has come from corporations and labor unions, have fundamentally divergent interests. Whereas this schism is reflected in very real and intractable issues such as "economic blackmail" (Bullard, 1987a), there are indications that this alone cannot fully explain the inaction of civil rights organizations on environmental issues. For example, the Congressional Black Caucus has been rated to be among the most progressive voting blocks on environmental issues (Taylor, 1984). An issue that has yet to be fully examined is simply the lack of familiarity on the part of civil rights community with such issues. In many respects, environmental issues are difficult to grasp, being highly technical and regulatory in nature. Poorer communities, lacking readily available pool of residents, such as doctors, lawyers and scientists, who are familiar with the nomenclature of environmental protection, are at a distinct disadvantage.

Accessibility to persons trained in environmental fields has been found to be a major element of success by communities confronting environmental problems. The article entitled "Citizen Action for Environmental Health: Report on a Survey of Community Organizations," reports the findings of a nationwide survey with grassroots environmental organizations:

> Identification and control of environmental health hazards have depended primarily on two strategies: scientific research and government regulation. In the last decade, a third strategy has emerged. In communities across the country, concerned citizens have banded together to attempt to force government or industry to reduce or eliminate a suspected hazard in their neighborhood (Freudenberg, 1984a).

As important and viable as this strategy has proven to be, it is only beginning to be recognized and used in African American and other racial/ethnic communities. There have been major developments, since the United Church of Christ Commission for Racial Justice study, on the part of both the environmental and civil rights movements that begin to address these issues. In early 1988, the National Sierra Club and the National Toxics Coalition co-sponsored the Southern Environmental Assembly in Atlanta, Georgia, the event which gave rise to the formation of the Louisiana Toxics Project. The event was aimed at impacting the 1988 presidential political campaign. While the organizers of this conference hired an African American organizer and sought to involve African Americans and showcase African American leaders such as Rep. John Lewis (D-GA), Lowery and Chavis, it was largely unsuccessful in obtaining African American participation. The delegation from Louisiana represented the bulk of the conference's African American participation. Nonetheless, as seen by developments in Louisiana and other areas, the conference did have a significant impact. An ongoing project, the African American Environmental Services project, based in Atlanta, Georgia, now exists. The Natural Resources Defense Council (NRDC) has devoted several articles of the *Amicus Journal* to minority issues, as will Environmental Action, which is planning to publish a major issue on minorities and the environment. NRDC is also beginning a project on environmental problems in minority communities in New York City.

Progressive African American leadership has begun to make the link between
environment and civil rights. Besides the United Church of Christ Commission for
Racial Justice's efforts, Jesse Jackson made the environment a major issue in his
1988 campaign. At the same time, growing restiveness around environmental
concerns such as global warming have combined with the commemoration of the
twentieth anniversary of Earth Day to create an upsurge of public interest in recent
years. The approach of environmentalists today has some significant difference
from that of 1970. Among the board members of the 1990 Earth Day committee was
Jesse Jackson. A tour by Jackson of minority communities with environmental
problems in early 1990 was also conducted.

There is an important ripple effect from this upsurge of activism around
environmental issues in minority communities. The issue is now a highly visible
one, reflected in the accompanying upsurge in press coverage. Such visibility not
only aids the work of local activists by making industry and government agencies
take their interests more seriously, but will cause political leaders to begin to see the
value of this issue as a part of their political platforms.

Academia

The United Church of Christ Commission for Racial Justice has placed great
importance on the following two recommendations from "Toxic Wastes and Race
in the United States":

1. Universities should give assistance to racial minority and ethnic students
    seeking training in technical and professional fields related to environmental
    protection such as environmental engineering, medicine, law and related
    fields. A special scholarship program should be jointly established by several
    philanthropic organizations to assist in this process (United Church of Christ
    Commission for Racial Justice, 1987: 27).
2. Universities should fully develop curricula in the area of "environmental
    sociology" that provide for the study of racial and socio-economic patterns
    associated with environmental pollution and related questions (United Church
    of Christ Commission for Racial Justice, 1987: 27).

It has been a fundamental premise of the United Church of Christ Commission
for Racial Justice that the training of racial minority persons for environmental
protection careers is a critical goal if we are to seriously address such problems in
racial minority communities. In 1988, when the U.S. Environmental Protection
Agency promulgated its Notice of Proposed Rule-making on "Worker Protection
Standards for Agricultural Pesticides," Hispanics made up about one percent of the
substantive policy-making positions in EPA, less than one-half of one percent of
Senior Executive Service (SES) positions, and none of the SES positions filled in

the past three years (United Church of Christ Commission for Racial Justice, 1987). The situation regarding African Americans and other minorities is no better. However important the inclusion of minority professionals is as a goal by itself, it must be complemented by the added goal of a strategy to marshall the technical expertise in academia and elsewhere to address pollution problems in minority communities.

Freudenberg's survey of community groups involved in environmental issues revealed that,

> after identifying the hazard, the next activity is to investigate it. More than half of the respondents reported that they attended conferences or meetings with scientific experts, read government reports, met with activists from other local or national environmental groups, read newspaper articles, or listened to television or radio reports in order to educate themselves. Contact with scientific experts was rated to be the most valuable source of information (Freudenberg, 1984a).

For these reasons, we were delighted to participate in a 1987 conference in Tallahassee, Florida entitled, "Community Toxic Pollution Awareness and Historically Black Colleges and Universities." This conference, sponsored by the Legal Environmental Assistance Foundation and Florida A & M University, drew approximately 75 participants from Historically Black Colleges and Universities (HBCUs) and non-HBCU faculty and administration, representatives of the U.S. Environmental Protection Agency and local communities. Dr. Ralph Turner, Chairperson of the FAMU Chemistry Department, noted that the conference was a golden opportunity to involve college science students in field work, further adding "many science students complain that their studies have little relevance to the 'real world,' and grow restless, or lose their sense of commitment" (Lee, 1987b).

The conference sought to fill a void in the area of minority educational opportunity for environmental fields. Seven years prior to this conference, the EPA contracted the publication of three reports on minority educational opportunities. The studies found minorities to be highly underrepresented in scientific professions related to the environment. In 1976, 6.6 percent of physical science majors and 9.5 percent of biological science majors who graduated from American colleges belonged to a minority group. Only 4.1 percent of agricultural and natural resource majors were minorities. Additionally, "there is widespread recognition that minority students and adults who counsel them are seldom aware of either the environmental problems affecting minority communities or those that affect the larger world" (Human Environment Center (HEC), 1981a; 1981b).

The conference pointedly revealed a continuation of this state of affairs. For example, the EPA has set aside significant research funds and internship opportunities for HBCUs. The Minority Institution Assistance Program is a special program to provide federal assistance to HBCUs. Faculty internships at the EPA for HBCU faculty are also available. However, in the summer of 1987, only 30 of the 114 available slots were filled (Debro, 1987).

Representatives were also present from the Student Environmental Health Project (STEHP) at Vanderbilt University in Nashville, Tennessee. In its seven year history, STEHP has provided technical assistance through summer interns to over forty communities, assisted over one hundred and fifty community labor and resource groups through its year round program and made service-learning opportunities available to over ninety students. STEHP's philosophy is based on two themes: (1) emphasizes the role of community-based leadership in building long-term solutions to health problems that affect chronically underserved communities, and (2) community settings provide excellent opportunities for experiential education (Vanderbilt University Center for Health Services, 1987). By definition, "chronically underserved communities" in the South are predominantly African American communities. A listing of such communities includes Greene County, Lowndes County and Sumter County in Alabama; Benton and Drakesboro Counties in Kentucky; Lexington, Mississippi; Pickaway County, Ohio; Greenbriar, Loudon and Nashville Counties in Tennessee; Washington County, Virginia; Minden, West Virginia; and Western Northern Carolina (Student Environmental Health Project, 1985; 1986; 1987).

A second model presented at the conference was that of the Center for the Biology of Natural Systems at Queens College (CBNS)/City University of New York. The Center's purpose was to analyze the "origins of environmental, energy and resource problems" and "to devise solutions which emphasize the improvement of the overall productivity, as well as the economic position and welfare of the affected social group." Based upon these goals, CBNS chose to concentrate on issues surrounding solid waste management and address the garbage crisis facing most urban environments today. In recent years, the center has completed a study on sources of plastics in trash, another study of intensive recycling of municipal solid waste, and a number of assessments of specific municipal solid waste strategies. The center has performed many of these projects with contracts from cities such as Philadelphia, Pennsylvania, San Diego, California; Minneapolis, Minnesota and East Hampton, New York (Center for the Biology of Natural Systems, 1987a; 1987b). By demonstrating the ability to generate funds and support itself based on services performed, the CBNS model can help to fulfill both the HBCU's developmental needs as well as providing needed services to minority communities.

In order for HBCUs to properly make use of these lessons, it is necessary to establish some preliminary context for these programs. Dr. Robert Bullard, in a paper prepared for the conference, advanced his interpretation of a workplan for advancing the research and public service mission of a proposed "Black Think Tank" with its hub in the HBCUs. The interdisciplinary focus of the Think Tank would be achieved through an aggressive and visible programmatic thrust which centers on five components: (1) policy-oriented research; (2) research findings dissemination; (3) community education and service; (4) technical assistance and training; and (5) demonstration models (Bullard, 1987b). Similarly, I presented the idea of a consortium of HBCUs to be the provider of environmentally related technical service to African American cities, townships and organizations (Lee, 1987b).

Subsequent to this conference, the United Church of Christ Commission for Racial Justice gave Bullard a small grant to conduct a survey of the environmental capabilities and attitudes of HBCUs. Bullard reported that, of the 57 institutions surveyed, the bulk of degree granting programs were undergraduate programs, i.e., 56 chemistry, 52 biology, and 24 allied health. There were only eight chemistry and eight biology programs offering advanced degrees. Only two graduate programs offered degrees in energy and environmental sciences, respectively. Although 21 institutions offered courses in environmental sciences, only nine undergraduate and two graduate environmental science programs existed.

The majority of faculty respondents saw "environmental discrimination" as a real problem facing the African American community, or saw the community "targeted" for various kinds of pollution. More than one half felt that the African American community had been treated unfairly in the enforcement of environmental and health regulations. Despite this, less than one fifth (17.9 percent) felt that their institution had taken an active role to reduce the threat of toxins in the African American community. On the other hand, eight of every ten persons surveyed (80.8 percent) would like to see their institution take a more active role in combatting environmental problems in the African American community.

A sizable share of the faculty had participated in academic activities related to the environment. Nearly two fifths (37.8 percent) had conducted research and one third had collaborated in research. A little over one fourth had provided technical assistance or served as a consultant. One fifth of the faculty had published in the area, received a grant or presented a paper at a professional meeting (Bullard, 1988).

Government

The United Church of Christ Commission for Racial Justice report made a number of recommendations to federal agencies, including the U.S. Environmental Protection Agency. These recommendations ranged from institutional reform, to educational initiatives and further investigation. Additionally, a set of recommendations were made to state and municipal governments.

With regard to institutional change within the federal government, we recommended the formation of an office devoted to minority environmental concerns as well as an advisory committee on this issue. We believed that there is precedence for such proposals, as the Department of Health and Human Services has set up an Office of Minority Health. In its initial response to the report, the EPA chose not to acknowledge the possibility that racial minority groups may face more serious or unaddressed risks from exposure to environmental pollutants.

This was voiced by J. Winston Porter, former Assistant Administrator for Solid and Hazardous Wastes, when he said that the EPA's decision making process is motivated by technical factors. According to Porter, "There's no sociology to it. It's strictly technical" (Porter, 1987). The EPA did, however, delineate programs which relate to minority concerns, including the following:

1. In the spring of 1986, the agency co-sponsored the "Conference on the Environment, Minorities and Women," aimed at universities and colleges with predominantly black, Hispanic, and female enrollments;
2. EPA's faculty internship program is designed to provide educators from Historically Black Colleges and Universities with experience at EPA and increase the black community's awareness of EPA programs and activities;
3. EPA has created an Indian Task Force with the goal of ensuring that Indians, particularly those living on reservations, are aware of and take advantage of EPA programs;
4. The EPA regional office in Dallas, Texas sponsored a regional conference in July 1987 to provide information about EPA and its efforts to protect communities from environmental pollutants; and
5. The EPA Office of Civil Rights is charged by federal law and by EPA policy to address allegations of unlawful discrimination and require corrective action where it is deemed necessary (Porter, 1987).

In contrast to the EPA, Dr. Hopkins of the Agency for Toxic Substances and Disease Registry responded to the report by saying that "it raises disturbing questions about the location of toxic waste sites in relation to racial composition of communities and persons at risk of exposure to hazardous substances from such sites." In addition, he spoke to two of the report's recommendations:

> Two of the report's recommendations that pertain to the Federal Government have implications for the Agency for Toxic Substances and Disease Registry (ATSDR). Recommendation 4 asks ATSDR to perform health assessments for a representative number of sites in racial and ethnic communities under the Superfund Amendments and Reauthorization Act of 1986 (SARA), irrespective of their inclusion on the National Priorities List. Recommendation 6 advises that the Department of Health and Human Services should conduct epidemiological studies to determine if hazardous wastes and other environmental pollutants are contributory factors in the development of known health problems in racial and ethnic communities (Hopkins, 1987).

Since then, ATSDR has undertaken an ambitious initiative around hazardous wastes and minority communities. As part of this initiative, ATSDR began in 1988 to conduct demographic analysis of sites in the South, to identify minority populations in surrounding areas so that it may begin developing strategies to address the needs of these populations. It has also begun to identify and consult with key individuals in the academic, scientific, environmental, and civil rights communities and with grassroots activists. In April, 1989, the ATSDR board of scientific advisors gave its support to such an initiative. ATSDR held a major conference around toxic pollution and minorities in the fall of 1990.

This effort represents fundamental policy decisions that recognize the existence of disparate levels of toxic pollution in racial minority communities and a distinctive, and in some ways unique, set of related health problems. This effort also represents fundamental policy decisions on the need to develop ways of conducting education and mobilization that conform with the social and political realities of racial minority communities.

When the United Church of Christ Commission for Racial Justice report was released, Dr. Barry Commoner commented that it showed that there is "a functional relationship between racism, poverty, and powerlessness, and the chemical industry's assault on the environment" (1987). The developments that I have outlined are cumulative in effect. Taken together, these changes have served to significantly change the balance of power in favor of minority communities confronted with environmental problems.

A final question was posed to me regarding changes in the siting and management of hazardous waste facilities since the report. The report did not directly address siting and management issues. Nor am I in a position to assess specific changes in these areas. However, I can definitely say that there have been major advances in the degree of public awareness and organization among minority communities that act as a deterrent to misconduct and abuse. As these increase, decisions made by corporations, government and others regarding their treatment of such communities will also take into greater account the concerns of minority communities.

3

Can the Environmental Movement Attract and Maintain the Support of Minorities?

Dorceta Taylor

For most of the 80s, the Reagan administration weakened environmental legislation, and this in turn has reduced the number of environmental victories. This trend has caused people within the environmental movement to examine the past, and re-assess strategies for the future. As preparations were being made for Earth Day 1990 (the 20th anniversary), many began taking a critical look at the movement, noting that three decades after *Silent Spring*, and two decades after Earth Day 1970, the established part of the the movement is still primarily white, middle class, and highly educated. Many are asking why this is the case, and how and when will it change?

Discussions about the composition of the environmental movement, in particular, and the continued absence of minorities,[1] have led to the development of numerous theories and hypotheses which attempt to explain existing patterns.[2] However, these explanations assume that the core composition of the movement will remain relatively unchanged in the future, and that if groups which are not currently participating want to participate, they will have to join the movement "as is." In other words, most of the costs associated with affiliation, cooperation, and coalition building will have to be borne by the people who aren't currently in the movement, because they will have to make the effort and adjustments necessary to participate.

Until now, this assumption has gone unchallenged. This paper, instead of assuming that potential joiners will fall in step with the existing structure, asks: "How can the environmental movement restructure itself in order to attract and maintain long-term support from minorities?" This question does not assume that the environmental future has already been defined, or that those within the movement have more power to shape and control events more than those currently

Dorceta Taylor wrote this article while she was a graduate student at Yale University. She specialized in Environmental Sociology and Organizational Theory and has strong research interests in the field of Sociology of Leisure, with a focus on ethnic variations in leisure patterns. She completed her doctorate in 1991 and is studying ethnic minority environmental groups in the United States, Great Britain, and Canada.

outside; it assumes that power, ideas, and the costs of including a wider variety of people can be equitably distributed or shared between potential newcomers and old timers. It is a question that is central because the environmental movement needs those who are not currently involved at least as much as they need the environmental movement, if the movement is to attain any real growth, diversification, maturity, and representative political power.

This paper also challenges the assumption that minorities— blacks in particular—have little or no interest in, or concern for environmental issues and have shown very limited participation in the movement per se.[3] It argues that there is much interest and concern in minority communities for environmental issues, and that minorities, are displaying increasing levels of political mobilization around environmental issues. However, minorities are responding to, and supporting only a limited part of the movement— what I will term, "the new grassroots." This paper analyzes and compares the characteristics of this emerging sector to that of others which remain unattractive to minorities, and discusses the implications of the current form and posture of each sector on future growth and membership support.

What is the mood within the established sectors of the movement? Is there a feeling that the issues being dealt with are relevant to minorities? What is the general outlook of people within the movement? The 1989 Conservation Leadership Project Survey[4] found that about 87 percent of the respondents agreed with the statement "many, perhaps most, minority and poor rural Americans see little in the conservation message that speaks to them."[5] While 80 percent of the respondents thought the conservation movement[6] was healthy, 57 percent thought it was fragmented, 54 percent thought it a political failure, and almost one third of the respondents thought there was no conservation movement. Forty-four percent thought there was leadership at the grassroots, 45 percent thought there were no new ideas in the movement, and 34 percent thought the national organizations were too professional.

It is clear that within the movement, there is an overwhelming sense that the message is not attractive to minorities and the poor, but as later discussions will show, organizations have resisted change by continuing to place high priorities on wildlife and preservation issues. There is also a sense of uncertainty about the health, the general direction of the movement, and the role of the grassroots in the future of the movement.

Finally, this paper examines the growing trend in the movement towards two kinds of groups or organizations: (1) those which have distanced themselves from direct action, and choose to serve a narrow range of constituents nation-wide, and (2) those which utilize broad-based, local community support to bring human environmental issues to the forefront. There is an analysis of the tensions that arise from making such choices, and the implications those choices have on the structure of the organization, and the membership that it is likely to attract in the long term. However, before one can answer these questions, one has to look at the history of the movement, and how that has influenced organizational or group structure, the types of issues fought, and the way in which they are fought.

Historical Background

The environmental movement can be described as a movement which developed in four stages: (1) the 1830s to the early 1900s; (2) the early 1900s through the 1950s; (3) 1960 through the 1970s; and (4) 1980 onwards. On the evolutionary scale, these stages mark the transformation of the movement from a cause championed by individual enthusiasts advocating preservation and conservation, to the formation of organizations to further those causes, to massive public support and broadening of the issues, and finally to radical redefinition of the issues and renewed growth.

Stage One

The environmental movement is a complex social movement that began in the early 1800s and was strongly influenced by Romanticism[7] and Trancendentalism.[8] In the decades between 1830 and 1860, there was no organized movement per se; individual philosophers, artists, writers, poets, and outdoorsmen, extolled the virtues of the natural environment, and sought to preserve it.[9] The federal government, the target of some of this environmental activism, played an interesting role in the acquisition, use, transfer and management of public lands during this period also. While on the one hand the government designated large tracts of land as national reserves and parks,[10] on the other hand, several land policies aimed at transferring lands from federal to private control and increasing use were enacted.[11]

As a result of rapid industrial expansion and exploitation of natural resources in the 1880s, environmental degradation became very apparent. Consequently, many outdoor enthusiasts began framing their dialogue less in Romantic and Transcendental terms, and more in ecological terms.[12] These wealthy conservation enthusiasts[13] had a strong interest in outdoor recreation, and as a result in the 1890s, they helped to form outdoor clubs like the Appalachian Mountain Club, the Sierra Club, the Boone and Crockett Club, and the Audubon Society. [14]

Stage Two

After the Hetch Hetchy[15] controversy of the early 1900s, the focus of the conservation movement was expanded to include wildlife protection,[16] and by the early 1920s, environmental organizations started to specialize: the Sierra Club was concerned with mountaineering and national park issues; the National Conservation Association dealt with forestry and power development; and the Audubon Associations focused on birds and other wildlife. However, as the decade drew to a close, overall attention was again focused on wildlife because of rapidly diminishing stocks, and loss of habitats.

The 1930s, the era of New Deal Conservation, was the period in which the Civilian Conservation Corps and the Tennessee Valley Authority were formed. Under Roosevelt, a staunch conservationist, the movement was realigned and became linked to political liberalism and the Democratic Party.[17]

Stage Three

The period between 1945 and 1960 was marked by unprecedented economic growth and development. This was accompanied by accelerated environmental degradation in air and water quality; pesticide use and contamination of the air, water, and land; and, in general, degraded landscapes. These environmental ills were quite visible, so the publication of Rachel Carson's, *Silent Spring,* in 1960[18] (which many believe was the catalyst that launched the birth of modern environmentalism), touched off a storm of controversy and environmental protest. The massive public outcry which followed not only energized the movement, but broadened the focus to include human welfare issues such as halting widespread pollution, the destruction of the environment, overpopulation, food production and distribution, the depletion of non-renewable energy resources, nuclear energy, and international fisheries.[19]

In addition to pushing for legislative reforms, other forms of protests, such as picketing, boycotts, and mass demonstrations were utilized. As the Sixties unfolded, and the anti-war and women's movements emerged, the environmental movement lost some forward momentum. By the end of the decade, however, the movement experienced renewed growth, as many young student activists, anxious for radical political reform, joined its ranks.[20]

These activists ushered in the Seventies with Earth Day (1970), and in the early years of the decade, the movement continued its rapid growth, with other young people who were formerly engaged in the anti-war movement, joining the environmental movement.[21] The Seventies was also a decade of environmental legislation.[22] On the one hand, it was a decade marked by the formation of radical, direct-action environmental groups which continued to use the tactics that proved successful in the Sixties, yet on the other hand, highly technocratic and legalistic groups emerged to fight the courtroom battles. At the same time, the recreational focus of the more established, traditional groups was deemphasized, as they, too, developed the technical and legal expertise needed to fight environmental battles.

Stage Four

As the seventies drew to a close, there was a noticeable decline in the number of legal victories, and the number of environmental laws being enacted. The environmental movement seemed to be running out of steam. At the same time, though, there was a subtle shift in the concerns of many. The air was cleaner, so was the water, but environmental toxins and solid waste disposal problems came to the forefront in a big way. Incidents at Love Canal (New York), Times Beach

TABLE 1   Classification of Environmental Groups

Categories of Environmental Groups	Examples of Groups in Each Category
Incremental Reformists	
Traditional Conservationists	National Audubon Society, Sierra Club, Izaak Walton League
New Conservationists	National Wildlife Federation, Wilderness Society
New Environmentalists	Friends of the Earth, Earth Island
Environmental Defense	Environmental Defense Fund, Natural Resources Defense Council
Land Trusts	The Nature Conservancy
Political Action Committee	The League of Conservation Voters
Energy	Environmental Policy Institute
Recreationists	Trout Unlimited, Ducks Unlimited
Radical Reformists	
Eco-activists	Greenpeace
New Grassroots	Citizens' Clearinghouse for Hazardous Waste, National Toxics Campaign
Consumer Advocates	Public Interest Research Group
Toxics	Citizens For a Better Environment
Anti-nuclear groups	Clamshell and Abalone Alliances
Deep Ecologists	New Alchemy Institute, Earth First
Green Parties	Green Program Project

(Missouri), and Triana (Alabama), helped to focus the nation's attention on toxic waste disposal.

These incidents helped to facilitate the birth of a new sector of the movement—the "new grassroots" groups concerned with stopping the proliferation of environmental toxins, and helping victims obtain compensation for exposure and illness. This new sector broadened the range of issues with which environmentalists get involved. It has also brought some racial and social class diversity to the movement, involving people who were not heard from before.

Niches Within the Environmental Movement

The large number of environmental organizations formed during the last three decades has resulted in greater "niche space partitioning" than ever before. Groups that occupy particular niches have developed separate and distinct visions of the present and future, organizational structures, strategies and tactics for mobilization and fundraising, positions on issues, and choice of issues in which to be involved. Such diverse groups as green parties, deep ecologists, anti-nuclear activists, environmental defense groups, bird watchers, anglers, hunters, hikers, land trustees, lobbyists, farm workers, appropriate technologists, and urban and rural grassroots coalitions all claim to be a part of the environmental movement.

To understand the development and continued existence of these different kinds of groups within one movement, one has to look not only at the history of the movement, but also at how it grows and recruits its membership, the structure of the various organizations and groups within particular niches and sectors, and how the existing movement holds itself together. This exploration also helps to provide an understanding of why the membership composition of most sectors of the movement remains relatively homogeneous, and why only a very small sector of the movement is attracting individuals from diverse backgrounds who have not participated in the movement in the past. Ultimately, this analysis puts us in a better position to address the question of how the movement should look if it is to attract and sustain widespread support from minorities.

Because of the diversity of environmental issues that can be tackled, it has been easy for groups to carve out niches by specializing. But these groups and organizations don't always work in a vacuum; they frequently form coalitions to fight certain issues, because many have their headquarters and lobbyists in Washington, D C. Environmental groups and organizations can be classified into general types: some can be categorized quite easily because of their program focus and their stand on issues, while others are much more difficult to categorize, because they tackle many issues in a variety of ways (see Table 1).

For the purposes of this analysis, organizations and groups are organized into two categories, viz., Incremental Reformists — those with a strong conservation orientation, and Radical Reformists — groups or organizations advocating direct action, and/or empowerment at the grassroots level.

Other foci, such as environmental education, population growth, apppropriate technology, food production and distribution, eco-feminism, Christian ecology, and international aid, could provide further types into which the movement could be dissected.

The following analysis attempts to demonstrate how the orientations of these two categories differ; it best describes "ideal types"[23] because such designations allow us to develop a general analysis of a wide range of organizations and groups.[24]

Incremental Reformists

The following characterization is probably most applicable to the traditional and new conservationists, but much of the analysis will be applicable to other types listed under this category. Incremental reformist groups tend to be large, centralized, and bureaucratic, with well-established chains of command, well-developed administrative structures, and standing committees. They have paid administrative program development and implementation staff, lobbyists, scientists, and technicians to reduce the uncertainty of total reliance on volunteer labor.

They believe there is still time to change the system, and so they seek legal and policy changes, bargains, and compromises, by working within the established political channels. These organizations are supported by large, mostly white, middle class professionals. Potential members are recruited through direct-mail appeals, or through local chapter affiliations; computerized mailings have taken precedence over, or substituted for, community organizing. Regardless of the mode of recruiting, these organizations engage in "homosocial reproduction," i.e., new members are recruited from a pool that closely resembles the existing membership in their racial and ethnic characteristics and socio-economic profiles. In addition, these organizations are supported by donations from wealthy individuals, endowments, tax exemptions, and federal and private grants.

Members are offered selective incentives[25] like four-color glossy magazines, journals, trips, and merchandise in exchange for their financial support and continued interest. In addition they get legal representation, congressional lobbies, and educational updates on issues that are pertinent to them, without expending much effort. Another less obvious, but nonetheless powerful, motivation to contribute is derived from traditional Romantic and Transcendental ideals — the idea of helping to conserve or preserve land and nature for one's own present and future use, or for future generations. Such use involves the ability to get away from it all; to transcend earthly worries, to escape, to commune with nature. The possibility of having a transcendental experience is strongly linked to the desire to save the places where such experiences are likely to occur.

Apparently these incentives are strong enough to maintain continued support despite the fact that the membership lacks any real decision-making capacity, or any real status within the organization. Depending on whether there are local chapters, and how these are organized, members may have little or no contact with other members of the organization.

On occasion, members are mobilized to send telegrams, make phone calls, contact their congressional representatives, support (vote on) key bills, run petition drives, and boycott products. Because these groups focus mainly on lobbying, litigation, education, and non-violent forms of obstruction, highly symbolic forms of protest might involve the members cutting up their credit cards or dumping the stocks of targeted companies.

Radical Reformists

The following characterization best describes the eco-activists, the anti-nuclear groups, and the deep ecologists, but it is also applicable to other radical reformist groups. In contrast to the incremental reformists, radical reformists rely heavily on volunteer support. They have few, if any, paid staff, and are kept going by the strong moral and political commitments of their membership, and the personal zeal they bring to the cause. They tend to be egalitarian, so they seek to minimize or eliminate formal organizational hierarchy, or the emergence of "leaders." If committees exist, they are organized on the task force model, that is, individuals choose to participate in whatever task they think they can accomplish rather than have the tasks delegated.

Radical reformist organizations or groups tend to be decentralized, with a number of local, regional, national, or international sister affiliates operating with the same program thrust. Group decisions are made democratically, but that often involves only those who are present at meetings, or are actively involved in projects. When a group convenes, if there are decisions to be made, instead of seeking the opinions of the entire membership, the people who are present make the decisions on behalf of the group.

Like the incremental reformists, their membership is mostly white and well educated, but they differ from the former in that many reject the world of money making and the climb up the corporate ladder. Instead, they seek alternative forms of employment that leave them enough time and resources for their political activism. These groups resist being "co-opted" and worry about being infiltrated; therefore, the group boundaries (members versus non-members) are very clearly defined. The purity of the group is partially defined by the strength of the personal commitments, and by the amount of effort members are willing to devote to the cause.

There is a tendency to define the group's position by attacking more mainstream environmental positions. The members believe that major environmental problems will only be abated by radical social changes, not through the small legal and policy changes sought by the incrementalists. Such changes are not drastic enough to avert the cataclysmic end with which the world is threatened. Combined with this vision of critical danger is a strong vision of what the world should be like. It is a vision in which humans coexist harmoniously with nature. They believe that there is no time left for compromises or bargains; therefore, they take a non-negotiable, often militant stance, because compromises are seen as bad — a dilution of the group's commitments. They are highly critical of big industry and high technology.

These groups, which are often small in size, rely heavily on the small donations from the membership and others sympathetic to the cause. They run highly symbolic campaigns in which members and supporters (who tend to move in and out of the groups as the need arises, or as moral pull becomes strong enough) participate in confrontational demonstrations, picketing, petition drives, boycotts, door-to-door canvassing, violent and non-violent obstructions, and even "monkeywrenching." Others take their commitments to very symbolic levels by adjusting their lifestyles to reflect the messages they preach, for example, wearing hand-woven clothes, making and using hand-made pottery, and eating organic food, to demonstrate their rejection of the technological dependence of modern societies.

Unlike the incremental reformists, these groups do not rely very heavily on offering selective incentives as a way of attracting and maintaining membership support. However, they too rely on the potency of the Romantic and Transcendental notions to attract members who have a strong sense of saving or creating better opportunities for the present and the future. As FitzSimmons and Gottlieb (1988) write, "these groups share, on the one hand, a fondness for nature over society[,] and on the other[,] a particular type of celebration of individualism, situating identity and growth not in the community or collective experience, but in the individual's experience of the natural."

The previous discussion has identified two basic types of organization, with differing styles and appeals, but neither has attracted the support of minorities or the poor. Numerous theories and hypotheses have been proffered to explain why this might be the case,[26] but the most pertinent is that very few groups in the environmental movement fight the issues that are most relevant to minorities and the poor.

Appealing to Minorities

As we have seen, environmental groups or organizations, as in any other social movement, recruit and sustain the support of their membership by offering selective incentives, by relying on strong personal moral commitment, by some combination of both, or by defining the issue in terms of survival. If the selective incentives are strong enough to keep the checks flowing in and to get a good showing when mass mobilization drives are called, then the reliance on heavy personal commitments of time, resources, fervor and zeal, can be reduced because the institution will have the resources necessary to wage a campaign without having to tax the strength of its members. However, if the organization is not in a position to offer or rely upon attractive selective incentives, and instead has to depend solely or mostly on the personal commitments of a small group of dedicated people, then it has to make moral appeals which are strong enough to keep people engaged in the struggle. In either case, the membership gets personal returns on the time, money, and effort they expend. Without any sort of returns, then the organization or group will fall prey to free rider problems. [27]

Since minority participation in the environmental movement is of primary concern, the preceding discussion on recruiting and maintaining membership support leads us to ask what it would take to make minorities want to join the movement. Would it take incentives, moral appeals, or relevant issues of survival?

If the selective incentives aren't ones that people value, or if they cannot afford the membership fees that render them eligible for these incentives, then the appeals will go unheeded. Similarly, if the group relies primarily on high levels of personal commitment, the issues have to be pressing and pertinent. Issues that are far removed from the life of an individual are not likely to elicit the kind of response necessary to sustain the commitment that a person needs to engage in any kind of struggle.

As I have discussed in an earlier paper, [28] the following factors are also important: (1) solidarity—a group or class of people having some sense of unity that produces or is based on common interest, objectives, or standards. The higher the levels of solidarity within a group or community, the more likely it is that people will respond to problems collectively. (2) The cognitive perception of reality— minorities tend to display low levels of political efficacy and do not always recognize advocacy channels in their communities. Without high levels of efficacy and the ability to recognize how to express one's needs effectively, persons perceiving a problem will be unable to do anything about it.[29] (3) The ability to mobilize resources (money, knowledge of the political system, scientific or technical expertise, and moral commitments). Groups need to mobilize these resources, in varying levels as the situation dictates, to remain viable.[30] (4) Psychological factors, such as ideology and discontent, and the degree to which a particular attitude is upheld, also play a part in determining whether people perceive a problem and respond to it. [31] (5) Groups are mobilized according to the degree of pre-existing group organization, i.e., groups with strong, distinctive identities and dense, interpersonal networks exclusive to group members are readily mobilized, while groups with weak identities, few intra-group networks, and strong ties to outsiders such as employers are less likely to mobilize.[32]

Does this mean that there are no environmental issues that will be appealing enough to minorities and the poor to get them to make such commitments? No. Indeed in this decade, and in the past few years in particular, there has been a surge of minority and working-class interest in environmental issues. Some of the issues of primary concern to them are toxins, pesticides, pollution, waste reduction, incineration, environmental health issues, the tradeoffs (and often the lack of choice) between jobs and health, lack of housing, recycling, and living and working in polluted neighborhoods. In short, they are concerned with human quality of life issues, particularly those which arise in the inner cities or economically depressed rural communities in which they are concentrated.

Organizations like the Citizens Clearinghouse for Hazardous Wastes (CCHW) and the National Toxics Campaign (NTC) alone work with over three thousand community groups, many of which are composed solely of blacks, Latinos, Asians, or American Indians, or other groups composed of coalitions of mixed social classes and racial groups.[33] In cities such as Los Angeles, and states like North Carolina, citizens groups from various racial and ethnic backgrounds are forming coalitions to support each other on environmental struggles which are going on in each region.[34]

Why are these groups being formed now? Why not earlier? Why are they supported by minorities — groups which are concerned with so many other basic life struggles that some would predict that they will not mobilize around environmental issues? Although Maslow's work has often been used to explain why these groups won't be motivated to mobilize around environmental issues, a careful examination of his work shows that the theory does not preclude potential activism by this group.[35]

It has been argued that blacks and other minorities are in a constant struggle to meet their basic needs and, therefore, do not place environmental issues at the top of their list of priorities.[36] This argument not only places environmentalism at the top of the hierarchy of needs, but it assumes that the ordering is permanently fixed. The argument does not allow for the possibility that environmental issues could become high-priority issues for minorities by redefining environmental issues in terms of basic needs, or that individuals might seek to meet high-order needs before all of their basic needs are met.

Because many of the environmental problems facing minorities are immediate and life-threatening, it is predicted that they will become involved in environmental organizations and groups, if and when these groups deal with issues of survival and basic needs. It should be noted that a person who is poor and deprived of many basic needs can still be concerned with higher order needs. In the same way that many such persons are sometimes concerned or preoccupied with status, aesthetics, and so forth, they can also be concerned with environmental issues. A problem arises when individuals have to convert that concern into action or activism. Too often such persons are suffering from low self-esteem or a low sense of personal efficacy, and lack the resources (money, knowledge) necessary to mobilize. Action becomes difficult and free-riding or apathy becomes common.[37]

These new grassroots groups have also succeeded in broadening and redefining the scope of the issues the movement tackles. Historically, the movement focussed on wilderness preservation. Even when the focus was broadened to encompass wildlife issues, the concern was primarily with diminishing stocks and the remedial steps that should be taken to reverse the trends. In the last three decades, however, the focus has been broadened to encompass a variety of issues pertaining to the biological environment. But despite the widened scope of the debate, the discussion is still limited.

A 1989 survey of 248 chief executive officers and other high ranking officials in environmental organizations nationwide shows that the program focus of the organizations they represent are primarily conservationist, educational, and preservationist. The highest percentage of the organizations' resources are devoted to: (1) fish and wildlife, (2) public land management, and (3) private land stewardship. Other top ten issues were: waterway protection, water quality, toxic wastes, land use, wilderness, agriculture, and air quality.[38]

The more established environmental organizations do fight issues of survival, and they use the survival theme to get the support of their members, but these are survival issues as they pertain to endangered species, national parks and preserves, threatened landscapes, animals, plants, and particular outdoor experiences that the membership enjoys. These survival debates are not linked to rural and urban poverty and quality of life issues.

If it is discovered that birds have lost their nesting sites, then environmentalists go to great expense and lengths to erect nesting boxes and find alternative breeding sites for them; when whales are stranded, enormous sums are spent to provide them food and shelter; when forests are threatened, large numbers of people are mobilized to prevent damage; but we have yet to see an environmental group champion the cause of homelessness in humans or joblessness as issues on which it will spend vast resources.[39] It is a strange paradox that a movement which exhorts the harmonious coexistence of people and nature, and worries about the continued survival of nature (particularly loss of habitat problems), somehow forgets about the survival of humans (especially those who have lost their "habitats" and "food sources"). If this trend continues, a vital piece of the web of survival will be missing—the humans (or, at least, that subset of humans who are the focus of this paper).

Environmentalists who rushed down to Brazil for consultations with the rubber tappers learned that the rubber tappers did not want nature preserves, they wanted extractive reserves. The same lessons are relevant in the United States: conservation and human survival[40] are inseparable. The environmentalists learned that, if they were going to get the support of the rubber tappers, they could not talk about saving nature without talking about saving jobs and improving the quality of life, because these issues were inextricably linked. The inner city is a jungle of another sort, but the same rules apply; it is unrealistic to expect someone subsisting at the margins of the urban or rural economy, or who is unemployed, to support wildlife and wilderness preservation if she or he has no access to or cannot utilize these resources. Similarly, she or he won't support plant closings if there is no other means of economic survival.

Another way in which the new grassroots movement, or "movement for environmental justice," as CCHW calls it,[41] are helping to redefine the environmental movement, has to do with the question of diversity. Here again we find the more established environmentalists practicing double standards. The same groups and organizations which preach biological diversity in nature, and which spend small fortunes to achieve this end, practice their craft in very homogeneous racial, cultural, and social settings. It is crystal clear that diversity in nature is superior to homogeneity; why isn't it obvious to the people advocating this position that such diversity is also desirable in human communities? Why isn't it understood that human diversity is necessary for this movement to grow and progress?

Some of the previous analysis helps us to answer these questions, or to see that even if environmentalists do realize that a diverse human community would make a more progressive environmental movement, they might be unwilling to diversify the staff and membership of the more established groups. As discussed earlier, the Romantic and Transcendental themes are powerful notions which serve to attract and maintain members. The membership of a particular group is bound by a commitment to similar metaphysical ideas as they relate to human-nature interactions, conservation, preservation, and outdoor, escapist experiences. Homosocial reproduction facilitates and perpetuates the commitment to similar metaphysics since members are recruited from similar backgrounds, education, socio-economic status, experiences, outlook, and commitments to causes. In such groups, there is a greater consensus on what the goals, structure, operation, and programming, and so forth, of the organization or group should be like, much more so than if the membership was derived by building coalitions across racial and class lines. To diversify such homogeneous groups or organizations, one would have to radically restructure the agenda, change hiring practices and staff assignments, redistribute resources, and redistribute the costs and benefits of environmental policies to accommodate the goals, interests, and metaphysical commitments brought to the table by various groups. These are costs that most environmental organizations seem unwilling to bear.

Some minorities are distrustful of many environmental groups, and doubt if such groups can or will resolve issues in favor of the former. They point to the fact that when many middle class neighborhoods or environmental groups say "not in my back yard," "not in my park," "don't block my view," "don't pollute my air"; then the waste dumps, smoke stacks, processing plants, factories, highways, and other pariahs end up on the front porches of the poor and the powerless. Many in the field, including researchers like Morrison and Dunlap (1986) who argue that the environmental movement is not elitist, have conceded that many environmental struggles have regressive impacts, i.e., the poor disproportionately bear the brunt of pollution and toxic contamination.[42]

Movement for Environmental Justice—The New Grassroots

What options do minorities have if they are faced with the choice of becoming more active in environmental issues? They could (A) join an existing environmental group, (B) form their own environmental groups and try to fight the issues on their own, or (C) form their own environmental groups but establish contacts with other groups to get expertise, advice, technical and financial assistance, and moral support. For reasons discussed above and elsewhere,[43] option A is not very viable. Groups that try option B quickly find that they need help from others who have done it before (be it another environmental group or another social movement group that knows the ropes), so option C in which the group tries to build a coalition or support network seems to work best for new groups.

In 1985, the Urban Environment Conference, an alliance of labor, minorities, and environmental organizations concerned with improving the environment and occupational health of minorities and working people, identified dozens of groups and organizations which participated in an "institute" dedicated to this cause.[44] The growth in the number of minority environmental groups and organizations dealing with minority communities can also be seen in the 1988 American Land Resource Association Survey where four hundred such organizations and groups were identified nationwide.

Today, clearinghouses like the National Toxics Campaign in Boston, and the Citizens Clearinghouse for Hazardous Wastes based in Arlington, Virginia, serve about 1300 and about 2000 citizens action groups, respectively. Both organizations work with numerous minority groups, most of which are based in the rural south; for CCHW, rural grassroots groups make up a big portion of its contacts. These clearinghouses provide direct aid and movement-building help like technical advice and analyses, legal services, research support, funding, organizing strategies, conferences, and workshops.[45]

What makes these new grassroots groups more appealing to minorities? Why don't minorities join incremental reformist groups or other radical reformist groups like the eco-activists, deep-ecologists, green parties, or anti-nuclear groups? The most obvious answers are:

1. These new grassroots organizations are fighting issues that are pertinent to poor communities—issues from which they will derive immediate and long term benefits;

2. In these newer groups, minorities and the poor can associate with others like themselves—instead of joining a group where there would be few or no other minority persons, these new coalitions offer the opportunity for single minority groups or coalitions to work together for a common cause;[46]

3. Even in the case where whites and other minorities join to fight an issue, minorities share and collaborate with whites, they don't expect to follow the directives of white leaders passively;

4. In many instances, the minority groups run the entire struggle with some, little, or no help from whites—something they couldn't do in more established environmental organizations under the existing structure;

5. Because of the high levels of involvement, minorities can attain in these groups through organizing themselves, and running, coordinating, or collaborating with others on campaigns, they become empowered—much more so than if they were just to send in a check for a few dollars to fight an issue, or to sign a pre-drafted letter to a Congressperson; and

6. Minorities can, through these groups, set, participate in, or define a new environmental agenda in which they have a real voice. Prior to the emergence of these new groups, the environmental agenda was set without

any consultation with these dispossesed groups. Just as in other areas of life where these groups are demanding that their voices be heard and their needs be taken into account, similar demands are now being made of the environmental movement.

To understand why these benefits can accrue in the new grassroots movements and not in the more established organizations, we will examine how the structure, composition, and ideology of these new organizations differ from the pre-existing ones. These new grassroots have similar structure, size, and employ similar activist strategies as the other radical reformist groups discussed earlier. However, they differ from the other radical reformists in the heterogeneity of racial and ethnic groups they attract, the broad class base of the membership, the relevance of the issues they tackle to minority and poor populations, and their reliance on certain kinds of metaphysical ideas to attract and maintain members.

The new grassroots groups are often formed by people with little or no prior experience of organizing or waging a campaign, or with no previously expressed interest in environmental issues. The coalitions are often working class, and many of the participants have had little or no history of participating in civic affairs. Many of these protest groups are spearheaded by women; often mothers who want to fight issues relating to the health of their families and the viability of their neighborhoods. There is often a strong coalition with labor and other occupational health and safety groups.

These coalitions and grassroots groups are emerging out of the inner city and the poor rural areas. Their campaigns, at the start, are issue specific—usually a "stop the…" campaign. They usually lack funding, the power of large numbers of supporters, experience in utilizing effective tactics, and the technical and lobbying expertise characteristic of more established groups. Their campaigns are highly visible; utilizing demonstrations, pickets, petitions, and obstructions.

They are very distrustful of the system or anyone deemed to be a part of it (even other environmentalists), and their protests are not designed to negotiate. They believe that they have been forced into this non-compromising position because, in the past, others have handled the negotiations, and they end up living with and paying the costs on a daily basis.

Through the process of waging a campaign, many of the people in these groups are exposed to others in neighboring areas with similar problems or other issues that they might choose to support. As time goes on, groups that start out with the express purpose of fighting an issue, broaden their scope and take on other issues that impact their membership (or others in a similar position) directly or indirectly. This is not always the case, however, as some of these groups, after getting involved in a campaign, disband either before the issue is resolved or right after (especially if they lose the campaign). This happens for any number of reasons: lack of resources, human capital, consensus on issues to fight in the future; differences in ideology, long term goals, and direction; or lack of time and commitment.

However, in the long term, these new grassroots groups will be able to attract and maintain the support of minorities and the poor because their structure allows for much flexibility. That is, if a potential member cannot afford the money required for membership fees or donations, then she or he can contribute time, or other non-monetary resources like phone lines, space to store materials, food, room and board for visiting organizers and supporters, and other supplies. Recruiting is not done from national mailing lists; people can, on the spur of the moment, recruit friends, families, or co-workers to participate. The commitment can be short-term, long-term, or intermittent, as time and personal resources allow.

People get to build support, friendship, camaraderie, goodwill, and fellowship with people they already know. If they have to form a coalition with others, it is not one person going cold turkey to deal with a group of unfamiliar people; it is a group of people who have already established some relationships with others whose interests might be similar, interfacing with another group.

Local issues are harder for residents in the community to ignore, so people in the group have a stronger calling card when recruiting members or support for the cause. Many people who belong to these groups have strong church or community group affiliations, therefore, the support network that such institutions offer can be quite useful. With such strong community-based ties, it is easier to utilize the bloc recruiting strategies employed in the civil rights movement,[47] whereby activists recruit in mass people of similar beliefs and affiliations who have a past history of interaction.

When minorities see other minorities initiating, organizing, and running a campaign with little or no help from others (the demonstration effect), they are more likely to join such movements than if help and directives are parachuted in from above. Minorities need to believe that they can wage such campaigns[48] before they are likely to join any group in large numbers and lend long-term support. Such opportunities are not yet possible in the more established environmental organizations. However, now that more and more campaigns have emerged with minority leaders, or with coalitions of minorities, poor, and others, the chances are good that minority participation in environmental groups will continue to increase.

This brings us back to the question of why minorities join the new grassroots groups and not other types of environmental groups, particularly the other radical reformist groups or the new environmentalists. As mentioned before, other radical reformist groups, on the one hand, share some characteristics (metaphysical calling) which are similar to that of the more traditional groups and organizations, and on the other hand, share structural and activist strategies with the new grassroots.

But these radical reformist groups have some characteristics which make them unattractive to minorities. Because they rely so heavily on strong personal commitments to a cause, they also rely on a strong metaphysical understanding, and similar interpretation and priority given to the cause, by all of its members. Consequently, these groups are not necessarily formed by building coalitions across racial and class lines, or by working with various interest groups and factions within a city or a community. Instead, they are formed by self-selected individuals who think like the existing group, who believe in the same goals, process, outcome, and ways of achieving certain ends, and thus they perpetuate another kind of homosocial reproduction.

The net result of this is a very homogeneous group—racially, class-wise, and ideologically—functioning on the metaphysics of perceiving an ill, or a threat to a Transcendental, Romantic experience, trying to stop it for present or future generations. Although these groups are formed out of a belief that their voices were being excluded from the environmental debate, they effectively exclude many from participating in their groups.

Most of the environmental organizations which are being formed in the fourth stage of the movement, represent a further break with the strong conservationist, and technical thrust of the more established organizations. These new grassroots groups perceive the established organizations as being alienated and estranged from their membership, and irresponsible to the needs of local communities. Their tactics are deemed ineffective in solving many of the environmental problems of the Eighties and Nineties.

The movement for environmental justice focuses on themes of fairness, justice, distribution of environmental impacts, and sharing the costs of environmental impacts. These themes are being used to mobilize community-wide coalitions built across race, ethnic, and class lines, and between interest groups and factions. They don't or can't rely on heavy personal commitments, as this could alienate much of the potential membership. Such commitments can be sought in later phases of the organizational or group development. These movements strive for true grassroots representation. The other radical reformist groups employ grassroots activist tactics, but they do not represent a true grassroots—at least not in the sense that the new grassroots tries to do.

Fairness and justice are issues that all can agree on as ones which are important in building a desirable society.[49] Therefore, they are ideas around which one can build broad coalitions. The radical reformists could be operating with these themes, also, but they don't use them as the primary means by which they build support for their groups or organizations. This is not to say that people in the movement for environmental justice do not or cannot operate on strong metaphysical calling to environmental struggles. They can, but these are not the criteria relied on to bring people into the movement, or keep them there. With such racial, ethnic and class diversity, it would be difficult, if not impossible for all to agree on a metaphysical calling strong enough to sustain the fervor needed for movement or group viability.

So instead of invoking the Romantic and Transcendental ideals to encourage people to join, the movement for environmental justice tends to focus on the more general, and widely accepted principles of justice and fairness. It tries to empower people to have a chance at these ideals. Such issues are easily placed at the top of the priority list of most people, so mobilization becomes a lot easier.

The activism of the new grassroots fits the McCarthy-Zald model of the entrepreneurial theory of resource mobilization wherein entrepreneurs representing deprived groups and disorganized collectives redefine long-standing (environmental) grievances in new terms. Changes in organizational style, level and type of resources, and the opportunities open to groups, give rise to movement formation, because such formations are linked to improvements in the status of aggrieved groups and improved likelihood of success. [50]

There are still many obstacles to increasing and maintaining membership support in the new grassroots groups and organizations. As mentioned before, some of these coalitions are formed to fight an issue, fizzle out and die before or after that campaign is complete. Such groups have to find a way to get members interested in issues beyond that which they are fighting in the short term. This is where contact with other more established environmental or other social movement groups can help (with education, exposure, contacts, strategies, identifying funding sources, and so forth).

The Relationship Between Minorities
and Established Environmental Organizations

A recent survey of minority organizations[51] dealing with natural resource issues, found water quality/ground water contamination, pesticides, sewage treatment, soil erosion, solid waste management, toxic waste disposal, and fisheries (for western Native Americans) were perceived as the most pressing issues affecting minority communities.[52] These concerns affected the communities in the following ways: through health, employment opportunities, environmental quality, land ownership, and agricultural practices. For Native American respondents, treaty rights, tribal revenues, overall tribal viability, and economic development, were pressing issues. When asked to identify reasons why minority groups do not work more closely with national environmental groups, the following reasons were cited most often: financial constraints, minority resource issues are local, there is no contact with national groups, shortage of people, and time constraints.

Minority organizations indicated that it would be easier to work with national groups if the national groups:

1. provided minority groups with more information about their activities;
2. worked on resource issues that were of concern to minority groups;
3. became more active in regional and local issues;
4. had minority representatives;
5. made greater outreach efforts to minority communities;

6. joined with minorities in coalitions;[53]
7. provided funding to minority groups;
8. were committed to treaty rights, and recognized tribal governments;
9. helped to cover the costs of travel to meetings, seminars, etc.;
10. accepted collect phone calls from local groups;
11. helped to develop solutions to local natural resource issues;
12. covered minority resource issues, campaigns, and problems in their publications;
13. helped to develop natural resource management plans; and
14. provided employment opportunities for minorities and the poor in their organizations.

Minority resource groups think they can be of help to national organizations by providing national groups with new information about local activities, making the national groups more aware of concerns that are common between both the minority and national groups, and by joining with them to create new coalitions.

A second part of this survey asked national environmental organizations to identify ways in which their interaction with minority resource groups could be enhanced. They expressed an interest in:

1. working with minorities in the field;
2. corresponding with minorities;
3. working on lobbying efforts with minorities;
4. helping with funding;
5. helping with educational materials;
6. providing technical assistance;
7. publicizing minority concerns;
8. providing training in resource management; and
9. helping with organizing.

National groups thought that minority groups could make themselves more accessible through newsletters, regular meetings with the staff of national groups, and by identifying a local representative with whom national staff can stay in contact.

From the preceding discussion, it would seem that the environment is fertile for a long and fruitful relationship between minority groups and national resource organizations. From the American Land Resource Association Survey, in many of the areas in which minorities needed help, the more established organizations said they were willing to help. What is preventing closer interaction? One key to understanding the blockage or low levels of interaction is the fact that within the minority organizations, there is a strong perception (and one that is not entirely false) that national groups have not helped minority groups in the past.[54] Also, the majority of the national environmental groups claimed that a minority group never asked them for help.[55] It is clear from the Conservation Leadership Survey discussed earlier that environmental organizations are not spending their resources in areas that are likely to have direct and immediate benefits in minority and poor areas. There are big differences between what the more established environmental organizations say they would like to do, what they actually do, and what they are capable of doing.

There is a feeling within minority communities that if they are going to get the issues pertinent to them on the agenda, they either have to wage those fights themselves or within the framework of the newer grassroots coalitions. They believe that if the more established, national environmental groups want people to really believe that they are committed to minority issues and issues related to the poor, then those organizations have to restructure themselves radically before large investments of time, human resources, and money are put into forming closer bonds.

In a recent round table discussion of minority leaders in the environmental field, the view was expressed that there have to be reforms within established environmental organizations if such organizations are going to attract any measure of minority support. If these organizations continue to express the desire to work with minorities, then this working relationship can be enhanced only if the following changes occur:

1. Minorities should have a real chance of making substantial changes in the environmental agenda of these organizations.
2. The possibility that such changes can materialize will be increased if greater numbers of minorities are hired in middle and upper level management positions. Currently the few minorities that are hired to fill the secretarial and janitorial pools of these organizations cannot make the kinds of changes necessary to restructure these organizations.
3. Minorities should not be offered job opportunities with blocked career paths. If there is no real opportunity to get to the top levels of the organization, then nothing has changed, or will change.
4. Minorities should sit on the boards of these organizations.
5. One minority individual or a few strategically-placed minorities will not satisfy these criteria. There is a need for minorities to lead program development, lobbying, funding, and research staffs, etc.
6. Resources should be earmarked for education and training which includes everyone from grammar schools to college students and grassroots community workers with little or no schooling. In addition to education and training, provisions should be made for employment opportunities.
7. Paid internships should be offered to minorities who cannot afford the high costs of volunteering (especially in the nation's capitol). The few internship slots that some organizations now have are woefully inadequate to meet the needs of this community.

8. Mentoring programs should be established so that interns can acquire useful skills, and gain an understanding of the issues; if interns are used as "gofers," that is not particularly helpful for them.

9. There are minority students already in the university system who are well qualified to work in the environmental field, but they are burdened with debt. If environmental organizations are serious about hiring those students, then they should institute a loan pardon program (tied to a number of years of service in the field) to facilitate the entry of those students into the field.

10. Scholarships (tuition, room, board, stipends) should be offered to help train future minority environmentalists.

11. Summer employment should be offered to interested people, and job offers should be made, either after graduation, or after a person has acquired certain skills.

12. Environmental organizations often say that they have no minorities on staff because there are none in this field, or they can't find them. If resources are earmarked for recruiting, then such organizations will be in a position to identify minorities who could work in this field.

13. Environmental organizations should fight local issues in minority communities in a way that will benefit these communities.

Many of the minority leaders at the round table expressed the concern that some environmental organizations had already siphoned off some of the best minority prospects, and that this could divert valuable human resources away from campaigns that could be of more benefit to minorities. They did not believe that the more established organizations were about to change in the ways suggested above any time soon. Instead, minorities would be better off networking amongst themselves; developing a minority environmental agenda and political-action platform, forming coalitions where necessary, concentrating on furthering minority environmental interests.

This raises an interesting question which is beyond the scope of this paper but should be addressed in the future: "Should minority environmental professionals and academics put their efforts into large established environmental organizations with the hope of effecting some change in the system (to make them more responsive to minority needs), or should they put their efforts into working with smaller, minority-oriented groups in an effort to help make changes at the local and community level?"

Where Do We Go from Here?

Does that mean that we will have two parallel movements: a middle class, mostly white environmental movement with a conservation-preservation thrust, and heterogeneous class and racial coalitions for environmental justice? The widening gap between the agendas of the new grassroots and that of the more established environmental organizations is due in part to the institutionalization of environmental issues. That institutionalization occurs in four ways: (1) in expertise; (2) in the establishment of a complex bureaucracy; (3) in the adoption of a corporate structure; and (4) in the adoption of corporate modes of action.[57]

Unless there is some flexibility on both sides, we will continue to see this trend. Unless the more established organizations are willing to share power, broaden the scope of their agenda and re-prioritize issues, include minorities in decision-making, share some of the impacts caused by environmental regulations or actions, offer opportunities to advance in their organizations, and be more sensitive to minority issues, then very little discussion will take place between both groups. On the other hand, minorities have to learn that not all established environmental groups are cut from the same cloth. Some, more than others, are sensitive to minority issues and are quite capable and willing to work with minorities. Minorities, therefore, have to identify such groups and develop contacts with them.

A growing, vibrant movement should be able to combine scientific and technological know-how with organizational, lobbying, educational, and fund-raising expertise, and with the spirit of humans ready to rally for a cause, to build a healthy movement. From the preceding discussion, all sides could learn and benefit from some of the characteristics that the others have. One organization doesn't have to dominate another, nor do all organizations have to be carbon copies of each other, but they can certainly put more effort into helping each other attain certain goals.

Notes

1.   The criticism of homogeneity and elitism does not necessarily apply to the new grassroots (movement for environmental justice), which is discussed in a later section of the paper.

2.   See Taylor, 1989: 175-205; Morrison and Dunlap, 1986: 581-589; Cotgrove, 1982; Coombs, 1972: 35-39; Devall, 1970: 123-126; Harry, Gale, and Hendee, 1969: 246-254; Mohai, 1985: 820-838; Sills, 1975: 1-41; Taylor, 1984: 51-52; Van Liere and Dunlap, 1980: 181-197; Buttel and Flinn, 1974; Cotgrove and Duff, 1980: 333-351.

3.   Because blacks and other minorities are not found in the established sectors of the movement in large numbers, the assumption is that they are not concerned with environmental issues and so, exhibit low levels of participation in the environmental movement. Research has shown that these groups are concerned about the environment, but that problems arise when that concern has to be converted into environmental action. See Taylor, 1989: 175-205; Lowe and Pinhey, 1982: 114-128; Lowe, Pinhey and Grimes, 1980: 423-445; Mitchell, 1979a: 16-20;

Buttel and Flinn, 1974: 56-69; 1978: 443-450; Buttel, 1987: 465-488; Van Liere and Dunlap, 1980: 181-197; Van Ardsol, et al., 1965: 144-153; Mohai, 1985: 820-838.

4.   See the Conservation Leadership Project's "Conservation Staff Survey," 1989. Statistics by Joe Floyd.

5.   Respondents were not asked if they thought there was actually anything in the "conservation message" for minorities and the poor; and they were not asked why they thought minorities and the poor saw "little" in the message for them.

6.   The survey asked about the "conservation movement," instead of the "environmental movement."

7.   Romanticism refers to an enthusiasm for the strange, the remote, the solitary, and the mysterious. In nature, Romantics prefer the wild, so wilderness areas hold special appeal because one can escape from civilization. Primitivism is an aspect of Romanticism, in which people believe that a person's happiness and well-being is decreased in more civilized settings. See: Lovejoy, 1955: 228-253; 1941: 257-278; Nash, 1982; Fairchild, 1931; Curti, 1951: 238-242; Lovejoy and Boas, 1935: 1-22; Boas, 1948: 1-14; Whitney, 1934: 7-68.

8.   Transcendentalism refers to the complex of attitudes linking humans, nature, and God. Transcendentalists believe in the existence of a reality higher than the physical, and that there is a correspondence or parallelism between the higher realm of spiritual truth and the lower one of material objects. Natural objects are important, therefore, because they reflect universal, spiritual truths. People's place in the universe is conceived to be divided between object and essence; by their physical existence, people are rooted to the material, but their soul gives them the power to transcend this condition (Nash, 1982).

9.   Henry David Thoreau was the leading spokesperson of the time. Paehlke, 1989: 14-22; Nash, 1982; Fox, 1985. For other histories see: Devall and Sessions, 1985; Pepper, 1986; Fleming, 1972.

10.   Arkansas Hot Springs was designated a national reserve in 1832, Yosemite Valley a public park in 1864, a national park bill was considered in 1871 by the Congress, and the two-million-acre Yellowstone National Park was designated in 1872 (Nash, 1982; Hays, 1959).

11.   Homestead Act of 1862 (repealed in 1976); General Mining Act of 1872; Timber Culture Acts, 1873 (repealed in 1982); Desert Land Act of 1877.

The federal government was also involved in the removal of native peoples from exploitable land and the annexation of territories (Hays, 1959).

12.   George Perkins Marsh, John Muir, and Aldo Leopold were among the first to make this adjustment by stressing the importance of understanding the link between natural resource use and long-term, adverse environmental impacts. Marsh (1801-1882) has been credited with coining the term "ecology" which he defined as the "study of the interrelationships between organisms and environment" (Russell, 1968: 3-5).

13.   The movement, today, is still supported by people who are primarily from

the upper and middle classes. Paehlke, 1989: 14-22; Fox, 1985: 103-217; Devall, 1970: 123-126; Mohai, 1985: 820-838; Taylor, 1989: 175-205; Harry, Gale, and Hendee, 1969: 246-254; Buttel and Flinn, 1974: 56-69; Hendee, Catton, Marlow, and Brockman, 1968; Faich and Gale, 1971: 270-287; Morrison, Hornback, and Warner, 1972: 259-279; Lowe, et al., 1980: 423-445.

14. During the 1890s, federal legislation, such as the 1897 Forest Management Act was enacted. Also, between 1901 and 1907, over 15 million acres of land were set aside for national parks, forests, and wildlife sanctuaries (Nash, 1982; Fleming, 1972; Hays, 1959).

15. Facing chronic water shortages, as early as 1882 San Francisco's city engineers recognized the possibility of damming the Tuolumne River at the end of the Hetch Hetchy Valley. In 1880, the act creating Yosemite National Park, designated Hetch Hetchy a wilderness preserve, making it more difficult for the city to get the plan approved. In the first two decades of the 1900s, while San Francisco sought to develop the valley for water supply and hydro-electricity, conservationists, preservationists, and the Congress fought a pitched battle over the future of Hetch Hetchy. Finally in December, 1913, the city was granted permission to develop the valley. See Nash, 1982: 161-181 for more details.

16. This shift came at a time when the movement was experiencing increased growth. Although the environmentalists had lost the Hetch Hetchy battle, they had succeeded in bringing the plight of wilderness preservation to the attention of the public. There was a massive public outcry, and many decided to be a part of the movement. Environmentalists also learned to lobby Congress, use letter writing campaigns, and the media as means of getting public support for their cause. At this time also, wildlife was in a state of decline, and since many of the outdoor clubs were primarily hunting, fishing, and bird watching clubs, the membership was ready and willing to extend its activism to wildlife protection.

17. Fox, 1985: 103-217.

18. "Silent Spring" first appeared in *The New Yorker* in 1960 and was later published as a book in 1962 and 1970.

19. Paehlke, 1989: 14-22.

20. As the politics of the Civil Rights Movement changed, and there was less of a role for young white student activists in the emerging Black Nationalist Movement, many turned to the environmental movement (Gale, 1972: 280-305).

21. Most of the former anti-war activists concentrated their efforts on fighting nuclear energy.

22. For example, the Wilderness Act of 1964; the National Environmental Policy Act of 1969; the Clean Air Act of 1970; the Federal Water Pollution Control Act of 1972; the Resource Conservation and Recovery Act of 1976; the Federal Pesticide Act of 1978; the Noise Control Act of 1972; the Endangered Species Act of 1973; and the Toxic Substances Control Act of 1976.

23. Weber utilized this methodological approach to allow him to consider

extreme and "pure" cases in detail—variations fell in between the extremes. See Gerth and Mills, 1946: 45-74, 267-301, 323-330.

24. See Douglas and Wildavsky, 1983.

25. Groups can use two types of incentives to attract members: instrumental—public goods which are obtained by the group for the benefit of members and non-members alike; and expressive—personal benefits exclusively reserved for group members (Dennis and Zube, 1988: 229-245; Gordon and Babchuk, 1959: 22-29; Jacoby and Babchuk, 1963: 461-471).

Mancur Olson, in his 1965 book, *Logic of Collective Action*, argues that selective (expressive) incentives provide the inducements necessary to entice individuals to join groups. See also Dennis and Zube, 1988: 229-245; Clark and Wilson, 1961: 129-166; Salisbury, 1969: 1-32; Truman, 1971; Wilson, 1973; McFarland, 1976; Berry, 1977; Mitchell, 1979b: 87-121; Moe, 1980; Goodwin and Mitchell, 1982: 161-181.

26. Such theories cite economic constraints, marginality, alienation, societal stage of development, and relative deprivation as reasons for low levels of concern. See Taylor, 1989: 175-205; Commoner, 1971: 207-208; Meeker, Woods, and Lucas, 1973; Mohai, 1985: 820-838; Van Ardsol, Sabagh, and Alexander, 1965: 144-153; Van Liere and Dunlap, 1980; Mueller and Gurin, 1962; Kreger, 1973; Frazier, 1957; Drake and Clayton, 1945; Maslow, 1954: 63-154; Morrison, et al., 1972: 259-279; Hershey and Hill, 1977-78: 439-458.

27. See Olson, 1965; Walsh and Warland, 1983.

28. Taylor, 1989: 175-205.

29. Eisenger, 1972: 123; Sharp, 1980: 362-376: Orum, 1974; Smith, et al., 1980.

30. McCarthy and Zald, 1973: 1212-1241; Walsh and Warland, 1983: 764-780.

31. Walsh and Warland, 1983: 764-780; Mohai, 1985: 820-838.

32. Tilly, 1978: 62-63; Jenkins, 1983: 527-553.

33. Stephen Lester of CCHW; Michael Stein of the National Toxics Campaign; Suro, 1989: 18; Collette, 1987: 44-45.

34. Dick Russell, 1989: 22-32. See also Hall, 1988; and Labalme, 1987.

35. Taylor, 1989: 175-205; Hershey and Hill, 1977-78: 439-458; Van Ardsol, et al., 1965: 144-153; Kreger, 1973: 30-34; Maslow, 1954: 63-154.

36. Taylor, 1989: 175-205; Hershey and Hill, 1977-78: 439-458; Kreger, 1973: 30-34; Van Ardsol, et al., 1965: 144-153.

37. Sharp, 1980: 362-276; Eisenger, 1972: 123; Verba and Nie, 1972; Taylor, 1989: 175-205; Mohai, 1985: 820-838; Walsh and Warland, 1983: 764-780; Orum, 1974; McCarthy and Zald, 1973: 1212-1241.

38. See the Conservation Leadership Project "Conservation Staff Survey," 1989. Statistics conducted by Joe Floyd.

Of the 248 respondents, 72.8 percent were C.E.O.s or Executive V.P.s or V.P.s; 17.9 percent were Program and Regional Directors; 1.6 percent were Chairpersons 2.4 percent were Administrative Assistants; and 5.3 percent "other."

39. True, there are some environmental groups that got involved in international issues in Ethiopia and Sudan which involved massive starvation and population displacement, but these groups overlook similar problems in America's inner cities and rural hinterlands.

Friends of the Earth is beginning to become involved in housing and jobs issues for poor and low-income communities.

40. That is, survival as it relates to access to and availability of resources; control and use of resources; a say in how resources are used, managed, and distributed; and a balance between utility and conservation.

41. Citizens Clearinghouse for Hazardous Wastes, 1989.

42. See Bullard, 1983; 1988, for case studies of black communities trying to fight the practice of placing waste dumps in their neighborhoods. See also, Russell, 1989: 22-32; Commission for Racial Justice, 1987; Pollack, Grozuczak, and Taylor, 1984; Silver, 1984: 36-37; U.S. General Accounting Office, 1983; Zwerdling, 1973.

43. Taylor, 1989: 175-205.

44. See the Urban Environment Conference's 1985 resource book, *Taking Back Our Health, An Institute on Surviving the Toxics Threat to Minority Communities, and Environmental Cancer, Causes, Victims, Solutions.*

45. Five Years of Progress 1981-6, CCHW history (1986); NTC's Toxic Times; Hall, 1989; Collette, 1987: 44-45.

46. See Faich and Gale, 1971: 270-287 for research that shows that members of environmental groups join for fellowship with others like themselves, recreational opportunities, and representation on issues.

47. See Adolph Reed, Jr.'s, *The Jessie Jackson Phenomenon*, 1986: 41-60.

48. Mohai, 1985: 820-838; Taylor, 1989: 175-205.

49. Rawls, 1985: 50-83.

50. McCarthy and Zald, 1973: 1212-1241; Jenkins, 1983: 527-553.

51. Conducted by the American Land Resource Association and the Natural Resources Council of America, January 1988.

52. Respondents were given a list of fifteen issues from which they chose ones most affecting their communities. The actual issues chosen and the priorities given to each might have been different if the list had been respondent-generated.

53. When asked if they were aware of any instance where a national natural resource organization had successfully worked with any minority resource organization, 69.8 percent of the respondents said "No." The report does list some cases where this has occurred.

54. For example, CCHW history, *Five Years of Progress 1981-86*, documents how new grassroots groups have sought help from more established environmental organizations with no success.

Black activists in the anti-LANCER (an incinerator proposed for a South Central Los Angeles neighborhood) found no help forthcoming from established environmental groups when they first tried to organize their campaign. Greenpeace later helped.

55. The survey did not ask the minority organizations if they were ever approached by national groups which wanted to offer their help.

56. The Conservation Leadership Project, Seattle, Washington, August 1989.

57. Fitzsimmons and Gottlieb, 1988: 114-130.

4

The Environmental Voting Record
of the Congressional Black Caucus

Henry Vance Davis

The League of Conservation Voters is a national, non-partisan committee formed in 1970 to help elect conservation-minded candidates to office. The League supports candidates based upon their environmental voting record. It has been called the political arm of the American environmental movement. The League's board includes leaders from major national and state environmental organizations: the Environmental Policy Institute, the Natural Resources Defense Council, the Sierra Club, and the National Parks and Conservation Association are among them. In addition to the cash campaign contributions it gives, the League does extensive field organization in key races. It is an aggressive organization that has pledged to "replace senators and representatives who are placing short-term economic considerations ahead of the agenda; we need to preserve a healthy and livable world" (Blackwelder, 1988).

The "Message from the Chairman" in the 1987-88 issue of the *Scorecard* describes the *Scorecard* as offering "a clear picture of which members of Congress are choosing to protect our natural heritage and which ones are postponing what will be even more painful decisions for future generations." Brent Blackwelder, Chairman of the Board, continued:

> In the last year we have just begun to see how immediately and dramatically environmental pollution is changing the world we live in. The greenhouse effect could cause long term drought and climate change. Ozone depletion is increasing skin cancer by permitting ultra-violet radiation to reach the earth. These and other developments are reversible only through strong action in the very near future. Leaders who are willing to postpone difficult environmental decisions today may leave us with a world that will be difficult to live in tomorrow.
>
> In the next few years, the League will be redoubling its efforts to elect

Henry Vance Davis has a Ph.D. in History, specializing in the history of African Americans. He is presently an Assistant Professor of History at Western Michigan University. His research interests include African American newspapers, African American student protests, and African Americans and the environment.

members of Congress who are ready to meet the environmental challenge of this new and changing world (Blackwelder, 1988: ii).

Scoring

In the *Scorecard,* the League tabulated votes on a broad range of environmental bills and issues which were deemed to be the most important by the Board of Directors of the League of Conservation Voters. In addition to votes cast on the House and Senate floor, the scores included co-sponsorships of bills and co-signatures of letters on major environmental issues. For example, in 1986-87 the League used 16 bills on which to score Congresspersons. The bills covered issues pertaining to the Clean Water Act, the Clean Air Act, energy conservation, various nuclear questions, the Endangered Species Act, and acid rain.

Pro-environmental votes were designated with a plus sign (+), while anti-environmental votes were denoted with a minus sign (-). Members who were ineligible to vote at the time the vote was taken were assigned an (I), and these were not computed into the percentages. The percentages computed are based on the number of pro-environment votes versus the total number of votes cast.

Conservation History Overview

Conservation history has at least three stages (Bailes, 1985; Nicholson, 1987; Nash, 1989; Udall, 1988). The fear of using up the resources of the earth (scarcity) was the first rallying point for conservation-minded individuals. Next, there was concern that humans would make the resources unusable before they could be consumed (pollution). Thirdly, the most current concern is that humans are making large sections of the earth dangerous to life as we know it because of the disposal of the by-products of our "progress" (hazardous waste).

The *Scorecard* primarily deals with the first two stages of conservation history. It has only been in the last ten years of the twentieth century that we have been coming to grips with the ramifications of the fact that we know little about the disposal of the by-products of human "progress"; consequently, we are just beginning to question the role our elected officials play in this new arena, for the hazardous waste stage is, comparatively, still in its infancy.

Unlike hazardous waste concerns, concern with conservation has a long history (Schrepfer, 1983; Robbins, 1982; Petulla; 1977). Paul B. Sear's *Deserts on the March*; William Vogt's *Road to Survival*; Fairfield Osborn's *Limits of the Earth*; and Rachel Carson's *Silent Spring* are a few of the works that followed in the tradition begun by George Perkins Marsh. Marsh published *Man and Nature: or Physical Geography as Modified by Human Action* in 1864. He sounded the alarm that early conservationists would repeat time and again.

> Man has too long forgotten that the earth was given to him for usufruct alone, not for consumption, still less for profligate waste. Nature has provided against the absolute destruction of any of the elementary material of her works, the thunderbolt and the tornado, the most convulsive throes of even the volcano and earthquake being only the phenomena of decomposition and recomposition. But she has left it within the power of man irreparably to derange the combinations of inorganic matter and of organic life, which through the night of aeons she had been proportioning and balancing to prepare the earth for his habitation, when in the fullness of time, his Creator should call him forth to enter into its possession (Marsh, 1864).

The term "conservation movement" has been attributed to Gifford Pinchot, a Forest Service administrator and politician. In 1908, he called together governors, Supreme Court Justices, members of Congress, representatives of a number of national societies, and others to address the conservation of forests, minerals, soils, and water.

Even at this early stage, the balance between economic concerns and environmental exploitation was a central concern. By 1954, when *Brown vs. Board of Education* was fueling the civil rights movement in America, the conservation movement, due in large part to economic concerns, was under heavy attack.

> Consider what the situation was in 1954. The drive for the Upper Colorado Storage Project was in high gear, and the fate of Dinosaur National Monument and with it the sanctity of the entire National Park System was all but sealed. Conservation representatives were valiantly testifying before hostile senators from Utah and other Rocky Mountain states. Senator Watkins, for example, attempted with all the advantages of his official position to break the dignity and courage of David Brower, who was dramatically demonstrating the technical possibility of an alternative plan that would leave Echo Park untouched. One of the facts that Senator Watkins extracted was that the Sierra Club was an organization of a mere eight thousand members. In the Northwest, the Olympic Park had just been subjected to another of its periodic attacks. And in the Northwest, also just a year later, it became apparent that the North Cascades were marked for the sort of "intensive management" by the Forest Service that could only spell destruction of their unique values of wilderness and beauty. A handful of people met in a living room in Auburn, Washington, to discuss the problem; it was a very glum occasion (McConnell, 1970: 4).

Contrary to the picture of 1954, the movement did not die; it prospered. By the 1960s, unparalleled gains were made under John F. Kennedy and Lyndon B. Johnson. Among important conservation legislation passed then were the Land and Water Conservation Fund Act, the Wilderness Act, the Federal Water Project

Recreation Act, far-reaching fish and wildlife conservation measures, and the creation of the Redwood and North Cascades National Parks. A significant victory was won when President Johnson recommended immediate establishment of Redwood National Park.

By the 1960s, however, conservationists had become concerned that using up the earth's resources was less of a problem than those same resources becoming unusable. A new warning was sounded by environmentalists. Pollution became the concern.

> [L]andscapes scarred by freeways and open pit mines, urban and rural blight, deterioration of fish and wildlife populations, and a myriad other affronts to the quality of life.
>
> This man-made pollution is bad enough in itself, but it reflects something even worse: a dangerous illusion that technological man can build bigger and better industrial societies with little regard for the long-term cumulative impact of his actions upon the natural environment (Cooley, 1970).

However, the installation of the Nixon presidency saw the conservation movement stall.

> There is some indication that the close of the Ninetieth Congress late in 1968 may mark the end of this remarkable period in the history of conservation politics in the United States. Some members of Congress, as well as of the new Republican administration, have suggested that we are reaching the end of a long wave of significant and highly visible progress, and that the widely hailed "environmental crisis" has, in a certain sense, passed the peak of critical national interest and public concern (Cooley, 1970).

More recently, Ronald Reagan's era has been viewed as a setback to conservationists (Short, 1989). The current conditions of the environment justify concern. The Environmental Protection Agency, often taken to task for inaction, recently estimated that industry is currently releasing 22.5 billion pounds of toxic materials each year into the environment.

And so, now, a new concern is attracting attention, a concern that goes beyond how fast we use up the resources of the earth and the systematic pollution of the earth's resources. Now we face the growing problems related to the disposal of toxic by-products and the side effects of our rush for the newer, and bigger, and better and more profitable (Schuyler, 1986; Castleman, 1986; Petulla, 1980).

The Congressional Office of Technology Assessment has warned that chemicals taint groundwater in all fifty states. The National Academy of Sciences reports that cancer-causing pesticides used on crops imperil the nation's food supply. Blue-ribbon commissions are looking at the chemicals used in refrigerators, air conditioners, and in making plastic coffee cups to see what their role is in the depletion of the planet's ozone layer and in the warming global climate. Top scientists have discovered that the government's own nuclear weapons plants are contaminating the countryside around them and have proved that acid rain from utility plants in the Ohio Valley is killing forests and lakes from New England to the Carolinas (McEntee, 1989).

We must now confront a litany of increasingly critical problems. The concern for the condition of our environment has gone from concern for the scarcity of the earth's resources to concern for life-threatening environmental conditions. It is this environmental climate that members of the CBC faced during the period under discussion.

The CBC Voting Patterns

With the history of conservation issues thus defined, the ramifications of the voting patterns of black Congresspersons, indeed Congresspersons in general, with regard to environmental issues are of critical significance in the 1990s.

The League of Conservation Voters 1980–1986 report on the energy and environment voting patterns of Congress provide a gauge of conservation voting. From the beginning of the study, the Congressional Black Caucus ("CBC") had the highest average of support of conservation issues of any group surveyed. The other groups, in descending order, were House Democrats, Senate Democrats, Congresswomen, House of Representatives, Senators, House Republicans, and Senate Republicans. At the opposite end from the CBC, House Republicans are exceeded only by the Senate Republicans in their failure to support environmental legislation.

The CBC not only outdistanced groups identified by political affiliation but its average was above the regional average of any section of the country. There were few state delegations with averages that exceeded the average of the CBC; no state delegations exceeded the CBC average in 1982. The CBC exceeded all but Vermont and Massachusetts in 1980; Rhode Island, Oregon, and Connecticut in 1981; and Connecticut, Delaware, Iowa, Massachusetts, New Jersey, Rhode Island, and Vermont in 1983. Only Massachusetts, Vermont, and Rhode Island had higher scores than the CBC in 1984. And in 1985-86, Delaware, Massachusetts, Rhode Island, and Vermont were the only state delegations that scored higher than the CBC. One should bear in mind that the larger the state delegation the more meaningful the average score. The most supportive states were those in the New England area: Connecticut, New Jersey, Rhode Island, Vermont, and Massachusetts. These states' delegations were the only delegations that consistently rivaled the voting average of the CBC.

While more recent *Scorecards* are not available, the trend appears to be continuing. The average of the years 1985-1988 for current CBC members was 78 percent. Mike Espy, MS-2nd district, had the lowest average at 50 percent and

Henry Vance Davis

TABLE 1   Scorecard Voting Percentages, 1981-1986

House	House Dems.	House Repubs.	House Women	CBC	Senate	Senate Repubs.	Senate Dems.	Year
48	54	37	62	74	nr	nr	nr	1980
49	63	32	56	81	43	28	59	1981
55	71	55	65	85	44	30	61	1982
54	68	31	61	72	nr	nr	nr	1983
56	71	36	62	81	52	36	71	1984
50	64	31	56	77	51	39	64	1985-86

Mfume Kweisi, MD-7th district, had a 100 percent mark. However, both of these had only one year of votes to tabulate. Aside from these two, the range went from 66 percent (Edolphus Towns, NY-11th district) to 93 percent (John Conyers, MI-1st district). In the 100th Congress, 59 percent of the CBC members scored 80 percent or above, and none scored lower than 50 percent.

This record of leadership can and has played a critical role — not just nationally but internationally as well—in the evolving society of the twenty-first century.

The problems of conservation and hazardous waste are a worldwide phenomenon. The world situation is poor at best. In Brazil's once lush Rondonia Territory, 35 percent of the forest has been reduced to ashes or in some other way degraded since 1980 to make way for farmers. Deforestation in northern India and Nepal, as well as the construction of dams in India, contributed directly to the recent floods in Bangladesh that drowned thousands and left 8 million homeless. In China, tons of arsenic, lead, mercury, and other chemical wastes are dumped into the mighty Yangtze River each day. In Mexico City, winter-long smog sends thousands to city hospitals each year with severe conjunctivitis and respiratory problems (Grieves, 1988).

The world state of affairs reflects questions that must be faced on a local level. For example, often when a company requests permission from a community to dump waste in its vicinity it is because the economic situation of the area is so depressed. Area natives and politicians are asked to choose between unemployment and a dangerous environment.

This scenario is played out often in Third World countries. In February of 1988, Guinea Bissau signed a five-year contract to accept 15 million tons of European industrial waste for 120 million dollars a year—a sum that nearly equals Guinea-Bissau's gross national product of 150 million dollars (Editorial, 1988).

Members of the CBC have shown leadership in this area also. John Conyers introduced an amendment, in July of 1988, to the Solid Waste Disposal Act that would prohibit the United States from exporting any toxic wastes other than waste materials exported to Canada or Mexico under existing bilateral agreements. He wrote:

A ban on waste exports is the only way to ensure that our waste does not enter the precious drinking water of drought stricken countries, that children do not play on barrels of cancerous and lethal hazardous waste, and that we do not give birth to a new generation of problems in the Third World (Black Enterprise, 1988: 31).

Is the choice of many Americans so different? In one respect, poor people in America are no different than the poor people in countries of the Third World. Poor, African American communities are and will be vortices of hazardous waste sites because the sites often appear to alleviate poverty.

A number of direct links of hazardous waste landfill siting to African American and low income communities have been identified. Rep. Walter Fauntroy (D-DC) commissioned a General Accounting Office study that disclosed that three of four off-site waste landfills, designated by states for disposal of hazardous materials, are in communities with predominantly African American populations. The GAO study found that at least 26 percent of the population in all four communities have incomes below the poverty level.

One of the sites reviewed by the GAO in Sumter County, Alabama, was later determined to be the largest waste landfill in the nation. Nearly 70 percent of the county's 17,000 residents are African American—96 percent of whom live below the poverty level.

CBC members must also address other American concerns. The hazardous waste problems found in Jackson State Prison, which houses a large African American population, are not isolated. United States Environmental Protection Agency (EPA) officials estimate that up to 33,000 people in the Jackson area could be exposed to the prison's pollution via contaminated ground water and surface waters. Of course, the prison population is at greater risk. Among the problems: illegal storage of chemicals such as DDT and Agent Orange, a DDT-laced landfill that is polluting groundwater, and prison farms fouled by tainted sewage sludge applied over a 40-year period.

Even when identified, hazardous sites are not easily cleaned up. The Reagan Administration had less than a sterling record for toxic clean up. An article written in September of 1989 indicated that in eight years cleanup work had been completed on only about three dozen of the 1,194 sites scheduled for decontamination. The author, Liane Clorfene Casten, continued to take the EPA and the Reagan Administration to task:

> The EPA took action at Love Canal and Times Beach, reluctantly, only after reports of death and damage had become too persistent to ignore. In Jacksonville, the EPA approach is to go to the courts. A recent Congressional study indicates that the nation may have to spend 22.7 billion dollars cleaning up hazardous waste sites, more than double what Congress has designated for the cleanup of abandoned waste dumps ....

On December 9, 1987, the agency lowered its assessment of the cancer-causing potential of dioxin to one-sixteenth of its 1985 estimate, calling the substance a "promoter" of cancer rather than an initiator. These manipulations and dodges serve the Reagan Administration's political agenda and protect the interests of big chemical companies. But they cannot change the fact that in Jacksonville people are dying (Casten, 1988).

The importance—the critical nature—of expanding the CBC's role is underscored by Ms. Casten's last words, "people are dying." The members of the Congressional Black Caucus have realized this and have acted accordingly. They must spread their influence to other members of Congress, so that the incidence of "people dying" is reduced rather than increased.

Conclusions: Toward the Twenty-First Century

In conclusion, some interesting questions arise. First, why has the CBC consistently scored higher than other groups? Unfortunately, we can only speculate. According to an African American, 8-year Congressional aide, black Congresspersons do not put a lot of resources into conservation and hazardous waste issues. His theory is that their support is on the basis of a philosophical liberalism that is generally anti-big business and, consequently, pro-conservation (Matlock, 1989). It appears that among Black Caucus members there is little caucusing around hazardous waste or conservation issues. While they came down on the same side of the issues time and again, they did so without design. This researcher found no stated CBC policy, program, or position. Perhaps they did just vote their philosophy.

In any event, certainly, the future will be more demanding. Given their limited participation in the history of the congressional environmental movement, African Americans of the 1980s have less experience to draw upon—fewer favors to call in—than their counterparts. Obviously, African Americans played little or no role in Congressional conservation legislation through the mid-60s. Except for a brief appearance during the period after Emancipation (1865 to 1876), the African American presence in Congress awaited Adam Clayton Powell in the 1940s. Undoubtedly, these shortcomings will limit their role; nonetheless, they are in a position to make important contributions.

Today, fueled by the Civil Rights Movement of the 1960s, no doubt buoyed by the Jesse Jackson presidential campaigns of the 1980s, African Americans wield unprecedented power. By the mid-1980s, CBC members chaired five House standing committees, two House select committees and fourteen House subcommittees. Surely they will find ways to influence the future agenda of the administration's environmental program.

While the Congressional Black Caucus should be applauded for its excellent record of voting to support conservation issues as defined by the League of

Conservation Voters, there is more to be done. Given the propensity of hazardous waste sites to be located near poor and minority people, hazardous waste should not just be a Walter Fauntroy or John Conyers issue focused on the Third World. It should be a CBC issue for America. The CBC should have a clear, coordinated program for environmental and waste related issues. The public should know where the CBC stands and how to communicate with it when necessary.

Blind support is not enough. The CBC must play a key role in answering age old environmental questions. Has Congress really come to grips with the ethical questions raised by the modern conservation movement? Are recent acts of Congress likely to create conditions which will enable the people of the United States to enrich the quality of their lives? Have policies been formulated that will direct science and technology toward a future wherein humans will find satisfaction in sharing life rather than in destroying it? And what about the future? The CBC can play a leading role in answering these questions.

Research is a key. Following the lead of Walter Fauntroy, the CBC can help create the body of information needed to make the best decisions for our future. Case studies should be undertaken that follow the model outlined by Cooley (1970). What was the environmental problem that gave rise to the need for governmental action? How did legislation come to be introduced in Congress and what did it propose to do? How was the legislation influenced and modified as it moved through the various steps of the Congressional decision-making process? Undoubtedly, economic issues play a critical role in conservation and hazardous waste legislation. We need more answers to the role of this critical element in the equation. Do conservation groups—the League of Conservation Voters for example—donate to African American Congresspersons? The increase in cooperate donations that undoubtedly influenced older groups of Congresspersons will soon have a chance (if they have not already) to influence the CBC. Can the CBC resist? What are the strengths and weaknesses of the final legislative product? What can be said in a broader sense about the ability of Congress to respond to environmental issues?

Finally, this is an issue for the twenty-first century. Often it is a struggle between money, power, and lives. As the world becomes more populated, as humans become more adept and reliant upon money to galvanize power and distinguish themselves, as waste and other by-products of human progress increase exponentially, the value of lives will decrease. Someone will have to help African Americans and the poor to protect themselves lest the Third World dumping ground of the twenty-first century becomes "Poor and Blacktown, U.S.A." The conservation voting pattern of the CBC indicates that it is qualified to lead in this role and to take its rightful place in the history of conservation in the twenty-first century. There is no better time to begin that than now in the 1990s.

5

Toward a Model of "Environmental Discrimination"

Michel Gelobter

In the past sixteen years, a wide variety of studies have suggested that the most common victims of environmental pollution are minorities and the poor (Anderson, 1986; Asch and Seneca, 1978; Berry, 1977; Bullard, 1983; Bullard and Wright, 1985; Freeman, 1972; Gianessi, Peskin, and Wolff 1977; 1979; Gianessi and Peskin, 1980; Handy, 1977; Kruvant, 1976; United Church of Christ, 1987; Zimmerman, 1984; 1986; Zupan, 1973). This literature has indicated that these groups are likely to be exposed to higher levels of pollution than their white or rich counterparts and has also demonstrated that the economic costs of pollution control are borne more heavily by minorities and the poor than by other groups (Freeman, 1977; Gianessi, Peskin, and Wolff, 1979; Harrison and Rubinfeld, 1977).

Many of these studies have also predicted that inequities in the distribution of pollution would be reduced if not eliminated by legislation and regulation (Asch and Seneca, 1978; Freeman, 1972). Indeed the Clean Air Act (CAA), as well as most of the sweeping environmental regulations of the early seventies, promised uniform pollution control "regardless of where...persons reside"[1] across the land.

But what legislation says and what it does are two different things. Contemporary studies of the distribution of pollution have suggested that, despite the fact that minorities and poor people are more than paying their way when it comes to environmental protection, government intervention may serve rather to aggravate the already regressive[2] and discriminatory[3] distribution of pollution that they face (Gelobter, 1986; U.S. General Accounting Office, 1983; United Church of Christ, 1987).

To date, work on inequitable environmental outcomes has been restricted to measuring the effects of discrimination. Some additional work has sought to understand the race and class elements of environmental social movement organizations and, to a lesser extent, of environmental ideologies (Albrecht, 1972;

Michel Gelobter is an Assistant Commissioner for Policy and Planning for the New York City Department of Environmental Protection. His research interests include environmental racism, air pollution, global warming and solid waste management.

Buttel, 1985; Buttel and Flinn, 1978; Hare, 1970; Morrison, 1973; 1986; Morrison and Dunlap, 1980; Van Liere and Dunlap, 1980).

This paper seeks to fill the void in understanding the dynamics of environmental discrimination by exploring the connection between environmental regulation and discriminatory outcomes. The next section surveys the various ways of measuring distribution and/or discrimination that have been used in the environmental context and summarizes how these definitions may lead to different conclusions about the extent of environmental discrimination. Following this discussion of methodological questions, the third section develops a model of environmental regulatory activity that goes beyond measuring environmental inequities to actually understanding the discriminatory dynamics underlying them.

Measuring Environmental Discrimination

The first task of any effort to discern the specific mechanisms through which inequitable and discriminatory distributions of pollution arise is to define discrimination in the environmental context. Feagin has developed a broad definition of discrimination that makes few assumptions about the underlying dynamics. He suggests that discrimination is "actions or practices carried out by dominant groups, or their representatives, which have a differential and negative impact on members of subordinate groups" (Feagin and Feagin, 1986: 20-21).

Definitions of discrimination have been traditionally operationalized in the literature on discrimination by assuming that once certain demographic or social variables[4] have been controlled for, residual differences in measures of status like income or employment (Feagin's "differential and negative impact") are attributable to discrimination (Farley, 1984).

The choice of these measures and variables have always been central to the conclusions of studies on discrimination. This section explores which measures can be used to detect "differential and negative impacts" and which other explanatory variables should be accounted for in measuring environmental discrimination.

Environmental Pollution: Exposures or Costs?

Physical Measures of Discrimination: Most studies have examined the distribution of pollution and the equity of pollution control measures by attempting to measure the incidence of physical pollution (Anderson, 1986; Asch and Seneca, 1978; Berry, 1977; Bullard, 1983; Bullard and Wright, 1985; Freeman, 1972; Handy, 1977; Kruvant, 1976; United Church of Christ, 1987; Zupan, 1973). By correlating geographical indicators of this incidence, such as the location of dumps or the level of air pollution, with the socio-economic characteristics of surrounding communities, researchers draw conclusions about the extent of environmental discrimination.

Figures 1A through 1D, drawn from my own work on the distribution of

66

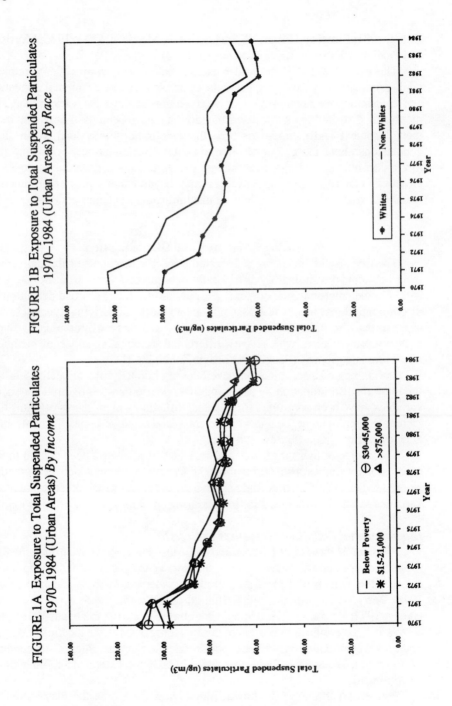

FIGURE 1A Exposure to Total Suspended Particulates
1970–1984 (Urban Areas) *By Income*

FIGURE 1B Exposure to Total Suspended Particulates
1970–1984 (Urban Areas) *By Race*

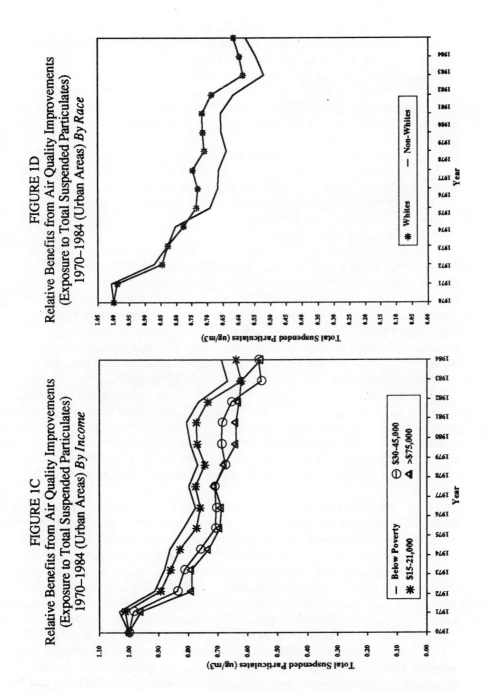

FIGURE 1D

Relative Benefits from Air Quality Improvements
(Exposure to Total Suspended Particulates)
1970–1984 (Urban Areas) *By Race*

FIGURE 1C

Relative Benefits from Air Quality Improvements
(Exposure to Total Suspended Particulates)
1970–1984 (Urban Areas) *By Income*

Sources: SEEDIS; SAROAD, 1986 (All Incomes in 1980$/Family)

outdoor air pollution, illustrates this approach. In this study I used a population-weighted index of ambient concentration as a measure of discriminatory results. I controlled for urbanization by examining the data for the country as a whole and urban areas alone. Figures 1A and 1B compare an absolute index of exposure to total suspended particulates (TSP) for six income groups and two race groups in urban areas from 1970 to 1984. Figures 1C and 1D compare relative improvements using 1970 as a base year.

These figures illustrate that, in urban areas, nonwhite-white inequities in average exposure by race are evident and exposure by income is slightly regressive. In general, however, urban differences in exposure to TSP by income group are small.

An important finding is that the poor experience a much lower relative decrease in exposure than the rich. Nonwhites appear to experience slightly greater relative reductions in exposure than whites.

The two different kinds of measures used in these figures (absolute vs. relative) illustrate the issue of how to measure change in discrimination. If we are to look at how environmental laws may be discriminatory, we must not only measure absolute levels of exposure (or whatever other indicator we choose), but we must measure the rate at which this indicator has changed for different groups as a result of regulation. Figures 1A through 1D illustrate one of the principle findings of my own air pollution study: the extent of differential exposure for different income groups varies from pollutant to pollutant, but all changes in exposure have been regressively distributed since 1970 (the year in which the Clean Air Act was adopted).

The data presented in Figures 1A through 1D represent part of the most extensive effort to date to measure the effects of discrimination in environmental protection programs. Most other studies of the physical incidence of pollution have examined only one or two years of data and have only hypothesized about the impacts of regulation. But among such studies there is general agreement that the distribution of pollution is regressive by income and discriminatory by race.

Economic Measures of Discrimination: To date, most of the analysts of the incidence of pollution and the inequity of environmental policy have been economists. As a result there have also been some efforts at determining the distribution of the costs of pollution (Gianessi, Peskin, and Wolff, 1977, 1979; Harrison, 1977).

The economic measures used by this type of study have provided authors with a great deal of flexibility in analyzing patterns in the distribution of pollution, but their results have varied widely. Some authors analyze only the distribution of the costs of one type of pollutant (Harrison, 1977). Others build economic measures of the distribution of multi-pollutant exposure (Gianessi, Peskin, and Wolff, 1977, 1979; Gianessi and Peskin, 1980), or first construct an index of the change in the physical environment and then calculate benefits by income or race based on willingness-to-pay[5] (Baumol and Oates, 1975; Freeman, 1972; Harrison and Rubinfeld, 1977). The latter method attempts to capture through economic

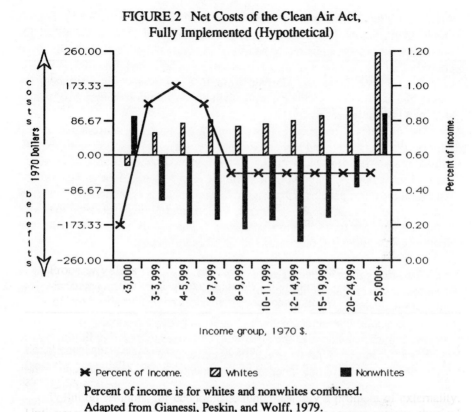

FIGURE 2   Net Costs of the Clean Air Act,
Fully Implemented (Hypothetical)

Income group, 1970 $.

✖ Percent of Income.   ▨ Whites   ▮ Nonwhites

Percent of income is for whites and nonwhites combined.
Adapted from Gianessi, Peskin, and Wolff, 1979.

Since the Act has yet to be *fully* implemented, the results of this study should be used with caution, but they are in general agreement with those sketched in Figure 1. The findings indicate that the costs of the Clean Air Act, as a percent of income, will be distributed regressively. They also indicate that the benefits of the Clean Air Act will outweigh its costs for nonwhites while the opposite is true for whites. This last finding reflects the fact that minorities were more exposed than whites prior to the Clean Air Act, but also contradicts the results in Figure 1 that indicate only a marginally greater improvement for nonwhites over whites.

measures the value of lost workdays, shortened lifespan and other impacts of exposure to pollutants.

The most ambitious effort to measure the distribution of the economic consequences of environmental regulation is summarized in Figure 2 (Gianessi, Peskin, and Wolff, 1977, 1979). The purpose of this study was to determine the ultimate distribution of costs and benefits arising from the full implementation of the Clean

Air Act. Using Census and Environmental Protection Agency (EPA) data on employment, automobile ownership, home heating, and their implications for emissions, the authors constructed estimates of regional[6] per capita benefits[7] from control of all regulated pollutants. Industrial, household, and governmental costs of pollution control (as also derived from EPA sector-specific estimates) are distributed among families in proportion to their consumption, automobile ownership, and tax burden respectively.

The differences between Figures 1 and 2 are probably attributable to two factors. First, as mentioned earlier, Gianessi, Peskin, and Wolff's cost and benefit estimates assume full implementation of the Clean Air Act. At present however, many cities remain out of compliance with the requirements of the Act. A second reason for the discrepancies is that Figure 1 accounts for geographic differences by analyzing only urban areas. Gianessi, Peskin, and Wolff's cost estimates as presented here are for the nation as a whole. The use of geographic factors in analyzing environmental outcomes will be taken up below.

Comparing Cost Measures and Physical Measures: Table 1 presents some of the measures, economic or physical, that have been or could be used in determining environmental discrimination.

An economic assessment of the distributional issues surrounding pollution can provide explicit valuations of the distributional consequences of pollution control measures. If properly done, these valuations can be used to assess the distributional trade-offs involved in implementing environmental policy (jobs versus environment, for example). Nevertheless, the valuation of environmental impacts, like increased morbidity or reduced wildlife diversity, remains one of the most problematic areas in economic cost/benefit analysis.

Physical measures of pollutant concentrations may not provide any more of an absolute scale by which to evaluate the benefits of pollution control than economic ones. Willingness-to-pay for environmental quality differs among individuals and is difficult to measure, but the same holds true for the human dose-response curve of most pollutants.

Physical measures, rather than cost estimates, of the distributional benefits of legislation such as the Clean Air Act may, however, provide a better basis for abatement strategies geared towards neutral or progressive redistribution. It is hard enough getting equal protection issues to be considered formally at the level of policy implementation without adding the difficulties of calculating and debating relative willingnesses-to-pay and the value of human life to the debate.

Asch and Seneca (1978) argue that an equal protection approach to pollutant regulation must be neutral to issues of income distribution. Such an approach, if applied to the regulation of pollution, may result in progressive redistribution since the poor and minorities not only may be expected to benefit from greater improvements in air quality but generally suffer greater health impacts from pollution.

TABLE 1 Measures of "Environmental Discrimination"

Economic	Physical
Benefits -expected reduction times willingness- to-pay	Exposure to Pollutants -absolute -relative/rate of improvement -proximity to pollutant sources
Costs -costs of abatement	-cumulative: multi-pollutant or multi-sources

Net Costs/Benefits
-costs of abatement minus
  damages
	Aesthetic Values
	-view
	-proximity to open space/
	   recreation/nature

Property Values -increased rent or housing values as result of improved environmental quality	Health Impacts -individual -community

This approach, however, must be tempered by economic analysis of distributional consequences to ensure that poor and minority communities are protected from the potentially serious economic consequences of environmental protection strategies.

Pollution remains, for economists, fundamentally a problem of externality. Until progress is made towards rationally internalizing its costs to society, physical measures are likely to be far more precise for the purposes of determining the distribution of pollution itself. Because they provide a more concrete tool for mobilizing concern, they are also likely to be far more useful in the debate about environmental discrimination.

Controlling for Confounders: The Time and Space Dimensions of Environmental Discrimination

Any explanatory scheme used to measure distribution must be sensitive to confounders: other variables that help explain some of the observed disparities. For example, variations in educational attainment or area of residence are sometimes taken into account when comparing statistics on earnings by race or class. In such studies of traditional discrimination, confounders are often themselves intertwined in complicated ways with the discrimination being measured. Similar problems complicate the choice of which variables associated with pollution should be "controlled for" when analyzing environmental discrimination.

Pollution has three important physical characteristics: magnitude, location, and duration. Magnitude can be represented as any one of the measures listed in Table 1. It is the measure we most often wish to use to describe environmental discrimination and is, therefore, usually the dependent variable.

Although the duration of pollution is important to determining the cumulative impact, it is not relevant to all measures of discrimination. The Safe Drinking Water Act (SDWA), for example, sets a maximum permissible concentration for various pollutants in water. In a study of the distribution by race of exposures to violations of the SDWA, it may be important to control for the amount of time spent by different groups at home and at the workplace. Such a study would then be able to distinguish between differences in exposure due to improper enforcement as opposed to differences in the time budgets of different groups. Both may be due to discrimination, but only the former is directly controlled by environmental regulation.

If, on the other hand, the study was concerned with the distributional impact of regulations controlling cumulative exposure (like threshold level values, or TLVs) then one would be less concerned with eliminating the influence of time from the analysis and more concerned with understanding its role in determining the effectiveness of regulation. Depending on the measure of discrimination to be used, time may, therefore, be a factor that should be examined separately.

Finally, pollution must be in a place. When designing a study of environmental discrimination, I believe that location is the most important variable to consider as a possible confounder.[8]

Prior to Gianessi, Peskin, and Wolff's work, no study had examined the distribution of pollution nationwide. The difference between their results and those of other researchers (Asch and Seneca, 1978; Freeman, 1972; Gelobter, 1986; Zupan, 1973) is due to their use of a geographically comprehensive database that spans the whole country rather than just a set of cities. Because the poorest environmental quality is found in urban areas, Gianessi, Peskin, and Wolff found that the poor (who live in greater numbers in rural areas) were paying less in pollution damages than the rich.

As another example, one of the findings of the Commission for Racial Justice's study of the distribution of hazardous waste sites is that approximately 24 percent of all minorities have one hazardous waste facility in their zip code area although they only make up 12 percent of the population. But because minorities make up approximately 24 percent of the urban population of the United States, it's possible that most hazardous waste sites are simply in urban areas. This study's measure of environmental discrimination would have been strengthened if it had controlled for urban- versus rural-located facilities.

Before controlling for even some form of geographic variable, it's important to have a conceptual model of the influence location may have in the distribution of the pollution being studied. Controlling for urban versus rural locations makes sense in certain cases because many polluting activities tend to be located in or near cities. But within urban areas, or for forms of pollution that move long distances like acid rain or low-level nuclear waste, it is harder to build a credible model of geographical factors that would coincide with a discriminatory outcome.

The "Residual": Proof or Description?

Farley states, in *Blacks and Whites: Narrowing the Gap?*: "A thorough examination of data can yield reasons for racial differences, but will seldom isolate the specific effects of racial discrimination" (1984:12). This section has explained how the selection of a useful environmental indicator of discrimination and a thorough examination of possible confounding variables can reveal a residual difference ("differential impact") between groups that may be a result of discrimination. But such descriptive work will often fall short of explaining the specific dynamics of discrimination. The following section will develop a model for uncovering and exploring the causal mechanisms underlying discriminatory outcomes.

Distributional Dynamics

Using any number of the tools described in the previous section, research on environmental discrimination has generally anticipated that environmental regulation, although regressive and discriminatory in its costs, would probably alleviate the distributional disparities in exposure and other measures of physical incidence. Recent work on this question, particularly my own, has cast some doubt on this assumption. It appears that, as Feagin puts it, "one important problem here is the otherwise legitimate social purpose which practices with [discriminatory] effects serve" (1977:196).

Discriminatory outcomes in pollution control do not appear to result solely from any inherently discriminatory rules and procedures for pollution control or as a result of the "prejudiced" behavior of individuals within the EPA. In the first case, environmental regulations would seem rather to guarantee more equal environmental protection because of their use of national standards and guidelines. In the second case, prejudice widespread enough to influence the distribution of pollution nationally must be placed in a broader context of organizational or institutionalized discrimination.

Despite the powers granted the newly created Environmental Protection Agency (EPA) in the 1970s, improvements in environmental quality and changes in its distribution cannot be solely attributed to EPA's regulatory activity. The period from 1970 to the mid-1980s was one of major restructuring of the U.S. industrial and urban-industrial base (Noyelle and Stanback, 1983) and there is no question that patterns of industrial change and relocation had an effect on the location of pollution sources.

Over the same period there have been equally important shifts in the composition of communities. Major changes in the ethnic and class composition of cities, along with shifting patterns of suburbanization, have also affected the distribution of pollution.

Nevertheless, most pollutant sources fell under the jurisdiction of the EPA in the course of the last two decades. In enforcing environmental laws, the EPA has had a substantial effect on the location and relocation of pollution and polluting activities. Furthermore, changes in environmental quality have influenced other factors, like rents and housing values, that are relevant to the demographics and composition of communities (Baumol, 1975; Harrison and Rubinfeld, 1978). Thus, although EPA activities are not the only factor influencing pollution, the Agency's role has been crucial to changes in environmental quality over the last 20 years.

Discriminatory outcomes should, therefore, be seen as the interaction of internal processes, external structures, and wider ideological and historical contexts and understandings. Only in this way can we understand the pervasiveness and persistence of discrimination despite changes at the institutional and individual levels in the last twenty years.

The framework I outline below for understanding discriminatory outcomes draws on three distinct bodies of work. First, recent literature on institutionalized racism has usefully categorized the types of discrimination that underlie activities at different social (personal, group, organizational, etc.) and motivational levels (intentional, unintentional, intent-to-harm, etc.) (Feagin and Eckberg, 1980; Rex, 1986; Williams, 1985). They have also suggested ways in which these different levels interact to produce the forms of discrimination that we observe (Feagin and Feagin, 1986; Williams, 1985).

Second, neo-Marxist theories of politics and the state have provided some important insights into the power/class struggle dynamics of the capitalist state. Skocpol (1981) and Block (1977), in particular, have provided a basis for understanding the state's and state bureaucrats' roles as autonomous agents of change. These contributions are important for understanding the context in which environmental issues arise in apparent contradiction with the state's more traditional role as guarantor of the accumulation process. These theories also provide us with tools with which to analyze the specifics of class struggle as it occurs within state apparatuses like the EPA.

Finally, this framework is also informed by the approaches of Crenson's, *The Unpolitics of Pollution: A Study of Non-Decisionmaking in the Cities* (1971) and Logan and Molotch's, *Urban Fortunes: The Political Economy of Place* (1987). Both offer hybrid understandings of the role of existing power structures in directing government action. These authors seek to explain the combined role of structural, community, and group factors in the determination of local policy outcomes. They also explore the importance of nondecision-making and of non-participation as a form of resistance to power structures. These perspectives will be important in analyzing how environmental regulations could have a serious impact on minority

FIGURE 3   A Model of Institutionalized Discrimination
in Environmental Protection Agencies

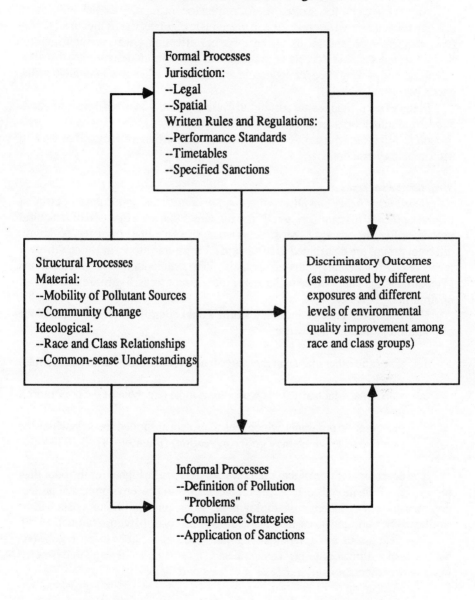

and poor communities even while these groups' participation in the process was minimal or non-existent (Morrison, 1986; Van Liere and Dunlap, 1980).

Any framework for analyzing discrimination in regulatory behavior must account for at least two factors. First, it must relate regulatory activities at all scales (national, regional, and local) to other factors affecting environmental quality. Second, it must isolate the role of enforcement activities in determining distributional outcomes from broader economic and social changes that may have influenced outcomes as well.

Many of such changes are part of the cycle of institutionalized discrimination. While retaining a broader structural view, the model laid out in Figure 3 attempts to isolate important dynamics within environmental bureaucracies that lead to discriminatory outcomes.

Structural Processes

Economic Theory and Discriminatory Dynamics: Economic theory pertinent to environmental discrimination relies on dynamics that are a function of structural processes like the market.[9] Most economists theorize that, prior to regulation, different groups are distributed according to a Tieboutian model in which different levels of environmental quality are available in a continuum of different locations (Tiebout, 1956). The poor, less able to buy into cleaner areas, live in areas with poor environmental quality.

Environmental policies in such a world would control the physical incidence of pollution in one of three ways:

1. taxes and other universal measures that affect all areas (and most people) equally;
2. standards, which affect the worst areas most (e.g. benefit the poor more); and
3. preservation programs, which seek to protect unspoiled areas (in which the rich live or to which they go for recreation) (Baumol, 1974: 202).

The costs for all three of these policies are likely to be higher for the poor than for the rich. Transitional costs, as the market adapts to new environmental protection measures, may increase unemployment. Long-run equilibrium costs will be similar to consumption taxes, increasing the overall cost-of-living (Baumol, 1974).

The benefits of environmental regulation are also likely to be regressive. Measures of willingness-to-pay have indicated that the rich will reap more benefits from environmental quality because of at least two factors:

1. they are likely to realize higher rents[10] on properties in cleaned up areas; and

2. they are more willing (or able) to pay for improvements in health than the poor (Harrison and Rubinfeld, 1977).

Zimmerman (1984, 1986) has done extensive theoretical work on the economic distribution of environmental pollution in both the United States and West Germany. The following six points made in his most recent work illustrate the degree of inequity that he has found to be almost "built in" to the structure of environmental regulation:

1. the distribution of environmental damage shows sharply regressive trends with respect to income groups;
2. the distribution of environmental benefits moves from proportionality to progressivity as the concept of the environment is extended (recreation, use of national parks, etc.) and as environmental benefits become more income-elastic;
3. an environment improved through environmental policy may lead to price effects (land values, rents) which virtually perpetuate the regressive structure of environmental damage;
4. the monetary costs of environmental policy, in particular in the United States, are regressively distributed to a marked extent, not only in particular areas of American environmental policy but also in total;
5. any direct distribution effects due to interference with or failure to achieve other economic goals as a result of environmental policy measures... also tend to be regressive; and
6. the net impact of environmental policy on monetary costs and benefits, even within the broadest concept of effects, is consistently regressive and becomes even more so the more regressive the financing system becomes and as more emphasis is given to "luxury components" of environmental policy (Zimmerman, 1986: 96).

The assumptions about the dynamics underlying most economic/Tieboutian analysis are stated in a quote from economist Robert Bish:

> Four basic assumptions of economic analysis are common in recent application of economics to political phenomena.... They are the assumptions of scarcity, methodological individualism, self-interest, and individual rationality in the use of scarce resources. [(Bish, 1971) as cited in (Newton, 1975)]

He later adds an assumption of perfect competition to the list.

Structural Approaches to Discriminatory Dynamics: The model in Figure 3 represents an attempt to explain discriminatory outcomes with a more realistic analysis of the social forces that drive markets and bureaucracies. By examining those factors external to environmental enforcement agencies that influence pollution, like demographic changes and locational patterns of polluters, we can begin to understand the relationship between material structures and the bureaucracy.

In *Race, Class and State Housing: Inequality and the Allocation of Public Housing in Britain*, Henderson and Karn point out that:

> Organizations can adequately be understood only when theorized in relation to the other structures (such as the class structure) that constitute the society of which they are a part, and indeed which are inherent in the organizations themselves such that in key ways they constrain the operation of those organizations (1987: 16).

To study institutionalized discrimination within a bureaucracy one must also study ideological elements in its operation (Williams, 1985: 334). The ideological linkage between the environmental enforcement agencies and other structures can be established by examining bureaucrats' own common-sense understandings of the agency's role and actions. These understandings are drawn from and related to broader societal understandings and ideologies.

Formal and Informal Agency Dynamics and Their Relation to Discriminatory Outcomes

To explain the influence of regulatory activity on discriminatory outcomes, we must come to understand "how the terms of [the bureaucrat's] discourse are assigned to real objects and events by normally competent persons in ordinary situations" (Bittner, 1965: 247). Thus an understanding of institutional discrimination will also be dependent on an examination of the agency's informal processes and its interpretations of the formal statements of its goals and methods.

The distinction between informal and formal levels is not a clearcut one. Formal structures are often constructed and understood through unstated and informal understandings and rules. Also, processes that we may perceive as informal may well have the regularity and predictability we normally associate with formal structures.

The conceptual model in Figure 3, nevertheless, distinguishes between the contribution to outcomes of formal "programmatic constructions" (Bittner, 1965: 240) (timetables, performance standards, specified sanctions) and informal agency processes (problem definitions, compliance strategies, and sanctioning behaviors). The differences in the operation of these processes can explain how outcomes differ between minority and white areas and/or poor and rich areas within even the same enforcement district.

Formal Processes: Formal agency rules and constructions can be examined in two ways. First, written rules influence outcomes by setting the legal and jurisdictional context of the agency's approach to pollution control. But in environmental problems, as discussed earlier, scale or spatial configuration matter also.

Clark and Deary (1984) point out that the state functions to integrate power over heterogeneous space. Logan and Molotch (1987), and Newton (1975), in an article entitled "American Urban Politics: Social Class, Political Structure, and Public Goods" emphasize the importance of the spatial forms of jurisdiction and fragmentation in protecting upper class interests. The extent to which the definitions of spatial jurisdiction define working class and minority areas as "residual" phenomena must be theorized in an understanding of discriminatory outcomes (Logan and Molotch, 1987:197). Thus, a second approach to environmental enforcement agencies' "programmatic constructions" must be to examine the spatial organization of the agencies' jurisdictions (emissions trading options, regional guidelines, jurisdictional boundaries, the location of monitors).

Informal Processes; Enforcement in the Field: Knoepfel (1986) has shown for eight European nations that the implementation of air pollution policy can incorporate implicit distributional issues and tendencies independently of formal programmatic definitions. He believes that these issues enter into the implementation phase in two ways that may affect the distribution of pollution among population groups. First, implementation can be seen as a form of delivering a service from government to industry or citizens. These services are often distributed according to broader societal norms of race, class, and power.

Second, his research finds significant differences in the extent and efficiency of regulation in different regions. Fragmented governmental structures or marginalized locales are more likely to be ineffective in implementing and enforcing formal regulations.

In an analysis of the transformations that took place through the 1970s and into the 1980s in EPA air pollution policy (specifically the emissions trading measures), Meidinger (1986) uncovers a regulatory culture with tremendous bureaucratic discretion. Poor and minority communities are not at all represented by the actors in this culture. This fact alone is likely to increase the discriminatory effects of environmental policy.

But Meidinger also traces substantive elements in the culture that will further such inequities. These include:

1. declining importance of scientific values in favor of political negotiation/ expediency in policy formulation;
2. declining "public good" concepts of the environment, in which all are equal consumers;

3. increasing use of property rights to manage pollution, thus establishing markets essentially closed to poor and minority communities; and
4. increasing affirmation of the concept of property rights in environmental ideology, strengthening the hand of private property holders and shifting concern from distributional considerations.

Both of these authors illustrate how distributional agendas may be influenced and contested in the informal arena of regulatory behavior.

This model's description of the informal processes of regulation provides a way of discovering such informal activity and of analyzing the day-to-day operations of environmental protection agencies for discriminatory effects. The framework developed in Hawkins', *Environment and Enforcement: The Social Definition of Pollution* (1984) categorizes enforcement agents' duties into three broad areas:

1. the definition or identification of pollution "problems": how enforcement agents discover a "pollution" and come to define it as a problem;
2. the pursuit of compliance to remedy them: how agents seek to bring the polluting source into compliance; and
3. the imposition of sanctions where compliance strategies have failed: how agents seek redress to law (formal process).

At each phase, enforcement agents impose understandings of these tasks in poor versus rich and minority versus white areas and, in turn, insert structural understandings of race and class into the determination of pollution outcomes.

Conclusions

This paper has sought to explore both the methodological and theoretical issues surrounding environmental discrimination. The model described here provides an empirically verifiable framework for understanding discriminatory dynamics in pollution control efforts.

As discussed above, discriminatory outcomes are measurable. But there is a dearth of studies that analyze the risk to poor and minority communities of such outcomes. Too many studies of environmental and community health have neglected social variables.[11]

Structural processes at the material and ideological level have been analyzed previously but much more work needs to be done on the specifics of race-class-environment interactions. Finally, bureaucratic activity, formal and informal, can be disarticulated according to the components listed in Figure 3 in order to see how and why discriminatory outcomes arise. Very little work has been done in this last category, particularly to analyze informal agency processes. But it is this realm that holds the greatest promise for developing environmental control strategies that are inclusive, and that recognize the needs of all communities.

Notes

1. 42 USC Sections 1857c-4, 1957c-5 (1970), cited in (Asch and Seneca, 1978).

2. Throughout this paper the terms "regressive" and "progressive" are used in their economic sense. A regressive outcome is one in which the poor lose proportionally more than the rich, or gain proportionally less. Progressive outcomes are just the opposite, and neutral outcomes are equally beneficial or detrimental to all.

3. This paper uses Feagin's formulation of discrimination: "actions or practices carried out by dominant groups, or their representatives, which have a differential and negative impact on members of subordinate groups" (Feagin, 1986: 20-21).

4. Such as educational attainment or location of residence in a study of discrimination in earnings.

5. Willingness-to-pay is a measure of the dollar value households are willing to pay for an incremental quantity of a good like environmental quality. It is usually derived from surrogate measures like calculations of how much housing values change when air quality improves.

6. The regions used in the analysis were Census County Groups (CCGs) for the U.S., as well as subgroupings within them, Standard Metropolitan Statistical Areas (SMSAs).

7. Because damages are assumed to result purely from noncompliance with the National Ambient Air Quality Standards, benefits are considered to be equal to damages avoided when the pollutants are controlled to the levels prescribed in the standards.

8. Location is also an important variable because it defines the resolution at which environmental discrimination will be measured. Rather than measuring the level of pollution at the individual level, most studies have assumed that, over a certain area, pollution is equally distributed among residents. The validity of this assumption is linked to the geographic resolution used and the characteristics of the pollutant itself. The distribution of a volatile pollutant like benzene as measured at the county level will differ significantly from its distribution at the tract level.

9. Such theory addresses only the issues of distribution by income.

10. Used here in its economic sense.

11. Two blatant examples of this are the famous "Harvard University Six Cities Study" of indoor air pollution and the "Total Exposure Assessment Methodology" developed by EPA (Speizer, 1990; Pellizzari, 1984). Although the two studies took thousands of measurements of individual exposures to pollution, neither collected any information on the social status of study participants.

6

Environmental Blackmail
in Minority Communities

Robert Bullard

Environmental problems have become potent political issues, especially as they threaten public health (Mitchell, 1979; Van Liere and Dunlap, 1980; Dunlap, 1987). Social equity and distributive concerns, however, have not fared so well over the years. Many of the conflicts that have resulted among core environmentalists, the poor, and minorities can be traced to distributional equity questions. How are the benefits and burden of environmental reform distributed? Who gets what, where, and why? Do environmental reforms have regressive impacts? After nearly three decades of modern environmentalism, the equity issues have not been resolved.

Environmental Elitism and Job Blackmail

Environmentalism in the United States grew out of the progressive conservation movement that began in the 1890s. The modern environmental movement, however, has its roots in the civil rights and anti-war movements of the late 60s (Humphrey and Buttel, 1982). The more radical student-activists splintered off from the civil rights and anti-war movement to form the core of the environmental movement in the early 1970s. The student environmental activists affected by the Earth Day enthusiasm in colleges and universities across the nation had hopes of bringing environmental reforms to the urban poor. They saw their role as environmental advocates for the poor, since the poor had not taken action on their own (Hays, 1987: 269). These advocates of the poor, however, were met with resistance and suspicion. Growing tension between the environmental movement and the social equity movement contributed to environmentalism

Robert Bullard is an Associate Professor of Sociology, University of California, Riverside. For the past ten years Professor Bullard has focused his research on the politics of pollution and how blacks and lower income groups have been disproportionately impacted by environmental stressors. He is the author of Dumping in Dixie: Race, Class, and Environmental Quality.

being tagged an "elitist" movement (Morrison, 1980, 1986; Schnaiberg, 1983; Gale, 1983; Morrison and Dunlap, 1986; Bullard and Wright, 1987a, 1987b).

Morrison and Dunlap (1986) grouped environmental elitism into three types: (1) compositional elitism, i.e., environmentalists come from privileged class strata; (2) ideological elitism, i.e., environmental reforms are a subterfuge for distributing the benefits to environmentalists and costs to non-environmentalists; and (3) impact elitism, i.e., environmental reforms have regressive distributional impacts.

Impact elitism has been the major sore point between environmentalists and the groups who see some reform proposals creating, exacerbating, and sustaining social inequities. The root of this conflict lies in the "jobs vs. environment" argument. Embedded in this argument are three competing advocacy groups: (1) environmental groups concerned about leisure and recreation, wildlife and wilderness preservation, resource conservation, pollution abatement, and industry regulation; (2) social justice advocates, whose major concerns include basic civil rights, social equity, expanded opportunity, economic mobility, and institutional discrimination; and (3) economic boosters, who have as their chief concerns maximizing profits, industrial expansion, economic stability, laissez faire operation, and deregulation.

Economic boosters were somewhat successful in convincing social justice advocates that environmental regulations had regressive distributive impacts. It was argued that acceptance of many reform proposals would result in plant closures, layoffs, and economic dislocation. Kazis and Grossman (1982: 37) refer to this practice as "job blackmail." The public is led to believe that there is no alternative to "business as usual" operation. If workers want to keep their jobs, they must work under conditions which may be hazardous to them, their families, and their community. Black workers are especially vulnerable to job blackmail because of high unemployment and their concentration in low-paying (high-risk) blue-collar occupations.

There is inherent conflict between the interests of capital and those of labor. Employers are empowered to move jobs (and sometimes hazards) in a political economic world-system. For example, firms may choose to move their operations from the Northeast and Midwest to the South and Sunbelt, or they may move the jobs to Third World countries where labor is cheaper and where there are fewer health and environmental regulations. Moreover, labor unions may feel it necessary to tone down their demands for improved worker safety conditions in a depressed economy for fear of layoffs, plant closings, and relocation of industries (e.g., moving to right-to-work states which proliferate in the South). The conflicts, fears, and anxieties that are manifested are usually built on the false assumption that environmental regulations are automatically linked to job loss.

The offer of a job (any job) to an unemployed inner city worker appears to have served a more immediate need than the promise of a clean environment. There is evidence that new jobs have been created as a direct result of environmental reforms (Miller, 1980). The question is: Who got these new jobs? The newly created jobs are often taken by people who already have jobs or by migrants who possess skills greater than those of the indigenous workforce. More often than not, "newcomers intervene between the jobs and the local residents, especially the disadvantaged" (Bluestone and Harrison, 1982: 90).

Low income and minority residents can point to a steady stream of industries and jobs leaving their communities. Moreover, social justice advocates take note of the miserable track record that environmentalists and preservationists have on environmental problems in the nation's racially segregated cities, deteriorating urban infrastructures, and hazardous industrial workplaces.

Compensation and Victims

The application of economic trade-offs in mitigating siting disputes and environmental conflict continues to generate a wide range of discussion. This is especially true for poor and minority communities that are beset with rising unemployment, extreme poverty, a shrinking tax base, and a decaying business infrastructure. Compensation and monetary inducements have been proposed, for example, as an alternative strategy to minimize opposition to hazardous waste facility siting (Morell, 1987; O'Hare et al., 1983; Portney, 1985).

How does compensation work? Communities that agree to host hazardous waste and other noxious facilities are promised compensation in an amount such that the perceived benefits outweigh the risks. The economic inducements serve as "equalizers" to redress the imbalance. There are, however, risks associated with a policy of compensation. Moreover, the moral question pertaining to compensation has not been adequately addressed. That is, should one part of society (the affluent) pay another part of society (the disadvantaged) to accept risks that others can afford to escape. Obviously, the well-off can "vote with their feet." Compensation strategies taken to an extreme can only exacerbate existing environmental inequities. The Commission for Racial Justice (1987: 7) cautions us on the use of compensation in environmental disputes: "To advance such a theory [of compensation] in the absence of the consideration of the racial and socio-economic characteristics of the host communities and existing forms of institutionalized racism leaves room for potential discrimination."

Local community groups may be turned off by the idea of sitting around a table with a waste disposal giant, a government regulator, and an environmentalist to negotiate the siting of a toxic waste facility in their community. The lines become blurred in terms of the parties representing the interests of the community and those of business. Negotiations of this type fuel residents' perception of an "unholy trinity," where the battle lines are drawn along an "us" vs. "them" power arrangement.

Talk of risk compensation for minority communities raises a series of moral dilemmas, especially where environmental imbalances already exist. Past waste siting practices should not guide future policy decisions. A community "saturated with facilities may have less impact sensitivity to a proposed project than might an area having few facilities" (Edelstein, 1987: 186). Thus, any saturation policy derived from past practices perpetuates equity impacts. Facility siting becomes a "modern ritual for selecting victims for sacrifice" (Edelstein, 1987: 195).

A voluminous body of research now exists on public concern about noxious facilities, risks, and mitigation strategies (Morell and Magorian, 1982). Few of these studies, however, have looked at this problem in minority communities. Given the nature of economic booster campaigns and growth machine politics (see Logan and Molotch, 1987), city leaders may endorse trade-offs, while local citizens who live nearby may object to siting decisions, even when compensation is part of the package.

Who Benefits and Who Pays?

Poor and minority residents had the most to gain in the passage of environmental regulations such as the Clean Air Act since they lived closest to the worst sources of the pollution (Humphrey and Buttel, 1982). These communities, however, continue to be burdened with a disproportionately large share of industrial pollution problems, even after the passage of all the regulations. Uneven enforcement of environmental and land-use regulations is a contributor to this problem.

Zoning, deed restrictions, and other "protectionist" devices have failed to effectively segregate industrial uses from residential uses in many black and lower income communities. The various social classes, with or without land use controls, are "unequally able to protect their environmental interests" (Logan and Molotch, 1987:158). Rich neighborhoods are able to leverage their economic and political clout into fending off unwanted uses (even public housing for the poor) while residents of poor neighborhoods have to put up with all kinds of unwanted neighbors, including noxious facilities (Babcock, 1982; Bullard, 1983, 1984).

Public opposition has been more vocal in middle and upper income groups on the issue of noxious facility siting. The Not In My Back Yard (NIMBY) syndrome has been the usual reaction in these communities. As affluent communities became more active in opposing a certain facility, the siting effort shifted toward a more powerless community (Edelstein, 1987: 186-187). Opposition groups often called for the facilities to be sited "somewhere else." "Somewhere Else, USA" often ends up being located in poor, powerless, minority communities. It is this unequal sharing of benefits and burden that has engendered feelings of unfair treatment among poor and minority communities.

Facility siting in the United States is largely reflective of the long pattern of disparate treatment of black communities. There is a "direct historical connection between the exploitation of the land and the exploitation of people, especially black people" (Goldfield, 1987: 211-212). Polluting industries have exploited the pro-growth and pro-jobs sentiment exhibited among the poor, working class, and minority communities (Neiman and Loveridge, 1981). Industries such as paper mills, waste disposal and treatment facilities, heavy metals operations, and chemical plants, searching for operating space, found minority communities to be a logical choice for their expansion. These communities and their leaders were seen as having a Third World view of development. That is, "any development is better than no development at all." Moreover, many residents in these communities were suspicious of environmentalists, a sentiment that aligned them with the pro-growth advocates.

The sight and smell of paper mills, waste treatment and disposal facilities, incinerators, chemical plants, and other industrial operations were promoted as trade-offs for having jobs near "poverty pockets." For example, a paper mill spewing its stench in one of Alabama's poverty-ridden blackbelt counties led Governor George Wallace to declare: "Yeah, that's the smell of prosperity. Sho' does smell sweet, don't it?" (Goldfield,1987:197). Similar views have been reported of residents and community leaders in West Virginia's, Louisiana's, and Texas' "chemical corridor" (Franklin, 1986; Brown, 1987; Bullard and Wright, 1987b).

The 1980s have seen a shift in the way black communities react to the jobs-environment issue. This shift has revolved around the issue of equity. Blacks have begun to challenge the legitimacy of environmental blackmail and the notion of trade-offs. They are now asking: Are the costs borne by the black community imposed to spare the larger community? Can environmental inequities (resulting from industrial facility siting decisions) be compensated? What are "acceptable" risks? Concern about equity is at the heart of black people's reaction to industrial facility siting where there is an inherent imbalance between localized costs and dispersed benefits (Morell, 1987; Morell and Magorian, 1982). Few residents want garbage dumps and landfills in their backyards. The price of siting noxious facilities has skyrocketed in recent years as a result of more stringent federal regulations and the growing militancy among the poor, working class, and minority communities. Compensation appears to hold little promise in mitigating locational conflict and environmental disputes in these communities.

Environmental disputes are likely to increase in the future as tighter federal regulations take effect (1984 amendments to the Resource Conservation and Recovery Act). All states will soon be required to have the treatment and disposal capacity to handle the hazardous wastes generated within their borders. Currently, some industries ship their wastes across state lines. It is not yet known what type of siting pattern will emerge from the new federal mandate. States, however, will need to respond to the equity issue if they expect to have successful siting strategies.

Mobilizing Black Community Residents

A "new" form of environmentalism has taken root in America and in the black community. Since the late seventies, a new grassroots social movement emerged around the toxics threat. Citizens mobilized around the anti-waste theme. The movement has a number of distinguishing characteristics. It:

1. focuses on equity;
2. challenges mainstream environmentalism for its tactics but not its goals;
3. emphasizes the needs of the community and workplace as primary agenda items;
4. uses its own self-taught "experts" and citizen lawsuits instead of relying on legislation and lobbying;
5. takes a "populist" stance on environmental issues relying on active members rather than dues-payers from mailing lists; and
6. embraces a democratic ideology akin to the civil rights and women's movement of the sixties (Gottlieb and Ingram, 1988: 14-15).

These social activists or "toxics warriors" acquired new skills in areas where they had little expertise or no prior experience. They soon became resident "experts" on the toxics issue (Hamilton, 1985). They did not limit their attacks to well-publicized toxic contamination issues, but sought remedial actions on problems like "housing, transportation, air quality, and even economic development — issues the traditional environmental agenda had largely ignored" (Gottlieb and Ingram, 1988: 14).

There is no single agenda or integrated political philosophy in the hundreds of environmental organizations found in the nation. The types of issues that environmental organizations tackle can greatly influence the type of constituents they attract (Gale, 1983). The issues that are most likely to attract black community residents are those that have been couched in an anti-environmental blackmail framework (see Table 1). They include those that:

1. focus on inequality and distributional impacts;
2. endorse the "politics of equity" and direct action;
3. appeal to urban mobilized groups;
4. advocate safeguards against job loss and plant closure; and
5. are ideologically aligned with policies that favor social and political "underdogs."

TABLE 1   Type of Environmental Groups and "Issue
Characteristics" that Attract Black Community Residents

Issue Characteristic	Type of Environmental Group			
	Main-stream	Grass-roots	Social Action	Emergent Coalition
Appeal to urban mobilized group	-[a]	+[b]	+	+
Concerned about inequality and distributional impacts	-/+[c]	-/+	+	+
Endorse the "politics of equity" and direct action	-/+	+	+	-/+
Focus on economic-environmental tradeoffs	-	-/+	+	+
Champion of the political and economic "underdog"	+	-/+	+	-/+

[a]-:   Group is unlikely to have characteristic.
[b]+:   Group is likely to have characteristic
[c]-/+: Group in some cases may have characteristic.

Source: Adapted from Richard P. Gale, "The Environmental Movement and the Left:
Antagonists or Allies?" *Sociological Inquiry* 53 (Spring, 1983): Table 1: 194.

Mainstream environmental organizations, including the "classic" and "mature" groups, have had a great deal of influence in shaping the nation's environmental policy.   Classic environmentalists continue to have a heavy emphasis on
preservation and outdoor recreation, while mature environmentalists are busy in the
area of "tightening regulations, seeking adequate funding for agencies, occasionally focusing on compliance with existing statutes through court action, and
opposing corporate efforts to repeal environmental legislation or weaken standards"
(Gale, 1983: 184).   These organizations, however, have not had a great deal of
success in attracting poor and working class persons, including the large urban
black underclass (that is burdened with both poverty and pollution) in the nation's
central cities or the rural southern blackbelt. Many of these individuals do not see
the mainstream environmental movement as a vehicle that is championing the
causes of the "little man," the "underdog," or the "oppressed" (Jordon, 1980;
Taylor, 1984; Bullard and Wright, 1987a, 1987b; Taylor, 1989).

The emergence of grassroots environmental groups, some of which are affiliated with mainstream environmental organizations, have begun to bridge the class and ideological gap between core environmentalists and the various orbits around which the movement was built. In some cases, these groups mirror their larger counterparts at the national level in terms of problems and issues selected, membership, ideological alignment, and tactics used. Grassroots groups usually are organized around area-specific and single-issue problems. They are in many cases more inclusive than mainstream environmental organizations. Grassroots environmental organizations, however, may or may not choose to focus on equity, distributional impacts, and economic-environmental trade-off issues. These groups do appeal to some black community residents, especially those who have been active in other confrontational protest activities.

Environmental groups in the black community quite often emerge out of established social action organizations. For example, black leadership has deep roots in the black church and other voluntary associations. Morris (1984: 282) contends that the black community "possesses (1) certain basic resources, (2) social activists with strong ties to mass-based indigenous institutions, and (3) tactics and strategies that can be effectively employed against a system of domination." These indigenous institutions have led the opposition against social injustice and racial discrimination. Many black community residents have affiliation with civic clubs, neighborhood associations, community improvement groups, and an array of anti-poverty and anti-discrimination organizations. A protest infrastructure, thus, is already in place for the emergence of an environmental-equity movement in the black community.

Social action groups that take on environmental issues as part of their agenda are often on the political left. They broaden their base of support and sphere of influence by incorporating environmental equity issues as agenda items that favor the disenfranchised and dispossessed. The push for equity is an extension of the civil rights movement, a movement where direct confrontation and the politics of protest were real weapons. In short, social action environmental organizations retain much of their civil rights flavor.

The fourth type of environmental group that has appealed to black community residents grew out of coalitions between environmentalists (mainstream and grassroots), social action advocates, and organized labor (Pollack and Grozuczak, 1984). These somewhat fragile coalitions operate from the position that social justice and environmental quality are compatible goals. Although these groups are beginning to formulate agendas for action, mistrust acts as a limiting factor (Bullard and Wright, 1987b). These coalitions have memberships that cut across racial, class, and geographic boundaries. Compositional factors may engender less group solidarity and sense of "control" among black members, compared to the indigenous social action or grassroots environmental groups where blacks are in the majority and make the decisions.

Thus, environmentalists have had a difficult task convincing blacks and the poor that they are on their side. Mistrust is engendered among economically and politically oppressed groups in this country when they see environmental reforms being used to direct social and economic resources away from problems of poor countries toward priorities of the affluent. For example, tighter government regulations and public opposition to disposal facility siting have opened up the Third World as the new dumping ground for this nation's toxic wastes (Porterfield and Weir, 1987; Vallette, 1989: 7-16). Few of these poor countries have laws or the infrastructure to handle the wastes from the United States and other Western industrialized nations. Blacks and other ethnic minorities in this country also see their communities being inundated with all types of toxics (Bullard, 1983; Commission for Racial Justice, 1987). This is especially the case in the southern United States (e.g., one of the most underdeveloped regions of the nation) where more than one-half of all blacks live.

The civil rights movement has its roots in the southern United States. Southern racism deprived blacks of "political rights, economic opportunity, social justice, and human dignity" (Bloom, 1987: 18). The new environmental-equity movement is also centered in the South, a region where marked ecological disparities exist between black and white communities. The 1980s have seen the emergence of a small cadre of blacks who equate environmental discrimination with a civil rights issue. An alliance has been forged between organized labor, blacks, and environmental groups, as exhibited by the 1983 Urban Environment Conference workshops held in New Orleans. Environmental and civil rights issues were presented as compatible agenda items by the conference organizers (Urban Environment Conference Inc., 1985: 29).

A growing number of grassroots organizations and their leaders have begun to adopt confrontational strategies (e.g., protests, neighborhood demonstrations, picketing, political pressure, litigation, etc.) to reduce and eliminate environmental stressors. The national black political leadership has also demonstrated a willingness to take a strong pro-environment stance. The League of Conservation Voters, for example, assigned the Congressional Black Caucus high marks for having one of the best pro-environment voting records (Taylor, 1984).

Toxic waste disposal has generated protests in many communities across the country. The first national environmental protest by blacks came in 1982 after the mostly black Warren County, North Carolina was selected as the burial site for 32,000 cubic yards of soil contaminated with the highly toxic PCBs (polychlorinated biphenyls). The soil was illegally dumped along the roadways in fourteen North Carolina counties in 1978. Black civil rights activists, political leaders, and local residents marched in protest demonstrations against the construction of the PCB landfill in their community. Why was Warren County selected as the landfill site? The decision made more political sense than environmental sense (Geiser and Waneck, 1983: 13-17).

Although the protests were unsuccessful in halting the landfill construction, they marked the first time blacks mobilized a nationally broad-based group to protest environmental inequities. The protests prompted Congressman Walter E. Fauntroy (Representative from the District of Columbia), who had been active in the demonstrations, to initiate the U.S. General Accounting Office (1983) study of hazardous waste landfill siting in the South. The GAO study observed a strong relationship between the siting of offsite hazardous landfills and race of surrounding communities. Three of the four offsite hazardous waste landfills in EPA's Region IV were located in black communities, while blacks made up only twenty percent of the region's population.

Toward the Politics of Inclusion

Because exposure to environmental toxins varies across population groups, distributive politics have come to play an important role in explaining the vastly different action strategies employed by middle income white communities and lower-income black communities. The middle class dominated environmental movement of the 1960s and 1970s built an impressive political base for environmental reform and regulatory relief. Many environmental problems in the 1980s, however, had social impacts somewhat different from earlier ones. A disproportionate burden of pollution is carried by the urban poor and minority residents (see McCaull 1975; Kruvant 1975; Jordon, 1980; Kazis and Grossman, 1982; Bullard and Wright, 1986). The nation's toxic waste problem has been widely publicized in the hundreds of "Love Canals" (see Levine, 1982; Epstein et al., 1982; Edelstein, 1987).

Few environmentalists realized the sociological implications of the NIMBY (not in my backyard) phenomenon (Morrison, 1986: 187-200). Given the political climate of the times, the hazardous wastes, garbage dumps, and polluting industries were likely to end up in somebody's backyard. But whose backyard? More often than not, these locally unwanted land uses (LULUs) ended up in poor, powerless, black communities rather than in affluent suburbs. This pattern has proven to be the rule, even though the benefits derived from industrial waste production are directly related to affluence. Public officials and private industry have, in many cases, responded to the NIMBY phenomenon using the "PIBBY" principle, "Place in Blacks' Back Yards."

Social justice movements have begun to move environmentalism to the left in an effort to address some of the distributional impact and equity issues (Gale, 1983: 179-199). Documentation of civil rights violations has strengthened the move to make environmental quality a basic right of all individuals. Rising energy costs, a continued erosion of the economy's ability to provide jobs, and rising real incomes are factors that favor environmentalism of the left blending with the

objectives of labor, minorities and other "underdog" groups, and middle class
environmentalists (Humphrey and Buttel, 1982: 253).

Mainstream environmental organizations were late in broadening their base
of support to include blacks and other minorities, the poor, and working class
persons. The "energy crisis" in the 1970s was a major impetus that moved many
environmentalists to embrace equity issues confronting the poor in this country
and countries of the Third World (Morrison, 1980). Environmentalism, over the
years, has shifted from a "participatory" to a "power" strategy where the "core of
active environmental movement is focused on litigation, political lobbying, and
technical evaluation rather than on mass mobilization for protest marches"
(Schnaiberg, 1980: 366-367).

Institutional racism and discrimination continue to influence the quality of
life in many of the nation's black communities. For example, the ability to exit a
negative or health-threatening physical environment is directly associated with
affluence. Federal policies, for example, were key elements in the development
of spatially differentiated metropolitan areas where blacks and other visible
minorities are segregated from whites and the poor from the more affluent citizens
(Momeni, 1986). Moreover, the federal government is the "proximate and essential
cause of urban apartheid" in the United States (Kushner, 1980: 130). The end result
of the nation's apartheid-type policies on black households has meant limited
mobility, reduced housing options and residential packages, and decreased environmental choices. For example, air pollution in inner-city neighborhoods can
be found at levels up to five times greater than those found in suburban areas. Urban
areas, in general, have "dirtier air and drinking water, more waste water and solid
waste problems, and greater exposure to lead and other heavy metals than non-
urban areas" (Kazis and Grossman, 1982: 48).

What is the answer to this problem? A first step lies in the diversification of the
environmental movement. It makes a lot of sense for the organized environmental
movement in the United States to broaden its base to include more minority, low
income, and working class individuals. Moreover, the narrowly defined agendas
of the larger environmental and conservation organizations need to be broadened
to incorporate minority and working class community concerns. Diversification,
however, does not mean "quota-filling" or "check-writing" to fill membership
rosters. Diversification can only enhance the national environmental movement's
worldwide credibility in dealing with global environmental and development
issues, especially in Third World nations.

Many of the nation's environmental organizations now mirror corporate
America in structure and outlook. They also reflect an under-representation of
minority professionals at all levels. There are just a handful of minority environmental organizations in the country with paid staffs. The Center for Environment,
Commerce and Energy, or CE^2, based in Washington, DC, is just one of the few
black environmental organizations. Inclusion of more minority professionals

among the ranks of environmental, occupational, and health and safety organizations would have far-reaching benefits beyond the organizations and groups served. Such an inclusion would infuse egalitarian principles into a movement that still has to shake off its "elitist" image. In short, "only economic justice can bring environmental justice, but minority professionals rising through the management ranks of government and industry can give impetus to the process" (Human Environment Center, 1981: v).

The environmental equity movement has elements of the three dominant approaches to neighborhood organizing: social work, political activist, and neighborhood maintenance (Fisher, 1984). First, the social work approach uses "enablers" and "advocates" to secure needed community services. Environmental protection is viewed as a public service not unlike fire and police protection and garbage collection. Second, the political activist approach views community organizing as a means of empowering local residents to defend their space and develop a political base to influence decision making. Third, the neighborhood maintenance approach, usually associated with middle and upper class neighborhoods, organizes around improving and maintaining residential areas while opposing external and internal threats from hostile forces.

Grassroots organizing within the black community will likely continue to blossom, while the threat of environmental blackmail will likely lose its appeal as residents become aware of the health risks and siting inequities. As an aid in future neighborhood organizing, however, the following strategies are proposed:

1. link minority, working class, and middle class environmental activists on issues that cut across geographic boundaries and political jurisdictions;
2. develop inter-organizational linkages and organizations that cut across racial and class lines;
3. create organizing channels that cut across the political spectrum;
4. develop leader exchange programs designed to break down the legacy of mistrust and artificial barriers that separate people and hinder mobilization;
5. set up training and leadership development programs for emergent grassroots environmental equity groups; and
6. institute "adopt-a-community" programs at Historically Black Colleges and Universities (HBCUs) around environmental justice, and target minority communities threatened by environmental hazards.

It is also important for the victims of the toxics war to know that there have been some citizen victories. For grassroots groups, especially minorities and other "underdog" groups, knowing that others in similar circumstances have triumphed gives them an added incentive to keep up the struggle. Ghetto residents, for example, are routinely bombarded with messages reinforcing their powerlessness and marginal status. Strategies for improving communication networks include:

1. maximizing networks through the use of information channeled into larger information systems (e.g., Citizens Clearinghouse for Hazardous Waste);
2. exposing the impact of NIMBY by having policy makers deal with this phenomenon as a genuine concern of minority groups, not as an exaggerated or irrational fear;
3. instilling self-confidence in community residents and leaders;
4. communicating environmentalism as a universal equity issue. People must know when they have "won"; and
5. inter-organizational communicating that dispels prevailing myths and stereotypes on both sides (environmentalists and social justice advocates).

For minority, working class, and poor persons to give their support for environmental and conservation programs, they must feel they have a stake or vested interest in these issues while not jeopardizing their support and credibility on urban and industrial policy areas.

Conclusion

Black communities are beginning to incorporate environmental safeguards into their agendas for economic development. Although economically vulnerable (few business and employment centers are indigenous to the community), a growing segment within the black community has begun to demand an environment-development balance. Job blackmail seems to be losing ground mainly because the promise of jobs and a broadened tax base for local residents has been more promise than anything else. Many communities that host noxious facilities have been left to suffer from the tragedy of poverty, pollution, increased health risks, and lowered property values. Residents also must contend with the stigma of living in a "contaminated" community.

The solution to the current environmental dilemma does not reside in compensation. Proposals that call for those less fortunate to accept risks others can escape will only heighten environmental inequities between poor and affluent communities. Many poor and minority communities, because of economic necessity, would be forced to adapt to lower quality physical environments.

Institutionalized discrimination continues to affect public policy decisions related to the enforcement of environmental regulations. The politics of pollution have placed public officials squarely in the middle of environmental disputes and locally unwanted land uses as in the case of municipal garbage landfills and incinerators, hazardous waste storage and treatment facilities, and chemical plants.

Although the effects of pollution have no geographic boundaries, blacks and lower income groups are often "trapped" in polluted environments because of low incomes, housing discrimination and residential segregation, limited residential choices, discriminatory zoning regulations, and ineffective land use policies. Moreover, black communities are beginning to integrate environmental issues into traditional civil rights agendas and to develop viable action strategies to combat environmental degradation, discrimination, job blackmail, and public policy decisions that have disparate distributional impacts on black and poor communities.

The 1990s offer some challenging opportunities for the environmental movement to embrace social justice and other redistributive policies. Population shifts and demographic trends all point to a more diverse nation. It is time for the environmental movement to diversify and reach out to the "other" America.

7

Invitation to Poison?
Detroit Minorities and Toxic Fish
Consumption from the Detroit River

Patrick C. West

In major urban areas across the country there have been efforts to increase opportunities for urban outdoor recreation along the banks of major urban rivers. In Detroit a "greening" of the Detroit River waterfront has improved access to the Detroit River and associated outdoor recreation pursuits such as fishing. Yet the tragic irony is that this may have also created an "invitation to poison" when fish from polluted urban rivers are caught and eaten.

This article describes results from a pilot study of fish consumption from the Detroit River by a sample of Detroit residents. Levels of fish consumption are important to understand in relation to Michigan's Rule 1057, regulating point source municipal and industrial discharge of toxic contaminants into Michigan surface waters. Michigan's Rule 1057 uses an average fish consumption assumption in its standards setting process and thus does not account for variation in levels of consumption by different sub-groups of the Michigan population. One major concern has been that certain sub-groups such as minorities and the elderly may consume greater amounts of contaminated fish than the average for the general population. This pilot study compares minority and white consumption of four heavily fished species from the Detroit River: White Bass, Walleye, Sheephead, and Yellow Perch.

Study Methods

The study was a phone survey of a stratified quota sample of residents of Detroit. A major problem in phone surveys in urban areas is the fact that low income households tend to be under-represented because a greater proportion of these

Patrick C. West is an Associate Professor of Natural Resources/Environmental Sociology at the University of Michigan and the Samuel T. Dana Professor of Outdoor Recreation, School of Natural Resources. His specific research foci include natural resources and Native Americans, and urban outdoor recreation and minorities. This study was funded by the Office of Urban Forest Recreation Research, Chicago, Illinois, as part of a wider study of urban outdoor recreation in Detroit. Supplemental funding for a Minority Student Intern was provided by the School of Natural Resources.

households do not have phones. Because of the importance of low income inner-city minorities to the purposes of this study, we designed a stratified quota sampling scheme to gain greater proportional representation of low income households in Detroit. We first examined census data on phone ownership by income and found that households under $5,000 had much lower rates of phone ownership. Then, using census data on income and race, we established a quota sampling goal for a typology of race and income categories.

Within this quota sampling scheme we then used the standard random digit dialing method of sampling households in Detroit. We were successful in achieving the quotas for a total sample size of 481 in all cells except whites with under $5,000 income.

The survey took place from September 1985 to January 1986. Respondents were asked about their fish consumption from the Detroit River for the one year period prior to the date of the interview. Race was measured by a self identification question with the following categories: "black, Hispanic, white, and other." There were very few Hispanic and "other" respondents so the categories were combined into a "white" and "non-white" dichotomous variable for purposes of analysis.

Results

Seventy-four respondents (15 percent of the full sample) reported catching and eating fish from the Detroit River over the one year period. Of this sub-sample, whites tended to fish primarily for recreation, while minorities tended to fish for both recreation and food (Table 1). Fish consumed from the Detroit River are viewed as supplemental sources of protein by many minority residents of Detroit. This adds a dimension of nutritional necessity to the policy debates over the need to protect water quality to permit safe access to fishery resources in urban areas.

Table 2 shows differences in fish consumption for whites and minorities of the four species of fish caught and eaten from the Detroit River over the one year period. Of those who fish the Detroit River, a greater proportion of minorities consumed each of the four species of fish than did whites. However, due to the low sub-sample size (63-65) only the differences for White Bass and Sheephead are statistically significant. For these species we can generalize results to the full population of Detroit residents who fish in the Detroit River. Further analysis of these data by income level suggests that for White Bass, Yellow Perch, and Sheephead, minorities whose income ranges from $5,000 to $20,000 have the highest consumption of these species. Surprisingly, the lowest income minorities (under $5,000) are not the highest consumers of fish from the Detroit River, possibly due to the lack of access and economic means. Rather, low to moderate income minorities are at the highest risk.

While these findings suggest a relatively greater proportion of fish consumption by minorities, they are not (in this form) comparable to the average fish

TABLE 1   Relationship Between Race and
Motivation for Fishing in the Detroit River

Motivation	Race			
	White		Non-White	
	N	Percent	N	Percent
Recreation	(18)	78.3	(20)	40
Food	(0)	0	(1)	2
Both	(5)	21.7	(29)	58
Total	(23)	100	(50)	100

X2=9.3, df=2,p< .01. Cravers's V=.35

consumption assumptions used in Michigan's Rule 1057. The Rule 1057 average consumption assumption is 6.5 grams/person/day (for all species and all waters). While our pilot study covers only four species from only one river in Michigan, we wished to see how much consumption was occurring in grams/person/day for the species examined from the Detroit River in comparison to the total consumption assumptions in Rule 1057. To make this comparison, we utilized conversion tables that convert average fish size of each species into grams. We then multiplied this conversion factor by the number of each fish species consumed per household and divided the total grams consumed by the number of persons in the household. This was divided by 365 days/year to get average grams/person/day.

Combining the three species that have the greatest disproportionate consumption by minorities (Sheephead, White Bass, and Yellow Perch) the average among those who caught and ate at least one of these species during the one year period was 3.7 grams/person/day. This is slightly more than half of the 6.5 grams assumption in Rule 1057 for all species and all waters in Michigan. Breaking this average down by race, we found that the average consumption by minority respondents (4.6 grams/person/day) is substantially greater than that for white respondents (1.8 grams/person/day). Because of the low sub-sample size, the T-test for differences in means is not quite statistically significant (T = -1.86, df = 26.76, P < .07), but the sample results are suggestive in a provisional sense. For these three species alone, from just this one river, minority consumption is already over 70 percent of the 6.5 total average assumption for all species in all Michigan waters in Rule 1057 and is 2 1/2 times as much as white consumption of these species.

We are currently conducting a much broader survey of fish consumption among a random sample of all sportfish license holders in Michigan under funding from the Michigan Toxic Substance Control Commission. The survey covers all

TABLE 2   Percent* of Whites and Non-Whites Who
Catch and Eat Selected Species of Fish from the Detroit River

Species	Percent White	Percent Non-White	X2	df	Sig.	Craver's V	N**
White Bass	16.7	52.2	8.05	2	.05	.35	64
Walleye	30	35.6	.22	2	NS	.06	65
Sheephead	0	33.3	9.69	2	.01	.39	63
Yellow Perch	16.7	35.6	2.85	2	NS	.21	63

* Percent is percent of each category (white/non-white) who caught and ate at least one fish from the Detroit River during the one year period; it is not percent of the total sample.
** N varies due to missing data

species from all Michigan surface waters and the Michigan Great Lakes. If these findings from the pilot study are born out in this wider research effort, they will have major implications for revising the assumptions of using average fish consumption in the setting of point discharge standards. If minorities and other significant sub-groups of the population consume disproportionately larger amounts of fish, policy makers will need to face more squarely the problems of planning for "the average consumer." It may be a relatively harmless error for state park planners to plan for the "average camper who doesn't exist," but in the case of regulating the public's exposure to toxic chemicals, such errors can have far more tragic consequences.

A broader confirmation of these pilot study findings would also have implications for more intensive, focused "targeting" of fish consumption advisory communications to sub-groups such as urban minorities that are at greater risk due to disproportionate consumption of fish from polluted urban rivers, but who may be less apt to read and abide by standard fish consumption advisory brochures.

8

Minority Anglers and Toxic Fish Consumption: Evidence from a Statewide Survey of Michigan

Patrick C. West, J. Mark Fly, Frances Larkin, and Robert W. Marans

This paper reports on fish consumption patterns by minority sport fishermen and members of their families that eat fish. Concerns about toxic chemicals in Michigan surface waters (e.g. Foran et al., 1989; Humphrey, 1976, 1983) have raised the issue of risks incurred by sport fishermen eating fish, especially subgroups in the population, such as minorities and the elderly that may consume more fish than the average fisherman. Pilot research by West indicates that black fishermen consume more of three species of fish from the Detroit River than do white fishermen (see Chapter 7). This paper seeks to examine whether these differences between minorities and whites exist on a state-wide basis. Findings indicate that they do. Policy implications for the setting of fish consumption assumptions in state water quality standards and targeted communication of fish consumption advisories are discussed.

Patrick C. West is an Associate Professor of Natural Resources/Environmental Sociology at the University of Michigan School of Natural Resources and the Samuel T. Dana Professor of Outdoor Recreation. His specific research foci include natural resources and Native Americans, and urban outdoor recreation and minorities.

J. Mark Fly is an Assistant Professor of Outdoor Recreation at the University of Wisconsin, Madison. Dr. Fly has research interests in outdoor recreation and reverse migration and in toxic fish consumption and fish consumption advisories in relation to minorities and the elderly.

Frances Larkin is a Professor of Public Health at the University of Michigan School of Public Health. Her general research interests are in dietary assessment methodology related to nutrition and food consumption.

Robert W. Marans is a Professor in the Urban Planning Program and a research scientist at the Institute for Social Research at the University of Michigan. His research interests include Great Lakes issues, outdoor recreation and quality of life, minorities and urban recreation, and toxic fish consumption related to minorities and the elderly.

Data and Methods

Sample

The study was a mail survey of a stratified sample of sport fish license holders. The sample was drawn from a data tape of the passbook file of all Michigan licensed anglers, obtained from the Michigan Department of Natural Resources. The main bases for stratifying the sample were type of license and geographic residence, as indicated by zip code. The total sample size was 2,600. (For further details of the sampling see West et al., 1989a).

Because of the need to minimize recall error about very specific fish consumption information respondents were asked only to recall detailed fish consumption patterns for the seven day period prior to filling out the survey. The sample of 2,600 was then spread in 18 randomly drawn cohorts over the period from mid January to early June 1988. Weighting was then used to generalize to, and be representative of, the period of January to early June. (For details of the weighting see West et al., 1989a). Thus, the results presented below relate only to the winter-spring period covered.

Mail Survey Pre-tests and Return Rate

The survey was pre-tested using personal interviews and mailed surveys. The survey was then revised and pretested again using personal interviews. The survey was then revised a final time.

The sample was sent a sequence of a post card, survey, post card, and survey.[1] If people still failed to return the survey, they were called on the telephone and encouraged to return the survey.[2] Despite this five-wave strategy, the final response rate was only 47.3 percent. Thus a second phone-call, follow-up survey was conducted with a sample of respondents and non-respondents to test for non-response bias (West et al., 1989b). The non-response survey found that there was indeed a non-response bias in the mail survey—those who did not return the surveys tended to eat less fish. The main mailed survey found that average fish consumption was 18.3 grams/person/day. This had to be adjusted downward by a factor of 2.2 (to 17.1 grams/person/day) to adjust for non-response bias (West et al., 1989b). This figure of 2.2 can be used as a rough estimate for adjusting sub-group means but cannot be used as an exact adjustment factor because the non-response bias survey did not measure non-response bias for sub-groups, only an adjustment for the the overall mean (West et al., 1989b). Thus, the sub-group means presented below are unadjusted.

Aspects of Variable Measurement

Fish meal consumption information was gathered from all members of the household that eat fish. It is important to include other members of the household because the suspected higher levels of fish consumption by anglers will also hold for other household members who eat fish. It may be particularly important in relation to women and children who have lower body weight but who may consume similar portions leading to higher concentrations of exposure for these family members. Because of this we were not able to meet the criteria of full statistical independence.[3] A standard conservative way of adjusting for this is to decrease the P value for statistical significance. Therefore, in this paper we will designate P values of .05 as "marginally non-significant" in the text and denote them as ".05 (NS)" in the tables.

Fish meals included self-caught fish, market fish, restaurant fish, and gift fish. It is important to include fish consumed other than self caught fish because the total risk to these individuals is the combination of sport caught fish and fish consumed from other sources. The fish consumption assumption currently in use (6.5 grams/ person/day) is the standard of Rule 1057 which regulates the discharge of toxic chemicals into Michigan surface waters. Rule 1057 comes from a national study that is not confined to sport caught fish from just one state. Thus we have used a parallel set of assumptions in defining the appropriate fish consumption parameters.

To calculate fish meal size the respondents were asked to estimate the size of each fish meal by looking at an enclosed picture of "about 1/2 pound" fish meal. The picture showed both a fillet and fish steak of "about 1/2 pound." Respondents were asked to judge whether each fish meal was "about the same," "less" or "more" than the fish meal in the picture. This technique has been used previously by Humphrey (1976, 1983) in diary studies of fish consumption and exposure to PCBs in Great Lakes fish. These results were converted into gram estimates for calculating average consumption in grams/person/day.

Statistical Analysis

Our main purpose in this paper is to discover sub-groups, especially those involving minorities, with especially high and potentially risky fish consumption behaviors. We are less concerned with causal analysis. To do this we will rely on a two way ANOVA (analysis of variance) as our main statistical technique. It will show average fish consumption for different sub-groups (e.g.. older, black minorities). We will confine the analysis to two way ANOVAs because in higher N-way ANOVAs, cell Ns would get too low for meaningful analysis of sub-group means. Tests for statistical interaction will be shown.[4] Where interaction is not significant summary statistics from multiple classification analysis will be used to partial out effects of independent variables.

Results

Michigan's Rule 1057, which regulates the discharge of toxic chemicals into Michigan surface waters, currently assumes that average fish consumption is 6.5 grams/person/day. As previously indicated, our study found that average fish consumption for the winter-spring period for sport fishermen and members of their

TABLE 1   Average Fish Consumption by Race

Race	N	Average Consumption*	SD	95 Percent Confidence Interval	Maximum Value***
Black	69	20.3	26.8	13.9–26.8	122.4
Native American	139	24.3	33.3	18.7–29.9	163.3
Other Minority****	123	19.8	24.5	15.4–24.2	138.8
White	3339	17.9	26.5	17.0–18.8	224.5
Total	3670	18.3	26.8	17.4–19.1	224.5

F=2.8, d.f.=3, P<.05 (NS)

* Average consumption, confidence intervals, and maximum values are in grams/person/day.

** The confidence interval is a statistical measure of the probability of the population mean (as opposed to the sample mean) falling within these parameters. In line one, for instance, there is a 95 percent chance that the population mean for those under 11 years old would fall between 8.1 and 11.0 grams/person/day.

***Maximum value is the highest fish consumption (in grams/person/day) found for any individual in that age group. Few people in the sample consume at this high level.

****"Other Minority" includes Hispanic, mixed, and other.

TABLE 2   Average Fish Consumption by Age Groups

Age	N	Average Consumption*	SD	95 Percent Confidence Interval	Maximum Value
0–10	444	9.5	15.7	8.1–11.0	82.6
11–20	571	10.8	18.6	9.2–12.3	106.1
21–30	566	18.0	25.7	15.9–20.2	146.9
31–40	665	20.4	30.0	18.1–22.7	163.3
41–50	566	20.9	30.0	18.4–23.4	224.5
51–65	560	24.0	29.2	21.6–26.4	224.5
Over 65	269	25.2	28.5	21.7–28.6	138.7
Total	3641	18.2**	26.6	17.3–19.0	224.5

F=25.5, d.f.=6, P<.001

* Average consumption and confidence limits in grams/person/day.

** The overall mean consumption is somewhat different (.1 gram) than the main figure reported above due to missing data for the age variable. Note that the confidence limit for the overall mean consumption is between 17.3 and 19 grams/person/day.

families who eat fish was 18.3 grams/person/day. This had to be adjusted downward by 2.2 grams to adjust for non-response bias.

Minority sport fishermen and their families consumed 21.7 grams/person/day compared to 17.9 grams/person/day for whites. These differences are marginally non-significant (two-tailed t test: t= 2.1, d.f. =3576, P=.05, NS). Comparisons for different minority groups are shown in Table 1. Here it can be seen that the the overall average for minorities of 21.7 grams/person/day is partitioned into 20.3 grams/person/day for blacks, 24.3 grams/person/day for Native Americans, 19.8 grams/person/day for other (Hispanic, other, mixed), and again 17.9 grams/person/day for whites. These differences are again marginally non-significant. However, the grams/person/day figures in the sample for black and especially Native American minorities are over the average for the sample and way over the 6.5 gram figure currently used in the water quality standards in Michigan.

Table 2 shows that older anglers also have high fish consumption. Those over 65 have an average fish consumption of 25.2 grams/person/day. This is the highest consumption rate of all single variable analyses. Those between 51-65 consume 24 grams/person/day. Differences by age are statistically significant. In Table 3 we show the joint multivariate effects of race and age in an ANOVA. While interaction is not statistically significant, main effects are. We also see that those who are both older (over 50) and black have very high rates of fish consumption (31.9 grams/person/day), between 4 and 5 times the 6.5 assumption in current water quality standards.

Native American sub-groups in combination with age also have high rates of consumption but here the highest group is Native Americans who are between 31-50 years old (30.6 grams/person/day). Thus different age groups combine with different minority groups to produce the highest consuming sub-groups in the table. The F value of the effect of race when controlled for age becomes non-significant. This is reflected in the slight drop from an Eta (bivariate) of .04 to a Beta (partial) of .03. Age is the main contributor to the joint main effects with an Eta and Beta of .18.

Income does not have a statistically significant bivariate relationship with fish consumption (West et al., 1989a). In the multivariate relationship among race, income and fish consumption, both main effects and interaction are marginally non-significant due to the adjustment of P values for statistical independence. The highest fish consuming group in the sample was medium income, black sport fishermen and their families.[5] For this group, average consumption is 30.5 grams/person/day. In contrast, for Native American and other minorities the modal category was low income (below $15,000).[6] Native Americans with low income had the highest consumption of all sub-groups in this table, 33.7 grams/person/day, over 5 times the the 6.5 gram standard in current use in Rule 1057. It should be noted that, in contrasting black and Native American fish consumption patterns in the sample in relation to income, black patterns are curvilinear in one direction with low

TABLE 3   Average Fish Consumption by Age and Race

	Age		
Race	1–30	31–50	51–91 *
Black	14.1**	19.8	31.9
	(26)***	(25)	(17)
Native	16.9	30.6	21.7
American	(35)	(48)	(53)
Other	13.1	27.4	24.1
Minority****	(56)	(37)	(24)
White	12.9	20.4	24.4
	(1463)	(1120)	(730)

Main Effects: F=24.5, d.f.=5, P<.001   Race: F=1.3, d.f.=3, NS*****

Age: F=57.4, d.f.=2, P<.001

Interaction: F=1.5, d.f.=6, NS
Summary Multiple Classification Analysis Statistics
Race: Eta=.04, Beta=.03   Age: Eta=.18, Beta=.18

* Age categories were collapsed to get a larger cell N size. We do not wish to imply that a 51 year old person is elderly. Note, however, in Table 2, that older persons between 51 and 65 consume more than younger cohorts.
** Average fish consumption in grams/person/day.
*** Cell Ns (sub-sample size).
**** Includes Hispanic, mixed, and other.
***** F values for individual variables are for the effect of that variable controlled for the other independent variable (Norusis, 1986:172). Generally this can be compared with the bivariate one-way ANOVA in other tables to see the change in F values when controlling for the second variable. However, there may be differences due to other causes. Nie et al. (1970: 404) note that in the calculation of the F value in one-way analysis of variance in SPSS the variation due to some factor X is assigned to error variation, whereas in N-way ANOVA the effects of X are not included as part of error variation. Also, in some cases variables are collapsed into fewer categories for the multivariate analysis and this will affect the F value differences between the one-way and two-way ANOVAs.

TABLE 4   Average Fish Consumption by Race and Income

| | Income in Dollars | | |
Race	Below 15,000	15,000– 29,000	30,000 and Above
Black	16.3 *	30.5	16.0
	(6) **	(15)	(40)
Native	33.7	17.2	29.4
American	(23)	(53)	(52)
Other	31.3	15.6	18.9
Minority***	(9)	(21)	(82)
White	15.0	17.7	18.5
	(310)	(800)	(1967)

Main Effects: F=2.3, d.f.=5, P<.05 (NS)   Race: F=3.2, d.f.=3, P<.05(NS)
Income: F=1.5, d.f.=2, NS   Interaction: F=2.5, d.f.=6, p<.05 (NS)
Summary Multiple Classification Analysis Statistics
Race: Eta=.05, Beta=.05   Income: Eta=.03, Beta=.03
* Average fish consumption in grams/person/day.
** Cell Ns (sub-sample sizes).
*** "Other Minority" includes Hispanic, mixed, and other.

TABLE 5   Average Fish Consumption by Education Level*

Education Level	N	Average Consumption**	SD	95 Percent Confidence Interval	Maximum Value
Graduated H. School	1499	18.8	26.5	17.5–20.2	163.3
Graduated College	1685	18.6	27.9	17.3–19.9	224.5
Graduate School	474	15.3	26.8	13.2–17.4	138.8
Total	3658	18.3	26.8	17.4–19.1	224.5

F=3.4, d.f.=2, P<.05 (NS)
* Education level was determined by the education level of the highest educated person in the household, as this generally determines the status level of the household and associated "life style" patterns such as fishing and fish eating patterns.
** Average consumption, confidence intervals, and maximum value are in grams/person/day.

TABLE 6   Average Fish Consumption by Race and Education

	Education		
Race	Through High School	Through College	Post-Graduate
Black	17.7 *	24.2	0.0
	(41) **	(28)	(0)
Native	23.8	24.0	26.9
American	(77)	(43)	(19)
Other	20.4	14.2	35.3
Minority***	(73)	(39)	(11)
White	18.5	18.5	14.3
	(1320)	(1575)	(444)

Main Effects: F=3.0, d.f.=5, P<.05 (NS)   Race: F=2.7, d.f.=3, P<.05 (NS)
Education: F=3.3, d.f.=2, P<.05 (NS)   Interaction: F=1.9, d.f.=5, NS
Summary Multiple Classification Analysis Statistics
Race: Eta=.05, Beta=.05   Education: Eta=.04, Beta=.04
* Average fish consumption in grams/person/day.
** Cell N (sub-sample size)
*** "Other Minority" includes Hispanic, mixed, and other.

consumption for low and high income (with high consumption for middle income). Native American patterns are curvilinear in the opposite way—high consumption for low and high income, with low consumption for middle income. White patterns by income, in contrast, are almost flat, with few differences by income level.

Education has a marginally non-significant bivariate relationship with fish consumption (Table 5). Those with graduate education have lower fish consumption than those with lower education. When the multivariate ANOVA between race and education is shown (Table 6) we see that the pattern in Table 5 is primarily the pattern for white fishermen. For blacks, the modal category is for those through college, 24.2 grams/person/day. We cannot compare this with black anglers with post graduate education because there are none in the sample (and probably few in the population). However, for Native Americans and other minorities, post graduate education is the modal category, exactly the opposite relationship that exists for whites. Interaction is not statistically significant and main effects are marginally non-significant.

The summary Multiple Classification Analysis correlational statistics show that the bivariate Etas and the partials (Betas) are identical, indicating that each variable is making an independent contribution to the relationship. However, the F values for both variables (controlled for each other) are marginally non-significant.

TABLE 7   Average Fish Consumption by Place of Residence

Place of Residence	N	Average Consumption*	SD	95 Percent Confidence Interval	Maximum Value
Large City/Suburb (over100,000)	699	19.7	27.8	17.6–21.7	195.9
Small City (20,000–100,000)	870	15.8	24.1	14.2–17.4	163.2
Town (2,000–20,000)	724	19.2	29.3	17.1–21.4	224.5
Small Town (100–2,000)	345	16.5	24.5	13.9–19.1	118.4
Rural Farm	253	20.4	26.6	17.1–23.7	130.6
Total	3657	18.4	26.8	17.5–19.2	224.5

F=2.9, d.f.=5, P<.01
* Average consumption, confidence limits, and maximum value are in grams/person/day.

Table 7 shows the bivariate relationship between place (size) of residence and average fish consumption. The relationship is statistically significant but non-linear. Table 8 presents the two-way ANOVA showing the joint relationship between race, place of residence, and fish consumption. Main effects are marginally non-significant. However, interaction is statistically significant. The nature of the interaction relationship is as follows. The highest black consumption tends to be from cities (23.9 grams/person/day), while high Native American fish consumption tends to be from rural farm, rural non-farm and small towns (32.1 grams/person/day). Other minorities tend to have a less strong relationship with place of residence but there is a slight tendency for moderately high consumption to come from cities. Similarly there is only a weak relationship for whites, with a slight tendency for moderately high consumption to come from rural farm and rural non-farm populations.

Average consumption of fish by years of residence in Michigan is shown in the one way ANOVA in Table 9. It can be seen that the longer a person has lived in Michigan the more likely he or she is to consume greater amounts of fish. This relationship is statistically significant. The relationship between race, length of residence, and fish consumption is shown in Table 10. Here it can be seen that there is no statistically significant interaction. However, the combined main effects are statistically significant. While race controlled for years of residence is not statistically significant there is no decline in the correlation coefficient. Both Eta

TABLE 8   Average Fish Consumption by Race and Place of Residence

| | Place of Residence | | |
Race	City Over 20,000	Town 100–20,000	Rural Farm Non-Farm
Black	23.9 *	5.1	20.4
	(51) **	(12)	(6)
Native	13.1	29.9	32.1
American	(51)	(51)	(37)
Other	21.5	19.0	17.0
Minority***	(63)	(29)	(31)
White	17.3	17.9	19.2
	(1403)	(977)	(945)

Main Effects: F=2.4, d.f.=5, P<.05 (NS)   Race: F=2.8, d.f.=3, P<.05 (NS)
Residence: F=2.8, d.f.=2, NS****   Interaction: F=3.1, d.f.=6, P<.01
* Average fish consumption in grams/person/day.
** Cell N (sub-sample size).
*** "OtherMinority" includes Hispanic, mixed, and other.
**** Note that while Place of Residence is not statistically significant when controlled for Race, it does play a causal role in the interaction effect. (On this point see Norusis, 1986b: 168).

TABLE 9   Average Fish Consumption by Years of Michigan Residence

Years of Michigan Residence	N	Average Consumption*	SD	95 Percent Confidence Interval	Maximum Value
0–16	977	11.5	18.8	10.3–12.7	138.8
17–30	894	17.8	26.4	16.1–19.6	163.3
31–44	867	19.7	29.7	22.7–26.4	224.5
45+	939	24.6	29	22.7–26.4	195.9
Total	3677	18.3	26.4	17.5–19.2	224.5

F=40.3, d.f.=3, P<.001

* Average consumption, confidence intervals, and maximum values in grams/person/day.

TABLE 10   Average Fish Consumption by Race and Years of Residence

Race	Years of Residence in Michigan	
	0–30 years	31–91 years
Black	14.3 *	30.3
	(43) **	(26)
Native	20.9	25.1
American	(53)	(84)
Other	18.1	22.1
Minority***	(64)	(53)
White	14.2	21.7
	(1710)	(1606)

Main Effects: F=19.8, d.f.=4, P<.001   Race: F=1.9, d.f.=3, NS
Years: F=72.1, d.f.=1, P<.001   Interaction: F=.89, d.f.=3, NS
Summary Multiple Classification Analysis Statistics
Race: Eta=.04, Beta=.04   Years: Eta=.14, Beta=.14
* Average fish consumption in grams/person/day.
** Cell Ns (sub-sample sizes).
*** "Other Minority" includes Hispanics, mixed, and others.

and Beta are .04. Clearly, however, years of residence is contributing more to the joint main effects with an Eta and Beta of .14.

Summary and Implications

Recall that our main purpose is not causal analysis, but rather the identification of sub-groups, especially those involving minorities, that have particularly high rates of fish consumption. The patterns of results for our two main minority groups—black and Native American anglers—differed markedly. Overall, Native Americans in the sample consume more fish than blacks (24.3 grams/person/day compared to 20.3 grams/person/day for blacks). However, both groups consume more than whites (17.9 grams/person/day). In the analysis of race and age we found that older (51-91) black anglers in the sample had very high rates of consumption (31.93 grams/person/day). There was also a high fish-consuming sub-group of Native Americans, but this was for the middle age group (31-50 years). The consumption rate for this sub-group was 30.6 grams/person/day. Both sub-groups had much higher consumption rates than whites of any age group.

Black, moderate income anglers ($15,000 - $29,999) in the sample had high fish consumption rates (30.48 grams/person/day). For Native Americans the highest consuming sub-group (33.72 grams/person/day) in the sample was low income (under $15,000) Native Americans. Again both sub-groups had much higher fish consumption rates than whites of any income group. There was also a statistical interaction effect between race and place of residence. The highest black consumption rate (23.9 grams/person/day) was from urban blacks (cities over 20,000). The highest consumption rate for Native Americans (32.1 grams/person/ day) was for rural farm/non-farm, followed closely by small towns (29.9 grams/ person/day). Length of residence in Michigan was particularly significant in relation to black minorities. Black anglers who had lived in Michigan over 30 years had a fish consumption rate of 30.3 grams/person per day.

In sum, there were numerous minority sub-groups in the sample who had fish consumption rates exceeding 30 grams/person/day. However, in some cases, the relationships were marginally non-significant and cannot be generalized to the population. The patterns of interaction and combination with other socio-economic factors varied by type of minority group. These rates of fish consumption are almost twice as high as the average for all anglers in our study (18.3 grams/person/day) and almost five times as high as the 6.5 gram assumption in Rule 1057. We should recall that these findings are only for the winter-spring months. Data from summer-fall months would be expected to yield somewhat higher rates of consumption (West et al., 1989a: 25-28).

Implications

There are two general categories of policy implications of these findings: (1) implications for the revision of Rule 1057 and similar regulations in other compa-rable states; and (2) implications for the targeting of fish consumption advisories. The reader will recall that Rule 1057 is the State of Michigan's regulation that controls the discharge of toxic chemicals into Michigan surface waters. It currently assumes a fish consumption rate of 6.5 grams/person/day. Our data indicate that Michigan should increase this assumption at least into the range used by several nearby states. Wisconsin now uses 20 grams/person/day. Ohio uses 21.8 grams/ person/day. However, our findings suggest that there are sub-groups of the angling population that consume more than these averages. Only New York's standards would cover these high rates. Their fish consumption assumption is 32.4 grams/ person/day which would cover the fish consumption averages we report in this paper. However, it will be quite a struggle to get Michigan to increase its assumption into the 18-20 gram range, and it would be a monumental struggle to get the Midwestern States to increase their standards up to the the level of the New York standard. Data such as ours can be leverage in this struggle, but data in and of itself will not bring change. Political will amongst those in power, and mobilization of environmental and civil rights groups will also be needed, especially if the goal is to raise the standard above the 20 gram range.

Until and unless these objectives are achieved, both advocates and policy makers may need to rely on policies and strategies of intensifying educational efforts about fish consumption advisories. One implication of the data presented here is that educational efforts should "target" sub-groups with particularly high fish consumption rates. A student of the principal author is doing just that in her master's thesis. Using the data from this paper she is conducting a pilot study to target communications to a moderate number of black elderly people with moderate incomes in urban areas. The State Department of Public Health should consider similar programs on a broader scale.

However, the reliance on fish consumption advisories should be considered a temporary stop-gap measure until standards can be tightened and toxic contaminants already in surface waters are cleaned up. This is especially important for minorities because our previous research (West) found that minorities catch and eat fish for both recreation and food, while whites fish primarily for recreation. To rely on a policy of fish consumption advisories creates more of a hardship for minorities because a needed protein source is at stake, not just a chance to catch that big one that didn't get away.

Notes

1.   Shorett (1986: 41-42) conducted a methodological study that randomly assigned half of her sample to receive an initial post card, followed by three more waves— the questionnaire, a reminder postcard, and a final questionnaire. The other half of her sample received the standard four-wave sequencing of a questionnaire, postcard, questionnaire, postcard. Using her technique she was able to increase response rates by about 8 percent over the traditional method. Based on her results we adopted this approach.

2.   The University of Michigan Institute for Social Research (ISR) has pioneered and validated a procedure that involves using a final wave phone call for the final reminder. Using their trained phone bank interviewers, and some of our own staff trained by ISR staff, all residual non-respondents in the sample (whose phone numbers could be located) were called reminding them to return the survey. If the respondent had misplaced or thrown the survey away, the phone interviewer immediately sent another in the mail. One limitation we experienced with this technique was that we were only able to locate phone numbers for 39 percent of non-respondents (N=509 of 1311 non-respondents).

3.   We encountered the problem of statistical independence because, on the one hand we needed data about all members of the household, and on the other hand we were confined to a mail survey due to grant funding limits ($30,000). It is possible in phone surveys to randomize respondent selection within a household but it is almost impossible to do this (with compliance) in mailed surveys. We have designated P values of .05 as "marginally non-significant" to distinguish this adjustment from higher P values that would be non-significant in any case. We

make this distinction because going to a .01 P value is conservative (more than we might need to do).

4.   "Statistical interaction occurs when the relationship between two variables is contingent on the state of a third variable" (West, 1989: 24). For a good discussion of interaction in a two way ANOVA consult Norusis (1986: 167-168) and Hays (1963: 388-392).

5.   We found this same interaction relationship showing high fish consumption for black middle income strata in our pilot study in the Detroit River (West).

6.   The Native Americans in the sample are non-reservation Indians living primarily along the Great Lakes. Those who live on the reservation do not need a state fishing license to fish and are hence not in our sample. Given the high levels of fish consumption among Native Americans in our sample we are currently seeking funding for a reservation-based fish consumption study.

9

The Effects of Occupational Injury, Illness, and Disease on the Health Status of Black Americans: A Review

Beverly Hendrix Wright

Americans have made great strides in improving their health and longevity. Although improved, the health status of some minority groups has shown a persistent and distressing disparity in important health indicators when compared to those of their white counterparts. In 1983, the life expectancy of whites reached a new high of 75.2 years, while black life expectancy reached only 69.6 years. This difference in the life expectancy of whites and blacks represents a gap of 5.6 years. The present life expectancy of black Americans was reached by white Americans in the early 1950s, thus representing a lag of about 30 years (U.S. Department of Health and Human Services, 1985).

In 1980, there were 26.5 million blacks in the United States. This represents an increase of approximately seventeen percent over 1970 census figures. Approximately fifteen percent of the total U.S. population in the fifteen or under age category are black. However, by the time they are sixty-four the relative proportion of the black U.S. population decreases to eight percent (U.S. Department of Health and Human Services, 1985).

To What Do We Attribute the Cause of This Disparity in Life Expectancy Among Blacks as Compared to Whites?

Although many factors are presumed to influence black health status and life expectancy in America today, environmental and occupational exposures are increasingly considered sources of disease and illness (see Ashford, 1976; Bullard and Wright, 1986; Davis, 1977, 1981; Epstein, 1978; Kazis and Grossman, 1982).

Beverly Hendrix Wright has a Ph.D. in Sociology from the State University of New York at Buffalo. At present, she is an Associate Professor of Sociology at Wake Forest University in North Carolina. Her former appointment was at the University of New Orleans. She is the author of a series of articles and essays on racial group identification, achievement motivation, social stratification, generational teen pregnancies, and health and environmental issues in the black community.

There are approximately 100 million workers in America. Each year 100,000 die from occupational diseases while nearly 400,000 new cases each year are reported (Elling, 1986; U.S. Council on Environmental Quality, 1980). Approximately nine million persons each year suffer from severe work related injuries (Congressional Quarterly, Inc., 1981).

Blacks, however, have a thirty-seven percent greater chance of suffering an occupational injury or illness and a twenty percent greater chance of dying from an occupational disease or injury than do white workers. Black workers are also twice as likely to be permanently or partially disabled due to a job related injury or illness (see Urban Environment Conference, 1984).

Black workers in the United States represent more than 12 million people and constitute a major segment of this nation's work force. The black work force comprises twelve percent of the total number of employed individuals in the United States and represents thirty percent of all unionized workers. They constitute the highest proportional percentage of unionized workers in this country (Davis, 1981).

Since the establishment of the Occupational Safety and Health Act of 1970, improvements in the general safety and health of workers have been made. Particularly in the area of the identification of hazards and the establishment of controls for toxic and cancer-causing agents, substantial improvements in the workplace environment have been advanced. Blacks and other minority workers, however, have not benefited from these improvements to the degree that white workers have. Among this highly unionized group within the work force, historically, the injury, disease and death rates have been and remain disproportionately high as compared to their white counterparts in certain industries. The question thus arises: why is it that black workers have fared so poorly in the area of job health safety?

This paper investigates the effects of hazards in the work place on the health (i.e., general health status) of black Americans (see Davis, 1981). Specifically examined is the extent to which the life expectancy of blacks can be explained by occupational or job categories as opposed to only "intrinsic" (i.e., diet, smoking, drinking, etc.) racial or cultural differences between blacks and whites.

Many theories are offered to explain diseases. However, "social causation" theories assert the idea that "we cannot understand disease incidence without looking at the social context in which people live and die" (Hall, 1979: 30-31). This most interesting and useful theoretical approach explains possible relationships among disease causing agents as well as contributing factors within those relationships. From this premise, Hall (1979), in a study of health in inner cities, identifies three causes for disease among low income, inner city minorities: (1) physically-induced, (2) socially-induced, and (3) genetically-induced. All three causes provide insight into reasons why low income, inner city minorities (and other inner city residents) contract disease at a much greater rate than more affluent urban, suburban, and rural residents. Hall's model is easily adapted to the questions of this research effort and works well in explaining why black workers are at greater risk of injury, disease, and death than are white workers.

Three causal explanations for the excess risk of injury, disease and death among black workers are advanced in the literature: (1) Socially-induced diseases are those that result from social rather than physical, genetic or environmental causes. Most importantly, these illnesses are often beyond the individual's control. For example, one of the ramifications of race may be sources of disease. In the case of black workers, consequences of race could include job discrimination and job placement as well as numerous other stressors. (2) Physically-induced diseases (in this research also including genetics) are those that result from physical rather than environmental or social causes. Physically induced diseases are those that occur because of intrinsic, racial or cultural factors such as unhealthy diets and habits. Genetic factors are also classified as physical inducements of disease. Hall, however, does not include genetic inducement with physical inducement of disease. Stereotypes and myths about minority groups, as well as genetic differences between races, have often been used as sources of disease and as justification for singling out some groups for differential treatment. For example, in the case of black workers, the myth concerning their ability to withstand hotter temperatures has been used as justification for their being assigned to the extremely dangerous coke ovens within the steel industry. Certain cultural habits, such as diets and smoking, are also used as explanations of disease and injury in black workers. (3) Environmentally-induced disease, for the purposes of this research effort, are separated from physically-induced disease and are discussed separately. Environmentally-induced diseases are those that result from environmental rather than physical or social causes and are caused by the quality of the environment in which we live. These include our homes, communities, and work environments. Most often, environmental exposure is involuntary and individuals lack specific information on the hazards associated with their environments. For example, in the case of black workers, shipyard workers in coastal Georgia were found to have a disproportionately high lung cancer death rate. This incidence of cancer was shown to be related to job exposure (see Blot, 1978).

Socially-Induced Disease

Socially-induced diseases result from social rather than physical, genetic or environmental causes. Stress and stress-related illnesses are identified as socially-induced diseases. They can occur "from physical and psychological responses to a variety of social as well as pathological factors over which people have varying degrees of control" (Hall, 1979). Stress and stress-related illnesses represent a major health problem among black Americans since their origins are often due to social factors beyond the individual's control (Eyer, 1975). Hypertension is a stress-related disease and is primarily seen as one that is socially induced. Only ten percent of all hypertension occurs because of a secondary effect of problems such as pituitary or adrenal tumors (Hall, 1979). An examination of hypertension among black Americans and a review of stress-related diseases within certain industries where significant numbers of black workers are employed further illustrate the volatile position of blacks in the workplace.

Hypertension

Hypertension is defined as elevated blood pressure and is a major cause of organ damage and death in humans. It is believed to be the "body's response to its need to accommodate faster breathing and heart beat in response to stress and other factors" (Hall, 1979). Approximately 25 to 30 million Americans are hypertensive (Williams, 1975). Hypertension rates for black Americans of every age are nearly twice as high as those for white Americans (Weiss, 1976:165). Approximately six million of the 25 to 30 million Americans who suffer from hypertension are black. Hypertension death rates are higher for both black males (3.8 to 3.2) and black females (3.9 to 4.8) than for white males or females (Hall, 1979). Heart disease, which is hypertensive related, accounts for more deaths a year than any other single category. Black Americans experience an excess of 26,169 deaths each year from hypertensive related diseases. Although these statistics suggest an inherent or genetic propensity to hypertension among black Americans, hypertension rates for blacks who are not Americans and who reside in other countries are significantly lower than whites in those same countries (Hall, 1979).

Explanations for this increased risk of hypertension and related diseases among black Americans range from cultural habits (i.e., eating, drinking, smoking) to psychological stressors due to discrimination or genetics. A social factor contributing to this increased risk that is generally overlooked is stressors in the workplace. To what extent is stress or stress-related disease due to occupational environments?

Available data lend support to the contention that occupational environments play a far more important role than is presently realized in the causation of stress-related diseases. Studies show that working conditions within certain industries contribute to the increased incidence of stress-related mortality and morbidity. Black workers are also more likely to be employed in stress-related job categories within these industries than are white workers.

For example, studies of both iron and steel foundry workers and laundry and dry cleaning industry workers show an increase in the incidence of stress-related mortality and morbidity among black as compared to white workers (Blaire, 1979; Davis, 1981; Rockett and Redmond, 1976). Black iron and steel foundry workers are concentrated in the most hazardous of jobs within that industry—the coke oven operation. The job involves a process that releases dangerous gases and dust particles, including carcinogens, and exposes the workers to extreme heat. These conditions increase the risk of stress-related diseases and death. Laundry workers are also exposed to a number of hazards on the job, including excessive heat, which can cause exhaustion, cramps, rashes and heat strokes. Dry cleaning workers are exposed to many different solvents and heat from pressers. Working conditions and exposures in these industries where significant numbers of blacks are employed increase the risk of stress-related disease and death among black workers.

These data seem to suggest that the social practice of discriminatory job placement has resulted in the assignment of blacks to extremely hazardous jobs that are also stress inducing. Black workers, as compared to white workers, disproportionately suffer from stress-related illnesses and death. Although conclusive proof does not exist, these data do suggest that discriminatory job placement based on race has impacted the health of black workers in certain industries.

Physically-Induced Disease

Physically-induced diseases are those that occur because of intrinsic factors such as diets, smoking or genetics. Even more significant is the fact that the individual's behavior and/or characteristics are seen as the primary cause of disease. "Victim blaming" is often the end result.

Blaming the Victim

In the area of occupational health and safety, a number of "victim blaming" arguments are advanced to explain the higher injury and death rates of nonwhite workers. The basic assumption is that working conditions in the modern workplace are so safe that accidents are the result of worker error rather than the fault of the industry (Epstein, 1978). Consequently, the lower life expectancy and higher incidence of cancer and death rates incurred by nonwhite (especially black) workers is often attributed to either bad habits or genetics. For example, Paul Kotin, in an address to the American Occupational Medical Association, resurrected the "hypersusceptibility worker" notion that shifts the focus from cancer-causing agents to the biological susceptibility of humans (Epstein, 1978). Kotin's argument begins with the reasonable assumption that "all biological organisms, including humans, vary in their response to external stimuli such as toxic substances or carcinogens." Based on this assumption, he then asserts that management has a "right" to select sturdier workers for riskier jobs. This viewpoint supports management's "right" to continue discriminatory job placement practices that already exist in some industries. For example, in the iron and steel industry one study showed that 91 percent of all workers in the coke ovens were black and were exposed to (among other things) extreme heat (Williams, 1971). The industry justifies this practice on the basis of the myth that blacks have a much higher tolerance for intense heat (Davis, 1977). Similar practices based on myths were found within the electronics industry where "dark skinned" minority workers were regularly assigned to jobs using caustic chemicals because skin irritations resulting from job exposure are not as pronounced on dark skin as they are on white skin.

Consequently, "dark skinned" workers will have fewer complaints than their white counterparts whose skin irritations are more noticeable (see Davis, 1977).

A second blame-the-victim tactic shifts the responsibility for occupational injury and death from uncontrolled exposure in the workplace to the worker's own insidious life-style (Davis, 1981; Epstein, 1978; Urban Environment Conference, 1984). For example, management often assigns the cause for the high incidence of lung cancer found among workers in some industries to smoking habits rather than to overexposure to dusts and chemicals in the workplace. The facts are that smoking definitely increases the susceptibility of workers exposed to dust and chemicals (e.g., asbestos, rubber, and steel workers), but the risk to nonsmoking workers in such industries is still greater than that of persons who do not work in those environments (Epstein, 1978; Urban Environment Conference, 1984).

Black males have the highest reported incidence of lung cancer. In fact, the death rate for lung cancer among blacks is about 20 times higher than it was 40 years ago. Although smoking most certainly accounts for some of the increase in lung cancer among black males, this alarming increase cannot be attributed to smoking alone. The excess risks are more likely due to environmental factors including occupational exposures. Only recently are we beginning to uncover occupationally induced cancer problems that have existed for years. Present data reveal that a significant number of black workers in specific industries have been assigned to the most hazardous jobs that also exposed them to numerous now known carcinogens (Davis, 1977, 1981; Epstein, 1978). The degree to which excess risks of lung cancer in black males may be attributed to occupational exposure is reflected, for example, in the fact that the highest incidence of lung cancer among black American males is in Pittsburgh, Pennsylvania. This fact is not surprising when one realizes that a significant number of black males in Pittsburgh are employed in the most hazardous jobs in the steel industry—jobs which expose them to known carcinogens.

"Blaming the victim" is an industry management tactic that is used to justify inaction in areas of occupational health and safety. Myths or racist stereotypes are often used to camouflage discriminatory job placement practices resulting in the purposeful exposure of black workers to hazardous work conditions. Equally insidious is the "victim-blaming" tactic employed by industry that blames occupational illness and death on intrinsic, racial or cultural characteristics including alleged genetic deficiencies. This rationale then absolves the industry of any blame for disease or injury rates among workers.

Environmentally-Induced Disease

Environmentally-induced diseases are those that occur due to exposures in the environment. The work environments of some industries have already been shown to be extremely hazardous for workers, especially black workers. Not surprisingly, cancer rates for blacks are increasing at an epidemic proportion, and black workers experience disproportionately high cancer incidence and death rates.

Occupational Cancer

Although in 1949 the reported cancer rate for blacks was 20 percent lower than the rate reported for whites, by 1967 the number of deaths from all cancers increased twice as rapidly among blacks as it did among whites. Presently, black males have the highest reported incidence rate for all cancers combined. Blacks are experiencing a growing cancer epidemic with a 25 percent increase in the cancer rate over the last ten years. The American Cancer Society (1986) data show that the cancer mortality rates for blacks and whites were practically the same 30 years ago. However, the cancer death rate in whites has subsequently increased by 10 percent while the rate for blacks has astoundingly increased by 40 percent. Many factors have been cited as possible contributors to the high incidence of cancer among blacks. Here again, smoking, diet, and genetics are included. The relationship between occupational exposures and cancer has received only minimal attention by the scientific community. However, available data tend to support the relationship between some work environments and the incidence of cancer among workers.

The exposure of black workers to many of the chemicals that are now known as carcinogens began in the early 1900s when large numbers of southern blacks migrated to urban industrial areas to work. The status and nature of the jobs, however, were no different from those relegated to them in the South. Black workers were hired for the worst jobs. These often were the most strenuous and hazardous jobs that also exposed them to chemicals now known to cause cancer (see Davis, 1981). Studies of industries where large numbers of blacks have worked in jobs using or producing carcinogens suggest that this exposure is responsible for some excess risk of cancer among black workers (Davis, 1981; Hall, 1979; Urban Environment Conference, Inc., 1984). For example, a study of 6,500 rubber workers in a large tire manufacturing plant in Akron, Ohio found that twenty-seven percent of the black workers in the sample, but only three percent of the white workers, had worked in the compounding and mixing area. The compounding and mixing area is located at the front of the production line where workers are exposed to dusts, chemicals, ingredients, and vapors that contain toxins and is the most dangerous location in the plant. Black workers in this area showed elevations in cancers of several types as compared to white workers, including respiratory and prostate cancer (McMichael, 1976). An interesting fact is that the cities of Toledo, Cleveland, and Akron, Ohio have major rubber producing and fabricating plants. These cities also have significantly high prostate cancer rates for blacks (Mason, 1976).

A study of 59,000 steelworkers or sixty-two percent of all U.S. males working in basic steel production was conducted from 1953 through 1962 (Williams, 1969). The area of greatest hazardous exposure in this industry is the coke oven operation.

Workers are exposed (among other things) to dangerous gases and dust particles, including the carcinogen benzo (a) pyrene. The study revealed that eighty-nine percent of nonwhite coke plant workers were employed at the coke ovens while only thirty-two percent of white workers were employed in that area (Williams,1971: 55). The findings of the 1953-62 study revealed that nonwhite workers (mostly black) in the coke plant experienced double the expected death rate from malignant neoplasms. In fact, all of the excess deaths for nonwhite coke plant workers were due to cancer of the respiratory system. Although only 7.3 respiratory cancer deaths would have been expected among nonwhite coke plant workers, twenty-five deaths from this cause occurred among those employed at least five years in the coke plant. The comparable number of expected deaths for whites in this area was 8.4 with only seven actual deaths (Williams, 1971). Exposures to carcinogens and toxins were greatest among workers employed in full time "top side" jobs in the coke plant. Nineteen percent of nonwhite workers compared to only three percent of white workers were employed in this capacity. Significantly, almost all of the excess death rates from lung cancer were due to the death of men employed in full-time topside jobs at the coke plant. The lung cancer death rate among nonwhite full-time topside workers (19 versus 2.2) was eight times greater than expected (Williams, 1971).

Other illustrations of industry exposure of black workers to possible cancer-causing agents include the following:

1. the National Cancer Institute conducted a study of laundry and dry cleaning workers and found that blacks had higher death rates from cancer of the liver, lung, cervix, uterus and skin (Blaire, 1979);
2. a 1978 cancer mortality study of coastal Georgia residents found black shipyard workers to have a lung cancer death rate two times higher than expected (see Blot, 1978); and
3. a 1946-1950 U.S. Public Health study of chromate workers found that the respiratory cancer mortality rate for all workers was 29 times higher than expected. However, the actual expected respiratory cancer death rate was 14.29 for whites and 80.00 for blacks.

These data suggest that the excess risk of cancer that exists for black workers as compared to white workers may be due to greater exposure of black workers to carcinogens in the work place. Moreover, the placement of blacks in greater numbers than whites in the most dangerous jobs in certain industries may account for this overexposure.

TABLE 1   The 30 Industries with the
Highest Percentage of Nonwhite Workers (1978)

Industry	Percentage Nonwhite
Private households	31
Tobacco manufacturing	30
Taxicab service	29
Logging	28
Laundering, cleaning, and other garment services	26
Sanitary services	25
Welfare services	24
Services to dwellings and other buildings	23
Ship and boat building and repairing	23
Hotels and motels	22
Street railway and bus lines	22
Yarn, thread, and fabric mills	21
Agricultural chemicals	21
Residential welfare facilities	20
Confectionary and related products	20
Postal service	20
Hospitals	19
Convalescent institutions	19
Detective and protective services	18
Miscellaneous wood products	18
Water transportation	18
Federal public administration	17
Other primary iron and steel industries (includes foundries)	17
Apparel and accessories	17
Other primary nonferrous industry (includes lead and copper smelters)	17
Meat products	16
Employment and temporary help agencies	16
Motor vehicles and motor vehicle equipment	15
Health services, not elsewhere classified	15
Auto services except repair	15

Source: Morris E. Davis and A.S. Rowland. "Problems Facing Black Workers," in *Occupational Health: Recognizing and Preventing Work Related Disease.* B.S. Levy and D. H. Wegman, eds. Boston: Little Brown and Company, 1983, p. 420.

TABLE 2 Occupational Injury and Illness Rates in Manufacturing
Industries with the Highest Percentage of Nonwhite Workers(1978 and 1987)

Industry	Percentage Nonwhite	1978 Annual Injury and Illness Rate Per 100 Full-Time Workers	1987 Annual Injury and Illness Rate Per 100 Full-Time Workers
Tobacco manufacturing	30	9	9
Logging	28	26	20
Ship and boat building and repairing	23	21	22
Yarn, thread, and fabric mills	21	9 *	10
Agricultural chemicals	21	9	13
Confectionary and related products	20	15	13
Miscellaneous wood products	18	20 *	16
Other primary iron and steel industries	17	25 **	22
Apparel and accessories	17	6 *	8
Other primary nonferrous industry	17	18 **	23
Meat products	16	28	28
Motor vehicles and motor vehicle equipment	15	11	15

Average annual injury and illness rate per 100 full-time workers for all manufacturing industries is 13. For industries with over 15 percent nonwhite workers, it is 16.
* Computed by the U.S. Department of Labor, Bureau of Labor Statistics by special request.
** Approximations (made with the assistance of personnel in the U.S. Department of Labor, Bureau of Labor Statistics) due to incompatibility between industrial classification of the steel industry in the two sets of data.

Source: Morris E. Davis and A.S. Rowland. "Problems Facing Black Workers," in B.S. Levy and D. H. Wegman, eds., *Occupational Health: Recognizing and Preventing Work Related Disease.* Boston: Little Brown and Company. 1983. p. 419. Bureau of Labor Statistics. *Occupational Injuries and Illnesses Incidence by Industry, 1986 and 1987.* Washington, DC: U.S. Department of Labor, 1989.

Conclusion

There are numerous factors that contribute to the health status of black Americans. Occupational exposures, however, have received little attention. In fact, statistics on occupational safety and health are generally lacking, and race specific data is even harder to find. However, black workers represent over 15 percent of the total workforce in nearly 33 occupational categories. Unfortunately, a large percentage of the black work force remains over-represented in low-pay, low-skill, high-risk blue collar and service occupations. Moreover, blacks are concentrated in certain industries, many of which have above average injury and illness rates (see Table 1). They are, for example, over-represented in laundry and dry cleaning, tobacco manufacture, fabric mills, smelters, hospitals (as orderlies and attendants) and service industries. Available data on job placement patterns within certain industries suggest an even more serious health threat for black workers. Black workers are also overrepresented in the dirtiest and most hazardous jobs in certain industries (see Table 2). Generally, black workers are relegated by discriminatory employment practices to the least desirable jobs. Historically, racist attitudes or practices have exacerbated resulting health and safety problems. For example, the Gauley Bridge disaster (1930-31) in West Virginia was responsible for the disability of 1500 workers and the death of 500 mostly black workers. They were recruited to tunnel through a mountain with a high silica content. Overexposure to this substance usually causes a chronic lung disease. In the Gauley Bridge incident, 169 black men literally dropped dead on the spot and were hurriedly buried on the spot. The workers, who earned about thirty-cents an hour, were not told of the known hazards or given protective breathing devices. The disaster was not uncovered until 1935 and resulted in the amendment of the West Virginia compensation law, but not soon enough to benefit the dead, disabled, or family members of the victims of the Gauley Bridge disaster (Davis, 1977).

Similarly, in 1969, the textile industry denied the evidence that exposure to cotton dust could cause byssinosis or "brown lung" disease. The general sentiment of the industry on this matter was reflected in an editorial in the industry's journal: "We are particularly intrigued by the term 'byssinosis,' a thing thought up by the venal doctors who attended the last International Labor Association meeting in Africa where inferior races are bound to be afflicted by diseases more superior races defeated years ago" (Davis, 1977: 17).

Today, black workers are still relegated to the dirtiest and most hazardous jobs within certain industries. There is evidence to support the contention that working conditions in certain industries employing significant numbers of blacks are contributing to the increased incidence of injury, disease and death among black as compared to white workers.

Moreover, there is a great disparity between the general health status (as represented by important health indicators such as life expectancy, incidence of disease, and death rates) of black Americans as compared to whites. Available data,

although limited, suggest that occupational factors play a significant role in the causation of major disease and health problems among black Americans. That black Americans are in greater jeopardy of loss of life and susceptibility to disease. The effects on the general health status of black Americans seem ominous and is even more distressing in light of the inaction on our government's part to address this problem. Even more disturbing is the fact that there is much evidence to support the notion that blacks are generally not aware of the dangers in their work environment.

In sum, arguments that place the blame for the excess risk of injury, disease, and death of black workers on physical factors (such as their "hypersusceptibility") or those that place the blame for the excess risk of injury, disease, and death of blacks in general on intrinsic factors (such as diets, smoking, and genetics) are generally unsupported by the research. The data suggest that it is unlikely that physical or genetic characteristics are solely to blame for the increased health risk among black Americans. In fact, it seems much more likely that environmental causes, including the work environment, contribute far more to this increased risk of injury, disease and death among black Americans than has been realized.

Occupational injury and death statistics very quickly paint a picture of an "unofficial policy of benign neglect" for black workers. This highly unionized group has not been the focus of federal agency policies established for special targeted industries, occupations, substance, or exemptions for small business including agriculture (Davis, 1981). It, therefore, comes as no surprise that occupational injury, illness, and death rates are significantly higher among black workers as compared to white workers in certain dangerous industries. Black workers are in "double jeopardy" of loss of life and susceptibility to disease or injury due to racial discrimination. Because blacks have been assigned a lower social status within American society, black citizens have historically been relegated to the most hazardous jobs in dangerous industries with no possibility of advancement or improvement. Job discrimination has been a pervasive fact of life for most black Americans and the consequences of these practices on the health of black workers are ominous. Available data, although limited, very clearly suggest that the concentration of black workers in certain hazardous jobs within industries is responsible for excess disability and death rates among these workers.

10

Hazardous Waste Incineration
and Minority Communities

Harvey L. White

Hazardous waste represents one of the greatest health threats humans have ever faced. "It is polluting the air we breathe, the water we drink, and the food we eat." In at least one respect, it represents a more imminent danger than the deadly AIDS virus. An individual can take steps to control or limit his or her exposure to AIDS. However, an individual has virtually no control over the quality of the air breathed, water drunk or food consumed.

Hazardous substances can enter the body through skin contact, inhalation and ingestion. Entry through any of these routes may cause injury in other parts of the body. The immediacy of the threat to human health has become more evident each year. Reports indicate that thousands are exposed annually to toxic materials (Begley, Hager, and Hunt, 1989; Haurwitz, 1988).

Pollution associated with incineration of hazardous materials accelerates exposure to toxins and aggravates an already deadly situation. For example, the United States Environmental Protection Agency (EPA) calculates that extant air toxins alone cause more than 2,000 cases of cancer each year. The EPA has also reported that living near a chemical plant poses a lifetime cancer risk greater than 1 in 1,000 (Begley et al., 1989). Toxic emissions from hazardous waste incinerators can only increase the illness and death in affected communities.

Various epidemiological studies have revealed that toxins in the air are associated with increased morbidity and mortality rates. For instance, separate studies in England, the United States, Japan and several other nations have linked high levels of morbidity and mortality from bronchitis to pollutants in the air (Lave and Seskin, 1977). The data are quite convincing and suggest a need for alarm in communities that are the sites for hazardous waste incinerators.

Harvey L. White is an Associate Professor of Public Management and Policy at the University of Pittsburgh Graduate School of Public and International Affairs. His research interests are: waste recovery, risk management, bureaucratic behavior, economic development and budget theory. The attitudinal survey of residents in Alsen was conducted also by Mary Elizabeth Joseph, Landa L. Sloan, Mohan I. Jaisinghani, Karen Little, and Jalal Tabrizi.

TABLE 1   Top 10 Toxic Chemicals*

Chemical	(Annual Production)—Toxic Effects
Ammonia	(3,244,519 pounds)--irritates skin, eyes, respiratory tract; very high levels can be fatal.
Nitric Acid	(2,564,502)--contact burns skin; vapor irritates lungs and at high levels can be fatal..
Benzene	(2,531,438 pounds)--chronic exposure can cause leukemia.
Aluminum Oxide	(1,812,459)--irritates lungs; a "nuisance dust."
Sulfuric Acid	(1,741,263)--contact causes burns; vapor can cause serious lung damage, death.
Toluene	(1,218,287 pounds)--irritates eyes, nose, throat; damages liver, kidneys.
Kylene	(1,189,211 pounds)--irritates eyes, nose, throat; damages liver, kidneys.
Naphthalene	(1,100,208 pounds)--irritates eyes, nose, throat; may damage a fetus.
Zinc Compounds	(852,320 pounds)--dust particles can irritate eyes, throat.
Chromium	(760,006 pounds)--chronic exposure can cause lung and throat cancer.

* Source: U.S. Environmental Protection Agency, 1989

Similar studies have found high correlations between air pollutants and incidences of cancer (Haenszel et al., 1962; Hagstron et al., 1967; Stocks and Campbell, 1955; Winkelstein and Kantor, 1969). Pollutants in the air have also been linked to high rates of cardiovascular disease, respiratory disease, and infant mortality. After reviewing some of these studies, Lave and Seskin (1977: 466) concluded that "an objective observer would have to agree that there is an important association between air pollution and morbidity and mortality rates."

For the most part, studies referenced above do not report the particular pollutants in the air. They do make it unequivocally clear, however, that toxic emissions are hazardous to human health. In fact, the health effects of these emissions may be more acute than currently realized, because exposure to toxins in the air can only be estimated. Air pressure, wind velocity and air currents help determine exposure. Consequently, the quantity and dispersion of pollutants in the air and the length of human exposure are seldom known. Frequently, individuals are not even aware of their exposure to toxic emissions. Industry rarely, if ever, informs the public when it is incinerating or emitting toxic pollutants. Even when industry

TABLE 2   Incinerator Pollutants*

Pollutant	Health and Environmental Effects
Sulfur Dioxide	Aggravates respiratory diseases; ingredient of acid rain.
Nitrogen Oxides	Irritates respiratory system; ingredient of acid rain.
Hydrochloric Acid	Irritates respiratory system.
Dioxins	High exposure levels cause chloracne, a skin disorder, and altered liver functions; 2, 3, 7, 7-and TCDD form may cause cancer and birth defects.
PCBs	Can cause chloracne and liver disorder in high exposure.
Lead	Brain damage, especially in children, probable human carcinogen.
Cadmium	Probable human carcinogen; linked to kidney disorders.
Chromium	May damage liver, kidney, respiratory system.
Arsenic	May damage liver and kidneys; probable human carcinogen.

* Source: U.S. Environmental Protection Agency, 1989.

must do so after the fact, the public is often not informed of the possible health effects of those pollutants.

Table 1 describes 10 chemicals commonly emitted into the air which contain toxic pollutants. These chemicals are capable of causing a variety of health problems. Chronic exposure to large quantities of some can cause cancer, genetic damage, birth defects, reproductive disorders and nervous system damage (Haurwitz, 1988). The effects of these chemicals on individuals vary. For example, exposure to sulfuric acid may irritate the eyes, nose, throat and lungs or cause coughing, chest tightness, or sneezing. Higher levels can cause a buildup of fluid in the lungs which can be fatal (EPA Fact Sheet, 1989). Incineration of hazardous waste intensifies the number of dangerous pollutants in the air.

A variety of hazardous substances are found in air emissions from incinerators. As noted in Table 2, emissions, which include toxins like dioxins and PCBs, cause skin and liver disorders. Other toxins emitted by incinerators include lead, arsenic and sulfur dioxide. As Representative Waxman (D-CA) has pointed out, the "[h]igh levels of toxic releases are sure to be accompanied by high levels of human suffering" (Begley et al., 1989).

Data collected by the Environmental Protection Agency support Waxman's assertion. These data indicate that the air we breathe already contains millions of pounds of toxic substances and is becoming increasingly hazardous. According to a congressional report issued on March 24, 1989, at least 2.4 billion pounds of pollutants were released into the air in 1987. Included were 235 million pounds of neurotoxins; nearly 70,000 pounds of the nerve gas phosgene, which killed thousands of soldiers in World War I; and more than 140,000 pounds of methyl isocyanide, which killed over 3,000 people in Bhopal (Begley et al., 1989). Data on toxic pollutants led Representative Waxman to conclude that "[t]he magnitude of the problem exceeds our worst fears."

As more of this data is assimilated by those affected by incinerators and other sources of emissions, health problems which stem from the stress associated with a feeling of helplessness are also likely to develop. Reactions to the location of hazardous waste facilities are often emotionally charged. Assurances from public and industry officials are seldom effective in reducing hostilities and concerns. Further, residents are prone to attribute any health irregularities to the presence of a hazardous waste facility.

There is evidence that perceived health threats, whether imagined or real, can result in stress-related illnesses. Although few have attempted to evaluate stress-related problems associated with hazardous waste incinerators, many news reports have chronicled the anxiety and frustration experienced by individuals who believe they have been exposed to toxic pollutants. Discussing reactions to the Three Mile Island accident, Gary Tuma (1989) of the *Post Gazette* observed: "Panic, fear, confusion and anger ran rampant in Central Pennsylvania as news of the event spread. Eventually, more than 200,000 left their homes for days or weeks." This experience was certainly quite stressful for those involved. If this stress is short-lived, authorities suggest that it has little negative impact on the body. However, researchers have found that stress associated with exposure to hazardous materials is not short-lived. In fact, the fear and anxiety may last a lifetime (Edelstein, 1987).

Once exposed to toxic substances, people tend to remain stressed for a variety of reasons. They tend to be concerned about the long-term effects of this exposure, the possibility of further exposure, and other fears that leave them feeling out of control of their lives. Interviews with residents of the Three Mile Island and Love Canal areas revealed these concerns. In both instances, the immediate danger of further exposure had diminished but fear and anxiety were a constant part of their lives. Studies have also found that when the danger is thought to be constant, fear, anger, frustration and other sources of stress are more pronounced (Levine, 1983; Peele, 1980; White, 1989).

Research has repeatedly shown that extreme stress, like that suggested above, can weaken the body's ability to fight off potential invaders. Further, even the daily ups and downs associated with stress can make the task of the immune system more difficult (Robert, 1987). Joan Borysenko (1987) argues in her book, *Minding the*

Body, Mending the Mind, that people who feel in control of life can withstand an enormous amount of difficulty and thrive on it. "People who feel helpless can hardly cope at all" (Borysenko, 1987: 22). The link, argues Norman L. Shoaf (1989: 5) in his article on "Stress and Your Immune System," is "between a person's mind and his or her physical condition, including health." As Borysenko (1987: 20) also observed:

> The fact is that the body cannot tell the difference between events that are actual threats to survival and events that are presented in thought alone.... The mind spins out endless fantasies of possible disasters past and future. This tendency to escalate a situation into its worst possible conclusion is what I call awfulizing, and it can be a key factor in tipping the balance toward illness or health.

Another dimension of the hazardous waste health concern emanates from connections between the nervous system and the immune system. As noted earlier, air pollutants which are toxic can have direct and indirect effects on both the immune system and the nervous system of the body. If either system is damaged, the other is less effective in protecting the body from illness. As Robert Ornstein and David Sobel (1987: 48) observed in their article, "The Healing Brain," "[t]he numerous connections between the nervous system and the immune system allow the mind to influence resistance or susceptibility to disease." Further, the authors explained, "[s]cores of studies on humans show that various types of social instability and the lack of resources to regain stability are associated with subsequent illness." Whether damaged directly by toxins or indirectly through stress-related disorders, the nervous system and the immune system can be affected by emissions from waste incinerators. Such effects represent potential health problems which deserve serious consideration and evaluative research before siting hazardous waste facilities.

The Emphasis on Incineration

As mentioned above, minority communities have long been depositories for unwanted waste from other areas. Pollution from "open pit" waste incinerators were common occurrences just a few years ago. Noise from landfill equipment has also been prevalent in these communities. The recent closure of many of these landfills has represented a temporary reprieve. Concerns about deposits of toxins have focused new attention on these sites.

Landfills were not only the depositories for waste from human residents but for toxins from business and industry as well. As minorities are often tenants in public housing or renters with ambition for home ownership in more affluent communities, landfill and other botherations were tolerated as "ad interim" irritants. (As explained below, this tolerance helped make these communities favorable sites for hazardous waste incinerators.) Today these sites represent much more than irritants for area residents. They are the focus of major policy initiatives that have fostered the use of incinerators.

"Run-off" from waste facilities, ground water contamination, and the cost and shortage of available land in urban areas have made traditional depositories unacceptable for much of today's wastes. Cleanup of existing sites has become a national priority. Furthermore, the "Not In My Back Yard" (NIMBY) syndrome has led to politics that make locating waste facilities in some communities almost politically impossible. Whether a landfill or a recycling plant, public officials have been reluctant to site waste facilities in affluent areas (National Solid Wastes Management Association, 1988a). The problem is that there is little land in or near minority communities that could be utilized for landfills. The solution rapidly gaining acceptance is incineration.

In addition to the NIMBY syndrome mentioned above, several other factors are encouraging the move toward incineration. Most important are economic costs of equipment, transporting waste, and perpetual monitoring required of landfills. Politically, fewer people are affected and fewer political jurisdictions are usually involved in incineration decisions. The social costs are also less inhibiting. For instance, the health risks associated with transportation of waste are reduced and fewer people are displaced. While incineration represents "a solution" for the broader community's waste problem, it could be a tragedy for minorities (Bullard and Wright, 1986).

Incineration and Minority Communities

Publications on waste incineration note as advantages such factors as volume reduction, waste to energy conversion, and conversion of hazardous waste into harmless compounds (Rollins Environmental Service, 1986; National Solid Wastes Management Association, 1988b; de Castro, 1989). On the surface, these factors do not suggest that incineration facilities could be tragic for minority communities. Prevailing circumstances, however, are reasons for concern (Commission for Racial Justice, 1987).

Minority communities represent a "least cost" option for waste incineration. This is true primarily because much of the waste that is likely to be incinerated is already in these communities. This is particularly true for hazardous waste. Baton Rouge, Louisiana, the location of the case study presented below, is a prime example.

This can be seen by examining the number of hazardous waste sites in Baton Rouge's ten largest white communities and the number in its ten largest minority communities. The white communities have a combined population of 124,400. The minorities communities have a population of 110,100. Between these two sets of communities, there are 19 hazardous waste sites and the amount of hazardous waste per capita is estimated to be nearly seven times the national average (Gould, 1986).

TABLE 3   Ten Largest White Communities in Baton Rouge, Louisiana

Area by Zip Code	Size of Pop.	Percent White Pop.	Percent Minority Pop.	No. of Waste Sites*	Waste Per Capita**
70739	7,500	95	5	0	.0
70744	2,900	97	3	0	.1
70749	1,400	95	5	0	.0
70754	5,200	98	2	1	.0
70770	3,400	90	10	0	.0
70774	4,200	100	0	0	.0
70809	13,900	95	5	1	.0
70814	14,300	97	3	0	.0
70815	37,400	97	3	0	.1
70816	34,200	97	3	3	.0
Total	124,400			5	.2

Note: This table was constructed from data in Jay M. Gould's (1986) book *Quality of Life in American Neighborhoods*.
* Sites in communities with population under 1,000 were not considered.
** 1.0=883 pounds of hazardous waste per person.

This high concentration of waste sites and the volume of waste in Baton Rouge are reasons for concern. However, minorities should be petrified! Fifteen of the hazardous waste sites are located in their communities; only five are in the ten white communities. In other words, these minority communities have an average of one site per every 7,349 residents. White communities have only one per every 31,100 residents.

The difference in the volume of waste in these communities is even more shocking. The white communities have less than 1 percent of the hazardous waste (see Table 3). Even though the minority communities are significantly smaller, they have more than 99 percent of the hazardous waste (see Table 4). If the distribution of waste sites and volume of hazardous materials in these sets of communities are the norm, minorities have much to fear. This is particularly true given the current reliance on incineration and site remediation in the waste industry.

As Suellen Pirages (1989:48) points out in her assessment of trends in waste disposal, "[i]ncineration has come to dominate the other choices when hazardous waste managers choose among the treatment/disposal options." Estimates suggest that the amount of hazardous waste incinerated has more than doubled during the

TABLE 4   Ten Largest Black Communities in Baton Rouge, Louisiana

Area by Zip Code	Size of Pop.	Percent White Pop.	Percent Minority Pop.	No. of Waste Sites*	Waste Per Capita**
70722	5,300	0	100	0	.0
70723	2,400	33	77	1	30.1
70725	1,100	29	79	2	.0
70757	2,400	40	60	0	.0
70760	7,900	0	100	1	.0
70776	2,100	0	100	3	100 ***
70788	4,600	49	51	1	.0
70802	46,000	17	83	1	.1
70807	26,500	5	95	6	2.4
70812	1,800	47	53	0	.0
Total	110,100			15	132.6

Note: This table was constructed from data in Jay M. Gould's (1986) book *Quality of Life in American Neighborhoods*.
 * Sites in communities with population under 1,000 were not considered.
** 1.0=883 pounds of hazardous waste per person.
*** 100 indicates per capita hazardous waste generation greater than 100 times the U.S. average of 883 pounds per capita.

last three years (Washington Analysis Corp., 1988). The percentage of hazardous waste incinerated has also increased rapidly. Recent reports indicate incineration handled 43 percent of the solid hazardous wastes generated in 1986, up from 13 percent in 1981 (Pirages, 1989; ICF Inc., 1988). As the EPA enforces cleanup requirements for existing hazardous waste sites, the demand for incineration will continue to increase.

There are thousands of hazardous waste sites throughout the country that must be cleaned up. As suggested above, a disproportionately large number of these sites are in minority communities. The dynamics associated with hazardous waste sites have resulted in a major public outcry.

Soils outside the immediate site areas are being contaminated with toxic organics, and these contaminants are threatening surface and subsurface water supplies. No longer are these sites simply irritants for those who live on the "wrong side of the tracks." Cleaning them up has become a major public and private activity.

An increasing focus of this activity has been on-site incineration. Concern over the safety and aesthetics of site cleanup has made transporting wastes through neighborhoods to a disposal site less acceptable. Further, on-site incineration is often perceived as the least objectionable cleanup option. It limits liability and provides immediate results. Thermal treatment equipment can come to a site, incinerate hazardous wastes, and leave—all in a relatively short period of time (Brunner, 1988). Thus, it is likely to be the politically expedient method of hazardous waste site remediation.

Syndrome Behavior and Minority Communities

Several syndromes prevail that make incineration in minority communities politically expedient. In addition to the NIMBY syndrome described above, these include:

√ NIMBY	(Not In My Back Yard!)
√ NIMTOF	(Not In My Term of Office!)
√ PIITBY	(Put It In Their Back Yard!)
√ WIMBY	(Why In My Back Yard?)

These syndromes have caused politicians to wither in the face of their constituents. Siting delays associated with them have been extremely costly for several companies seeking to develop incinerators (Pirages, 1989). Any mention of waste incinerators usually results in a NIMBY syndrome in affluent communities, which in turn leads to NIMBY and NIMTOF behavior by elected officials. Pressure for a solution to the waste problem is forcing these officials to look for a compromise. The likely compromise is "Put It In Their Back Yard" (PIITBY).

This PIITBY compromise often results in a decision to place hazardous waste facilities in minority communities. Circumstances internal and external to these communities encourage their selection as sites for treating waste. The priority exhibited in site selection is one such circumstance. Principally, sites given the most attention will be those that affect more affluent communities. Such communities will have the resources, knowledge and contacts to sustain the symptoms of the NIMBY syndrome. As a consequence, residents from these communities are more likely to be proactive. They are, generally, the driving force which causes politicians to exhibit both the NIMBY and NIMTOF syndromes (National Solid Wastes Management Association, 1988a).

The NIMBY, NIMTOF and PIITBY syndromes are seen less frequently in minority communities. These communities are more prone to exhibit a WIMBY (Why In My Back Yard) syndrome. That is, they are more reactive than proactive in their response to waste siting decisions. This WIMBY syndrome emanates from social, economic and political realities which surround these communities.

Minority communities do not have the resources, or contacts, to initiate or sustain the proactive behavior found in more affluent communities. Nor do residents in these communities have the contacts in government and industry necessary to become involved during pre-planning and planning stages for waste sites. These factors and others have led to a "knowledge and information" gap in minority communities about hazardous waste. Perhaps, because of the tradition of having landfills and other waste facilities in their communities, there is also more of a "social acceptance" of hazardous waste incinerators (Edelstein, 1987). Thus, the activism or WIMBY syndrome in minority communities tends to be after facilities have been constructed or other crucial decisions have been made.

The WIMBY syndrome exhibited in minority communities is also far more congenial to the "Not In My Election Year" and the "Not In My Term Of Office" political behaviors than the NIMBY Syndrome. For politicians, it is safer to investigate "why something was done" than intervene "while something is being done." The "why" is less likely to affect voter decisions. Most of the politically sensitive decisions will have already been made when symptoms of the WIMBY syndrome become apparent. Decisions about zoning, building permits and franchise licenses can occur with little or no public outcry.

The greatest concern in minority communities is raised after facilities are operational. It is then that residents learn "incinerators are not just irritants to be tolerated." They pose serious health threats. Further, they can even disrupt normal educational, religious and social activities in the community. The consequence of siting the Rollins hazardous waste incinerator in Alsen, Louisiana is a clear "case in point."

A Profile of the Alsen Community

The Alsen Community is located in Central Louisiana ten miles north of the state capital, Baton Rouge. It is strategically located with geographical boundaries on the Mississippi River and along two major north-south highways. It is serviced by major rail lines and is only four miles from the Baton Rouge Metropolitan Airport.

Approximately two thousand people live in the Alsen community. Nearly all are black (98 percent). Based on social and economic indicators, Alsen should be a viable middle class community with a promising future. The average income is more than $15,000 a year. Nearly 80 percent of the population has at least some college training. More than half of the residents have lived in the community for ten years or more. Only 9 percent are over 65, the others are distributed fairly evenly among various age groups. These statistics suggest that Alsen is a wholesome place to live. Indeed, residents in this semi-rural community had few concerns until Rollins Environmental Services located its waste facility in the neighborhood.

The "Unfriendly Neighbor"

Although the Rollins facility in Alsen evolved from a landfill to its current status as a hazardous waste incinerator, it was viewed as an "unfriendly neighbor" shortly after arriving in the community. As noted by one Alsen resident:

> When Rollins purchased that land, they pursued their operations as an unfriendly neighbor because they started digging all over the place. Large holes were dug.... Large trucks with trailers began entering and exiting this facility with all types of materials and waste disposal. People who worked there from the Alsen Community were not allowed to touch the trailers.... Odorous vapors used to be seen and smelt throughout the community. This brought about the identification of the business Rollins was conducting (Joseph and White, 1986: 3).

Rollins' initial waste disposal facility in Alsen was established in 1971. It was developed as a landfill disposal unit for hazardous materials. By 1981, this facility included a hazardous waste incinerator. Landfills at the Alsen site proved to be problematic for Rollins. Contaminated surface water from landfill sites ran into the river and was absorbed by the soil causing a "topographical downgrade." As a result of a consent order with EPA, monitoring wells were installed from December 15, 1980 until February 1981 and a site remediation program was developed. Rollins subsequently installed an incineration method to dispose of PCBs. According to company informational materials, it disposes hundreds of pounds of hazardous waste at the site daily.

Although operations at the landfill were considered annoying, it has been activities at the incinerator that have led Alsen residents to exhibit behavior associated with the WIMBY syndrome. These activities have antagonized, frightened and frustrated local residents. They have also resulted in law suits and efforts to close the facility. Hazardous waste incineration has not led to fruitful consequences for the Alsen community.

Some Consequences of Hazardous Waste Incineration in Alsen

The consequences of activities at the Rollins' incinerator in Alsen illustrate why minority communities should be alarmed. The air has been polluted, church services disrupted and the health of preschoolers threatened. The quiet, serene and wholesome pre-Rollins community no longer exists.

Residents complained for a number of years of chronic air pollution and other environmental problems to no avail. They reported contaminated water, ill-smelling odors, eye irritations, and vegetation and property damage. It took a series of near disasters before public health officials began to investigate the consequences of activities at the hazardous waste facility (Joseph and White, 1986).

On August 5, 1985, the incinerator at the Rollins hazardous waste facility malfunctioned, sending heavy black smoke and odors throughout the community. Residents reported nausea, eye irritations and other afflictions. A church service at the Mount Bethel Baptist Church was terminated because of pollutants. According to Reverend W.L. Fontenot, he had to cut his sermon short during a revival meeting that night because he had a headache and his eyes were burning. Others at the church also experienced similar symptoms and discomforts (Editorial, 1986).

A similar incident on February 6, 1986, threatened the health of students and staff at a Head Start Center. According to a report in the *Times-Picayune* (Editorial, 1986: 28):

> [F]umes from a hazardous waste company apparently made pre-schoolers at a Head Start Center sick.... Rollins failed to report last week's incident to the State as required by State regulations.... Classes at the Alsen Head Start Center were disturbed Thursday by a foul odor that caused some of the 3- and 4-year olds to vomit.... The problem occurred about the same time as a release of fumes at the plant during a waste mixing operation.

In addition to the two incidents mentioned above, the hazardous waste facility has been cited over 100 times for violations (*Times-Picayune*, 1986). Such violations led to a state fine of $1.7 million. Health threats, as a consequence of activities at the facility, were the subsequent concern of state officials. George Cramer, an administrator with the Louisiana Department of Environmental Quality, noted: "It's been 2-1/2 years since the company got the first test results [showing contamination] and Rollins did nothing to rectify the situation. We are concerned that if it is not taken care of it will represent a risk" (Editorial, 1985: 6).

State officials had come to realize what Alsen residents had known for some tim—the Rollins facility represents a significant health risk and has reduced the quality of life in the community. A research study reported high concentrations of sulfur dioxide, nitrogen oxides, carbon monoxide, hydrocarbons and acids. As indicated above, extensive exposure to any of these can lead to severe health problems (Joseph and White, 1986).

The consequences of activity at the Rollins facility forced the community to seek relief in the courts. By 1986, nine law suits had been filed against Rollins by Alsen residents. The most renowned is McCastle II. McCastle II is reported to have been settled with an award of $350,000 to Alsen residents. Although the community has not been hesitant to take legal action against Rollins, it has not been able to prevent the incinerator from emitting toxic pollutants.

Rollins was under an injunction barring it "from emitting chemical fumes and odors that make the plaintiffs [McCastle, et al.] ill or cause serious discomfort" when the pollutants described above were released. Rollins' response to complaints was to take a more aggressive posture. In response to the February 6, 1986, incident, Rollins responded "by dispatching a lawyer, its local public relations official and a stenographer to the center to take deposition from parents and teachers" (Swartz, 1986: 6). Although Rollins defended this action by saying "it was trying to determine the facts and be a good neighbor" (Swartz, 1986: 6), residents suggested that this was just another intimidation tactic by the company. According to Alsen residents, the neighborly thing for Rollins to do was to close the hazardous waste facility.

Rollins has conceded that the plant does not have a model record (Freedman, 1986). However, even with its record of violations, Rollins has been able to resist efforts to close the facility. The latest attempt emanated from the equipment malfunction that occurred August 5, 1985, when the Louisiana Secretary of Environmental Quality ordered the facility closed. Rollins countered quickly with legal petitions and was able to get a court order to reopen the plant over the Secretary's objection. It was also able to get the Louisiana Supreme Court to bar her from serving as the hearing officer to determine the fate of the hazardous waste incinerator (Swartz, 1986). Although the facility has a record replete with violations and unneighborly activity, it still operates its hazardous waste incinerator in the Alsen Community. To say the least, the facility has had a major impact on residents and their perceptions of themselves and the community.

Attitudes and Perceptions of Alsen Residents

Surveys of perceptions and attitudes of residents suggest the presence of fear and hope. Mainly they suggest that siting the hazardous waste facility in Alsen may lead to the eventual destruction of the community. The overwhelming majority of the residents (76 percent) noted that they have become well-informed about environmental issues since Rollins located its facility in the community. Nearly two-thirds (66 percent) have become more active in civic affairs. Most of the residents (60 percent) want to remain in Alsen. These are hopeful signs. However, other attitudes and perceptions indicate that the hazardous waste facility has diminished the viability of Alsen and the will to revive the community.

Research findings suggest that few residents would be involved in economic ventures in the community. Very few, only nine percent, believed that the climate in Alsen would attract business. The majority also believe property values are declining. Most disturbing is that more than three-fourths (76 percent) of the residents surveyed indicated that, because of health concerns, they would encourage their children to move away from the community. Also disturbing is the fear and concern for their own health created by the incinerator. Nearly a third felt that their health had deteriorated because of the incinerator. The same percentage also categorized their feelings toward the industry as hostile. In general, Alsen residents no longer believe their community is a wholesome place to live (Snyder, 1985), nor do they believe the government has taken action to protect them.

The residents of Alsen seem to put little trust in public officials at any level of government. Neither branch of government was held in high esteem. Even though they have won substantial judgments, the overwhelming majority (90 percent) felt the courts have been biased in favor of the hazardous waste company. They also indicated that no elected official has represented their interests very well. However, residents (66%) indicated that they were more vocal in expressing their views to these officials. The same percentage also attend more public meetings. This suggests Alsen residents have become less dependent on others to protect their interests.

Conclusion

The Alsen community, as a case study, typifies many of the concerns expressed regarding the location of hazardous waste facilities in minority communities. Several of the social, economic and health concerns raised were actually present. Further, residents' behavior in response to the incinerator was reactive and thus exhibited symptoms associated with the "Why In My Back Yard?" syndrome. However, the consequences of activities at the hazardous waste incinerator have also led to proactive behavior.

Alsen residents seem to have narrowed the "knowledge and information gap." They have become astute participants in the public policy process in Baton Rouge. Residents of Alsen are networking with environmental agencies and other communities. They are focusing on state and national environmental issues. They have successfully challenged proposals to place additional hazardous waste facilities in their community. One can only wonder what might have happened if this proactive behavior had been there to challenge the decision to place the Rollins hazardous waste incinerator in Alsen. In any event, other minority communities might gain from Alsen residents' experiences. Their successes and failures offer valuable learning opportunities.

11

Environmentalism and Civil Rights in Sumter County, Alabama

Conner Bailey and Charles E. Faupel

Alabama is host to the nation's largest hazardous waste landfill, located in Sumter County near the small town of Emelle.[1] This paper examines the issue of hazardous waste and race through a case study approach. The paper is based on four years of field and archival research. It begins with a description of Sumter County and the economic impact of the Emelle landfill. This is followed by a discussion of black political empowerment since the 1960s. Next, the mobilization of local opposition to the landfill and the emerging alliance between environmentalists and civil rights leaders is described. The paper concludes with a discussion of the logic inherent in siting hazardous waste facilities and the likelihood that other minority communities would be selected as sites as a consequence of this logic.

Sumter County, Alabama
Demographic Characteristics

Sumter County can best be described as black, rural and poor. The population of Sumter County is nearly 70 percent black. With a 1982 population of under 17,000, average population density is 18.6 per square mile, compared to the state average of 76.7 (Table 1). Most of this population is concentrated in the southern half of the county in and around the towns of Livingston (pop. 3200) and York (pop. 3400). Most of the white population of Sumter County lives in these two small towns. The next largest community is Cuba (pop. 500), also located in the southern half of Sumter County. The hazardous waste landfill near Emelle (pop. under 300) is located in the more sparsely populated and predominantly black northern half of Sumter County.

Conner Bailey is an Associate Professor in the Department of Agricultural Economics and Rural Sociology at Auburn University. His research interests include the sociology of natural resources and the sociology of the environment. He has been involved in researching the social and political aspects of hazardous waste over the past five years.

Charles E. Faupel is an Associate Professor in the School of Social Work at Auburn University. He has done extensive research on the sociology of disaster and of drug use. For the past six years, he has been researching hazardous waste as a social and political issue.

TABLE 1   Per Capita Income and Percent of Black Residents in
10 Least Densely Populated Alabama Counties, 1980

			Per Capita Income	
County*	Density**	Percent Black	As Percent of State	Dollars
Washington	15.6	32.9	87	6481
Wilcox	16.7	68.9	70	5235
Bullock	17.0	67.7	81	6084
Coosa	17.3	34.9	79	5886
Green	17.5	75.4	69	5144
Choctaw	18.5	43.6	81	6027
Conecuh	18.6	41.4	75	5628
Lowndes	18.6	75.1	70	5258
Macon	18.6	85.0	71	5280
Sumter	18.6	69.5	74	5553
Alabama	76.7	26.2	100	7481

* Ranked by population density.
** Population per square mile.
Source: Alabama Department of Economic and Community Affairs, 1984.

Sumter County has experienced significant outmigration over the past 50 years. Between 1940 and 1982, the total population declined more than 40 percent from 27,000 to under 17,000 (Center for Demographic and Cultural Research, 1987). Between 1960 and 1970, over 5,400 people migrated from Sumter County, more than a quarter of the 1960 population. Between 1970 and 1980, the rate of outmigration continued at a slower rate. During this period, over 1,400 Sumter County residents moved away, 8.5 percent of the 1970 population (Alabama Department of Economic and Community Affairs, 1984). Outmigration has continued in the 1980s. Between 1980 and 1987, net outmigration from Sumter County totaled 1,100, or 6.5 percent of the 1980 population (Alabama Department of Economic and Community Affairs, 1989).

Economic Conditions
This pattern of out-migration reflects limited opportunities in the local economy. Agriculture, the historic base of the economy, has suffered declining fortunes due

to depletion of soil fertility associated with continuous cotton production in the 19th century. Soybean production briefly flourished during the 1970s but declined in the 1980s due to declining prices and inability of local farmers to compete with producers in the Mid-west. Between 1978 and 1982 the number of farms with over $20,000 in sales declined by 18.5 percent while total farm acreage in production declined by 20 percent (Alabama Department of Economic and Community Affairs, 1984). In 1982, cash receipts from agriculture in Sumter County totaled $18.2 million, slightly over half of which came from row crops (e.g., soybeans, cotton). Five years later, total cash receipts from agriculture in Sumter County had declined to less than $14 million. Row crops accounted for most of this reduction, declining from approximately $9 million in 1982 to less than $1.5 million in 1987 (Alabama Department of Economic and Community Affairs, 1989). By the close of the 1980s, cattle and timber had replaced row crop agriculture. Because both involve relatively extensive uses of the land, the effect has been to reduce employment opportunities in the area.

Sumter County is rural but not isolated, served by Interstate 59, an active railroad, and the recently opened Tennessee-Tombigbee Waterway. The combination of these transportation facilities and low wage rates made Sumter County an attractive place for manufacturers relocating out of the rust belt during the energy crisis years of the 1970s. Several industries moved into Sumter County during the early 1970s but moved out again a decade later, following a pattern experienced in many other small Southern towns (Falk and Lyson, 1988).

The result has been continuing unemployment and poverty. During most of the 1980s, the unemployment rate fluctuated between 12 percent and 22 percent. In 1984, Sumter County ranked 64th out of 67 counties in Alabama in terms of per capita income ($6,703, compared to $9,987 for the State and $12,772 for the nation as a whole) (Center for Demographic and Cultural Research, 1987). Almost 30 percent of the population of Sumter County was below the poverty line in 1980, though this was far better than the 45 percent poverty rate in 1970 (Alabama Department of Economic and Community Affairs, 1984).

The Hazardous Waste Landfill

The initial move to establish a hazardous waste landfill in Sumter County was made by a small group of regional investors known as Resource Industries, Incorporated. In 1977, when the landfill was established, it was not necessary for public hearings to be held. This group of investors quietly established the necessary political connections through James Parsons, the son-in-law of George Wallace, then Governor. Parsons introduced these investors to Drayton Pruitt, who acted as lawyer on their behalf in negotiating the purchase of 2,400 acres of land near Emelle. It is widely believed that Parsons also provided political contacts necessary to obtain an operating permit in 1977. In 1978, the land and permit were sold to

Chemical Waste Management, Inc. (CWM), which subsequently purchased an additional parcel of land bringing their total to 3,200 acres.[2]

The landfill at Emelle is owned by Chemical Waste Management, Inc. CWM is a major actor in the hazardous waste industry, owning four of the six largest hazardous waste landfills in the nation (EPA data, quoted in United Church of Christ, 1987). These four facilities account for over 50 percent of permitted hazardous waste landfill capacity in the United States. The Emelle facility alone represents nearly half of this total. CWM also owns a variety of other facilities, land-based hazardous waste incinerators and ships designed specifically for incineration of liquid hazardous wastes. CWM had corporate profits of $117 million on revenues of $700 million in 1988 (CWM, 1989). The *Wall Street Journal* (Dorfman, 1989) reported that CWM revenues account for 40 percent of the total for the entire hazardous waste industry.

Economic Impact of CWM on Sumter County

CWM is Sumter County's single largest employer, employing over 400 people with a 1985 payroll of $7.7 million (Keasler, 1986). In an area where underemployment and low wage rates are the norm, CWM provides large numbers of relatively well-paying jobs. CWM purchases local goods and services valued at $4.4 million in 1985. In addition, CWM pays to Sumter County a user fee (currently $5.40) on every ton of waste buried at Emelle. In 1989, approximately 700,000 tons of wastes were brought to Emelle, generating $3.8 million in revenues. These figures for payroll, local purchases and user fee revenues reflect the importance of CWM to the economy of Sumter County. Conservatively assuming that the figures for payroll and local purchases remained constant between 1985 and 1988, CWM operations directly channeled $15.9 million into the local economy. Using a multiplier of 1.6 to reflect local turnover for every dollar spent, the total economic impact of CWM on Sumter County's economy was $25.4 million, or (assuming a population of 17,000) $1,500 per capita. In 1986, average per capita income in Sumter County was $8,290. If CWM were suddenly to cease operations, Sumter County's economy would suffer a serious and immediate decline.

The importance of CWM to the local economy explains why most business and community leaders either support or accept the presence of the landfill in their midst. In the past ten years, CWM user fees paid to Sumter County accounted for $15 million in revenues. These revenues are distributed according to a formula established by Sumter County's representatives in the state legislature. Recipients of these funds include the city governments of Livingston and York, five smaller towns, ten civic organizations (e.g., library, rescue squad, water authority), the small local university, the county school board, and the county government's general fund. The mayor of York, noting that 30 percent of that town's revenues come from this source, has publicly expressed concern over local dependency on

144

FIGURE 1   Where the CWM Dollar Goes

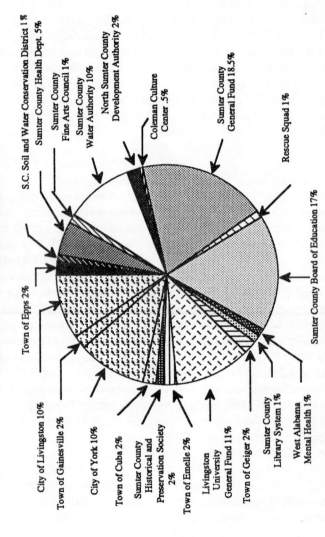

"How much will we get from Chem Waste?" That cry will be heard after this month as local agencies prepare budgets for the coming fiscal year. The above chart, courtesy of Chemical Waste Management, is a reminder of how much influence the world's largest Chemical Waste Facility has been in Sumter County life. The percentages represent the amount of money each agency or government gets from the total dedicated revenue of the CWM tax bill. CWM is the largest county taxpayer, generating about one-half of all public funds collected.

CWM. Local critics of CWM claim Sumter County has become a "hazardous waste junkie."

Black Political Empowerment in Sumter County

The majority black and the minority white populations of Sumter County live essentially separate social lives. Black and white residents of Sumter County go to separate churches, are buried in separate cemeteries, and send their children to separate schools. The public school system was segregated until 1969. In that year, a federal court ordered Sumter County public schools to desegregate. Ten months after that court order, the all-white Sumter Academy was established as a means of maintaining a segregated school system. Since 1970, the public school system has been almost exclusively a black system. Virtually all white residents continue to send their children to the private academy.

Race relations in Sumter County are flavored by the history of slavery and continued economic dominance by the minority white population. The white population of Sumter County controls most of the businesses in the area, from banks to retailers. In addition, most of the farm and timber land in the County is owned either by local whites or absentee landlords. Here, as elsewhere, economic power and political power go hand-in-hand. Unemployment and poverty are common black experiences in Sumter County, creating a situation of black dependence on whites for jobs and other small favors. These differences in economic circumstances reflect a history of racial discrimination and the contemporary reality of vastly different class positions separating the black and white residents of Sumter County. Hank Sanders, a leading black politician in west Alabama and state senator representing Sumter County, notes that white politicians from this area are among the most racist and ideologically conservative within the state (Sanders, 1986).

In Sumter County, the political status quo began to erode during the 1960s, when blacks finally won the right to vote. For the black citizens of Sumter County, the 1970s and 1980s were decades of struggle with an entrenched white political establishment (Sanders, 1986). It took until 1982 before the first black was elected to office in Sumter County.

In the early 1970s, the Federation of Southern Cooperatives established its main training facility in Sumter County. The stated purpose of the Federation was to encourage the development of cooperatives, strengthening small black and white family farms through technical and managerial training, and giving such farmers the advantages of economies of scale both in purchasing inputs and in marketing their production. In Sumter County, however, the Federation's most important impact was in strengthening local black political organization. The effect was to hasten the disruption of white political hegemony.

In 1979, the white political establishment struck back at the Federation. In what has come to be known as the "Cotton Patch Conspiracy" (Bethell, 1982), local political contacts in Washington, DC, were used to initiate a federal grand jury investigation of financial wrong-doing. This investigation had a chilling effect on the Federation for two reasons. First, private foundations which had provided an important base of support, adopted a wait-and-see attitude and withheld funding. Second, Federation leaders were required to devote considerable energies to defending themselves and their organization during the two year investigation. No evidence of wrong-doing was discovered. Local black leaders are convinced that the investigation was motivated by the white establishment's desire to undermine the Federation. More recently, Federal Bureau of Investigation agents began looking into allegations of vote fraud. In 1985, indictments were made against eight voting rights activists in neighboring Perry and Greene counties. The result was a handful of misdemeanor convictions. More importantly, these leaders had to defend themselves at considerable expense (Alabama Blackbelt Defense Committee, n.d.).

In the long run, these obstacles may have strengthened the civil rights movement in west Alabama and only briefly postponed black political empowerment. With few exceptions, the white elite has been unsuccessful in maintaining control over local affairs. Whites have continued to hold the positions of mayor both in Livingston and York. The white probate judge has been able to fend off the challenges of a leading black politician in the 1984 and 1988 elections, though by the slimmest of margins and through the use of questionable means.[3]

During the past two decades, politics in Sumter County has become largely a struggle between the white and black communities. Race always has been the key factor in determining political power, but only became an issue of contention when blacks gained the right to vote and began to organize politically. It has taken two decades for the black population of Sumter County to consolidate control over political life. This struggle for ascendancy absorbed the political energies of both groups, deflecting attention from other issues, including that of the rapidly growing business of CWM.

Mobilization of Opposition to CWM

The quiet manner in which the Emelle landfill was opened and operated in the late 1970s served initially to limit public opposition. "The thing was here in Sumter County before most people knew about it," remarked one of our respondents. Numerous rumors regarding the nature of the facility were circulating at the time. Some thought it was a brick factory, while others thought a cement kiln or a fertilizer plant was being established. A review of the weekly newspapers published in York and Livingston between 1978 and 1988 shows that the landfill attracted little notice during its first years of operation (Faupel, Bailey, and Griffin, 1990).

The presence of CWM did not entirely escape local notice, however. Black leaders of Sumter County played an important role in alerting the public to the presence and dangers of the Emelle landfill in 1981. In that year, Wendell Paris led a loosely knit black organization called the Minority People's Council in organizing a demonstration at the gate of the facility, protesting unsafe working conditions at the plant. This demonstration generated unwanted media attention for CWM. CWM's response was two-fold: improve worker conditions, and mount a high-visibility public relations campaign to portray CWM as a good corporate neighbor.

A very different approach was taken by an organization called Sumter Countians Organized for the Protection of the Environment (SCOPE), organized shortly after the facility opened. SCOPE was a largely white and essentially moderate organization which sought more rigorous monitoring of landfill operations, greater accountability to the public, and free public access to reliable information on landfill operations. Several public meetings were organized by SCOPE. The activities of SCOPE significantly decreased when it gave rise to a more radical faction, Alabamians for a Clean Environment (ACE). ACE has taken the lead in local opposition to CWM. Like its predecessor, ACE is a largely white organization. ACE claims a membership of over 300, but has a core group of less than 10 individuals. ACE claims of broad public support are hard to verify given that few local citizens have attended ACE rallies and demonstrations. ACE leaders note that many local people are afraid to speak out in an area where so many jobs and so much of the economy is linked to CWM.

ACE's primary goal is simple: shut down the CWM facility. Because of this radical stance, many Sumter County residents do not regard ACE very seriously, viewing them as, at best, a small band of highly idealistic, utopian environmentalists. One of our respondents described them as "a little local group.... As far as their having any effect, it's about like a mouse trying to stomp an elephant."

The importance of this group as a political force in the County has been greatly underestimated by local leaders, however. First, while ACE is outside of the traditional power structure in Sumter County, it is tenacious in keeping the issue of the environment before the public. "They (CWM) have often reacted to ACE like it was a pesky fly you keep swatting around," observed one of our respondents, adding "anytime you can get someone to keep reacting to you, then you're powerful." Moreover, while ACE has been characterized as a small local group, its influence and recognition extends far beyond Sumter County. This group is associated with other nationally based environmentalist groups ranging from the Sierra Club to Greenpeace and the Citizens' Clearinghouse for Hazardous Wastes. These groups provide ACE with both a greater resource base and higher level of visibility, legitimacy, and technical expertise. ACE leaders were prominently featured as speakers and organizers at a region-wide meeting of environmentalists (Southern Environmental Assembly '88) held in Atlanta. ACE also gained recognition when the past president of the organization was named Alabama Volunteer of the Year by Governor Guy Hunt in 1988. Just weeks later she was one of a dozen individuals nation-wide honored by President Reagan for voluntary service, an award made on the basis of environmental activism associated with ACE.

Emerging Alliance

Black leaders played a key role in early opposition to CWM, but during much of the 1980s the black community's attention to this issue was deflected by the struggle for civil rights and black political empowerment. Because of this larger struggle, black leaders and the black community itself remained on the sidelines as CWM became entrenched during the early and mid-1980s. ACE, CWM's chief source of opposition, was and remains essentially a white organization within an overwhelmingly black setting. ACE attempts to get black leaders to oppose CWM were largely unsuccessful until 1987.

In that year, a rally was held in Montgomery, Alabama, followed by a caravan and demonstrations in Livingston and at the gates of the Emelle facility. The rally was organized by ACE with assistance from Greenpeace and the Citizens Clearinghouse for Hazardous Wastes. The theme was the "Toxic Trail of Tears," an explicit attempt to link hazardous wastes and minority populations. Alabama's Creek Indians were forcibly resettled in Oklahoma during the 1830s, and Sumter County was an assembly point for the original Trail of Tears. Native American and black speakers protested the disproportionate presence of hazardous waste sites in minority communities. Civil rights songs and chants were mixed with those of the environmental activist movement. Wendell Paris, a key leader of Sumter County's black population, played a prominent role in the proceedings.

ACE's social and political position outside of the traditional white power structure makes it much more amenable to forging a strong working relationship with the black community. "The only meaningful contacts with whites as equals comes with the people from ACE," claimed one of the black leaders in Sumter County. Since then, civil rights and environmental activists have begun to work more closely together, a pattern noted by Bullard and Wright (1987) to be occurring elsewhere as well.

Nonetheless, the alliance between civil rights and environmental activists in Sumter County remains an unrealized goal, largely because ACE is a single-issue organization while black civil rights leaders are pursuing broader goals. With the exception of Wendell Paris, most black leaders in Sumter County remain reluctant to speak out against CWM. On February 1, 1990, Representative Lucius Black, a black leader from Livingston representing Sumter County in the state legislature, spoke against proposed tax increases on CWM's business because of the possibility that this would reduce employment opportunities available to his constituents. Other black leaders also have reservations about opposing CWM operations. Blacks control the public school system and the county government, both of which depend on CWM payments to finance a substantial portion of their operations. In addition, a large number of black residents of Sumter County work for CWM, which by local standards pays its employees extremely well. These workers, their families, and many of their kin, are understandably reluctant to support actions directed at shutting CWM down.

This is not to suggest that black residents of Sumter County are not concerned with the environment. In a mail survey conducted during 1988, black respondents from Sumter County viewed hazardous wastes as an even more serious threat to their own community than did their white counterparts (Bailey et al., 1989).[4] Nonetheless, for most black political leaders, opposition to CWM is a no win situation. Speaking out against CWM would be seen by some as undercutting the only positive economic development to occur in the last decade. Taking an anti-CWM position carries with it considerable risk of losing support for an uncertain political gain. Few have had the courage to speak out against CWM, and those who have (mostly white ACE members) have suffered social ostracism and public ridicule. Outside of ACE, opposition to CWM in Sumter County is muted. Indeed, not a single politician, even Wendell Paris (the one black leader who has spoken out against CWM), has run an election campaign where hazardous waste was a significant issue.

In contrast, hazardous wastes are an important political issue at the state level. In 1986, one candidate for governor complained that Alabama had become "the nation's pay toilet." The current governor and attorney general, likely opponents in the 1990 gubernatorial race, began staking out their claims to the environmentalist mantel soon after the 1986 election. Hazardous waste issues featured prominently in the 1989 state legislative session and as of this writing (February 1990) also has been a major issue during the 1990 session.

Why Sumter County?

There is much evidence that black and other minority communities in the United States have a disproportionate share of hazardous waste sites in their midst. Three out of four major hazardous waste management facilities in the southeastern United States have majority black populations (GAO, 1983). This pattern is repeated elsewhere in the United States for blacks and other minority groups, especially Mexican-Americans (Russell, 1989; United Church of Christ, 1987). Minority communities are targeted because "those communities which are poorer, less informed, less organized, and less politically influential become more likely targets for abuse from polluters." (Charles Lee, quoted in Russell, 1989: 25) "There is a functional link between racism, poverty and powerlessness, and the chemical industry's assault on the environment." (Barry Commoner, quoted in Russell, 1989: 25)

From the preceding discussion, it should be obvious that the issue of race pervades virtually all social, economic and political aspects of life in Sumter

County. In this section, however, the question is: "Did race play a role in the decision to site the Emelle facility?"

CWM and EPA claim that Sumter County became the site of a hazardous waste landfill primarily due to the presence of the Selma Chalk. In 1974, the EPA issued a report that identified the Selma Chalk formation as having favorable qualities for hazardous waste disposal due to geological stability and the physical characteristics of the formation itself. The Selma Chalk formation cuts a swath through the middle of Alabama, extending from Selma westward through Sumter County and into Mississippi.

The Selma Chalk is a marine sedimentary formation best described as a dense clay comprised of calcium carbonate materials. In Sumter County, the formation lies near the surface, often protruding where the topsoil has eroded. Two physical characteristics of the Selma Chalk were responsible for making it attractive as a site for disposal of hazardous wastes. First, the Selma Chalk near Emelle has an average thickness of 700 feet. Second, the density of the formation was thought to provide long-term protection against movement of chemical contaminants into the under-lying Eutaw aquifer, an important source of water for large portions of Alabama and Mississippi.[5]

Another attractive feature of Sumter County was the relative sparseness of the population. Large hazardous waste facilities like Emelle typically are not found in the center of major metropolitan areas for two simple reasons: first, competing uses drive up the cost of land; second, a large population would be placed at risk. Sparsely populated rural areas are therefore the logical locations of such facilities. From a human ecology perspective, population density can be related to natural resource endowments and economic opportunity. Among Alabama's 67 counties, the 10 with the lowest population densities also have average per capita incomes well below the state average (Table 1). Blacks, who account for 26 percent of Alabama's total population, are a majority in six of these ten counties and have above average representation in the remaining four. Six of the counties listed on Table 1 are among the 10 counties in Alabama with the lowest average per capita incomes.[6] All six have black majorities ranging from 69 percent to 85 percent.

These figures show that a sparse population often is a good indicator of poverty. In the context of Alabama, and the South generally, the population of poor and sparsely populated rural counties is likely to be mostly black. It follows that criteria for siting hazardous waste facilities which include density of population will have the effect of targeting rural black communities that have high rates of poverty.

Communities which fit this description are likely to be politically marginal at the state and federal levels. Politicians and officials are more likely to respond to citizen concerns from a wealthy white suburb of Birmingham than from a sparsely populated, politically powerless area such as Sumter County. Lacking political clout, poor rural black communities are unable to mobilize effectively to oppose a hazardous waste facility or to make sure they are adequately compensated for the risks associated with such a facility. Government agencies and private companies in the past have tried to take advantage of this relatively weak political organization to site hazardous waste and other similar facilities (Cerrell Associates, Inc., 1984). Not only is Sumter County politically marginal within the state, it is divided by internal rivalries between the white and black populations. These rivalries serve to deflect attention from serious public debate regarding the long-term consequences of the CWM presence.

Conclusion

Both white and black residents of Sumter County are concerned about the impact of hazardous wastes on public health and the local environment. Active opposition to the CWM facility, however, has been limited to a small group of white environmentalists. This group has tried, with increasing success, to link their concerns to those of black civil rights leaders in Sumter County. However, the broader struggle for civil rights and black political empowerment continues to absorb most of the energies of these leaders. The saliency of these issues has deflected local attention of both black and white residents from the hazardous waste issue.

Opponents of the CWM facility claim that it is not so much geology as race that led to siting of the Emelle landfill. This view is only partially correct. We contend that race was not a determining factor in the initial decision to locate a landfill in the Selma Chalk formation. Neighboring counties to the east and west which share the same geologic conditions also share common demographic characteristics. The issue of race enters when population density is used as a criterion for siting. This criterion tends to be selective of poor minority communities.

Although race may not have been the primary consideration behind selection of Sumter County, the history of the Emelle landfill cannot be understood in isolation from the issue of race. Local controversy surrounding operation of the nation's largest hazardous waste landfill to date has been dissipated by pre-existing struggles for black empowerment, control over education policy, and efforts to boost a flagging economy. In the context of a racially divided population, local opposition to this landfill has had little effect on regulatory agencies or CWM. The consolidation of black political power and increasingly successful attempts by ACE to draw black leaders into environmental activism could have the effect of focusing greater attention on the hazardous waste issue by the local population. Some local black leaders seem to realize the potential of environmental justice as a focal point for political action by the black community.

Notes

1. In 1989, the Emelle facility received over 788,000 tons of hazardous wastes.
2. Only 300 acres of this total are permitted for landfill operations. The remainder serves as a buffer and is managed as wildlife preserve.

3.   The Probate Judge is an administrative rather than judicial position and is responsible for, among other things, certifying candidates eligible to be placed on ballots. A controversy over certifying black candidates, including the challenger to the current Probate Judge, contributed to the challenger's defeat in 1988. In 1982, the white monopoly of political power was broken when a black man was elected District Judge. Black politicians now represent Sumter County in both the State Senate and House of Representatives. Blacks also have a majority on the Board of County Commissioners (responsible for budgetary and policy matters) and the County School Board.

4.   Response rate to our Sumter County questionnaire was disappointingly low (35 percent). Black respondents accounted for only 29 percent of our total, though they are nearly 70 percent of the population. The mail survey technique typically yields a low response rate from a poor and the non- or marginally-literate population. The sample itself was drawn randomly from a list of registrations for private automobiles. These problems prevent us from speaking from our survey data with great confidence. In early 1990, we will be involved in face-to-face interviews with 500 low-income households in Sumter County, that portion of the population missed in our mail survey. For further details on the mail survey, see Bailey et al. (1989).

5.   Subsequent research suggests the possibility that the Selma Chalk may be less perfect as a final repository of hazardous wastes. This formation was extensively fractured by a large earthquake that occurred some 20 million years ago. A 90 foot displacement known as the Livingston Fault Line was created by that quake and runs in a northwest to southeasterly direction less than two miles from the Emelle landfill. The fractures caused by this quake may have recalcified under pressures of depth, though research on this question is inconclusive (Bittner, King, and Holston, 1988). As a marine sediment, the Selma Chalk is laced with numerous sand lenses. If chemical contaminants were to exploit a fracture connected to such a sand lens, they would move horizontally, increasing the possibility of coming in contact with additional fractures.

The reality that all landfills leak is generally accepted. Chemical Waste Management, Inc., owner of the landfill, claims that it would take 10,000 years for one drop of water to percolate through the Selma Chalk. However, chemical wastes, not water, are being disposed of at Emelle. Although it is no longer legal to landfill liquid wastes, between 1977 and 1985 a variety of liquid wastes (including industrial solvents) were buried in steel barrels. How these wastes will react with the calcium carbonate materials of the Selma Chalk formation and how this will affect the fate and transport of chemical contaminants from the disposal cells was not considered in the original 1974 EPA report, nor have there been published studies on this issue. There is, however, research which suggests that organic chemicals of the type commonly disposed of at Emelle will have the effect of expanding fractures in the Selma Chalk through shrinkage of the clays (Brown and Thomas, 1987). The safety of the Selma Chalk became a matter of public concern and legislative debate during early 1990 (Lewis, 1990).

6.   The other counties (Blount, Cleburn, Hale and Perry) also had black majorities.

12

Uranium Production and Its Effects on Navajo Communities Along the Rio Puerco in Western New Mexico

Wm. Paul Robinson

Uranium mining and milling technology typically involves the generation of large volumes of waste, called mine and mill tailings, which contain significant concentrations of hazardous and radioactive chemicals and are produced when the uranium values are separated from the rest of the ore. Uranium mining, the removal of naturally occurring uranium ore from the ground, is restricted to areas where uranium is found in significant concentrations. Ore containing uranium in the 0.10 percent to 1.0 percent (occasionally as high as 5.0 percent) range is frequently exploited, resulting in 100 to 1,000 times as much waste tailings as the produced product.

Uranium milling, where chemical separation of the natural uranium is conducted, is found next to or in the general region of the ore deposits. Mill tailings are usually disposed of at or near the mill site, using a wide range of technologies with varying degrees of success. The mill tailings produced by this processing operation typically contain 85 percent of the original radioactivity of the ore, and essentially all of the heavy metals, frequently found in hazardous concentrations in the uranium ore, as well as toxic mill reagents disposed of along with waste rock.

The radioactivity found in uranium mill tailings results from uranium decay series radionuclides found with the uranium, such as thorium-230, radium-226, radon-222 and associated radon decay products. The heavy metals found in association with uranium vary in different locations and include arsenic, lead, molybdenum, selenium and copper in New Mexico ore bodies. Toxic mill reagents also vary for different operations but include sulfuric acid, ammonium chloride, and other hazardous organic chemicals such as tertiary amines and diesel fuel, for conventional uranium mills.

Wm. Paul Robinson is the Research Director of the Southwest Research and Information Center located in Albuquerque, New Mexico. Southwest is a nonprofit educational organization working on various natural resources, environmental and consumer interests. Activities include educating people and agencies about toxic and nuclear waste, air pollution, agricultural development, land use, economic development and health.

Uranium has been mined to provide energy for two dominant applications, nuclear power reactors and nuclear weapons. As a result, essentially all the uranium mining on the planet has occurred since 1945. Though this uranium mining activity has occurred since the Second World War, a significant portion of the world's uranium resources has been exploited on land still retained by aboriginal or other land-based communities. Those native or traditional community lands are the lands left for aboriginal communities after the major land acquisitions by government and private interests in the 19th and early 20th centuries.

A list of locations where significant uranium reserves have been found and mined on aboriginal lands includes:

1. Australia—particularly the Arnhem Land Area of the Northern Territory, home to a large existing aboriginal community;
2. Canada—particularly in northern Saskatchewan area inhabited by Cree-Dene Native Americans;
3. Southwest Africa—Namibia—under South African mining concessions in the "last colony in Africa"; and
4. United States—on Navajo, Laguna Pueblo, Havasupai, and Colville Confederated Tribal Lands, along with pre-1848 Hispanic Land Grants at Cebolleta and San Mateo Springs.

This list identifies important uranium producing regions on land retained by native communities within the four largest uranium producing countries (the Namibian production is included as part of South Africa's uranium within this context).

At uranium operations near native communities, uranium has been extracted for commercial nuclear power operations or weapons applications far removed from any direct economic or social needs of the residents of the mining regions. For the mine and mill operators, the political, environmental, economic and health impacts of uranium extraction on native and traditional communities have been of far lesser importance than the short-term economic value of the production of a strategic raw material like uranium. As with many other extractive operations on native lands, resource extraction for raw materials export—a "raw materials colony" relationship—has a devastating effect on the health, economic conditions, and cultural viability of the native community.

The case of Navajo people living near the Rio Puerco of western New Mexico illustrates the diverse long-term impacts of resource extraction, particularly uranium mining, on native people. The actions of the people of the area to counter the cultural and health impacts of the mining operations illustrates the responses available to native people to protect themselves and their children from the long-term effects of uranium production and other resource extraction wastes.

Uranium Production in Navajo Country, Focused on the Churchrock Area

The Navajo Nation is the largest Native American tribe, as measured by either reservation size or population, in the United States. The reservation covers 17,000 square miles, the size of West Virginia, in New Mexico, Arizona and Utah; but many of the approximately 200,000 Navajo live in the "Indian country" surrounding the reservation. Some of this surrounding area includes lands allotted to individual Navajo or their families, not the tribal government. Several areas of the reservation, as well as "allotments" off the reservation in the Eastern Navajo Agency of New Mexico, have produced large quantities of uranium, as well as oil and gas and coal.

Uranium has been mined and milled at several locations in Navajo Country— Cameron, Mexican Hat, and Kayenta Chapters (a Chapter is a local government unit, about the size of a county, in the Navajo governmental system), in Arizona; Shiprock, Red Rock and Cove Chapters, near the Four Corners; and Churchrock, Crownpoint and Becenti Chapters, in New Mexico. Mining at Cameron, Mexican Hat, Kayenta, Red Rock and Cove occurred in the 1950s and 1960s to supply uranium for nuclear weapons. Mining at Becenti and Crownpoint occurred in the late 1970s and 1980s for nuclear power applications. The longest sequence of mining in Navajo country took place in Churchrock Chapter and took place during the period 1954-1986.

Each of these communities, as with other mining communities worldwide, has its own individual history of mineral rights ownership and development, economic impacts, waste generation and management and local concern over chronic health effects. However, among these cases, the effects of uranium mining at Churchrock are uniquely severe and very revealing. Churchrock Chapter is located east of Gallup, New Mexico and includes part of the watershed of the Rio Puerco, a tributary of the Colorado River. Geologically, part of the Southern San Juan Basin, the Churchrock area comprises a mining district in the Western part of the Grants Mineral Belt, the source of 45 percent of the uranium ever mined and milled in the U.S.

The Churchrock area, and the Puerco Valley, have been home for Navajo sheepherders and farmers since well before the U.S. acquisition of the region after the Treaty of Guadalupe-Hidalgo in 1848. As a result of military campaigns in the 1860s and 1870s and the completion of the railroads in the 1880s and 1890s, Navajo people, along with other tribes in the United States, had their lands defined by U.S. government treaties and laws. These legal formulas have been modified frequently and identify the legal status of tribal reservation lands and individual allotments within a highly complex mix of surface and subsurface ownership — much more complex than the "checkerboard" nickname often applied to the region.

Navajo people had no central government prior to 1923. At that time, oil and gas interests sought approval from Navajos for leasing of tribal lands for exploration. The current government of the Navajo Nation derives from the Navajo Tribal Council created for these lease approvals in the 1923 period and still serves as a vehicle for resource development leasing. The uranium mined near Churchrock has come off of leases issued for tribal land, not individual allotments. As a result, lease income has gone to the tribal government for use and distribution, not to Navajo individuals in the Churchrock area directly impacted by the mines.

Further distancing the Churchrock residents from tribal government is the location of the community outside the formal boundaries of the Navajo reservation. Since off-reservation Navajo such as the Churchrock residents have individual allotments, and off-reservation Navajo are a minority among their own people, tribal government provides significantly fewer services to off-reservation, rather than on-reservation, chapters. A significant result of this political relationship is that the tribal government leased land to the uranium mining companies without the consent or active involvement of the local residents and collected mineral revenues without directing them to the communities directly affected by the mines.

Uranium was first identified at Churchrock in the early 1950s along the north side of the Rio Puerco Valley, where uranium bearing rock is exposed at the surface. Exploration for commercial quantities of ore lead to leasing and subsequent drilling for core samples in a northerly direction from the uranium-bearing outcrops towards deeper and deeper ore zones. Significant commercial reserves were discovered in the Churchrock Chapter along the Pipeline Arroyo, a tributary of the North Fork of the Rio Puerco.

Sporadic uranium production in the area occurred in the 1950s and 1960s, prior to the most recent U. S. uranium boom of the 1970s. Fueled by anticipated development of new nuclear reactors, the Navajo tribal government held a series of uranium exploration and development lease sales for tribal government lands in the area. Two companies acquired leases and developed mining plans for specific ore bodies, United Nuclear Corporation and Kerr-McGee Nuclear Corporation. After mine plan approval in the late 1960s and early 1970s, these companies sank mine shafts into the ground to provide access to ore found in the mineral rich rock 1,000-1,800 feet below the surface. Kerr-McGee extracted uranium ore from its leases and transported it by truck to its mill at Ambrosia Lake, 50 miles east of Churchrock. United Nuclear successfully worked a land exchange with the State of New Mexico which provided the company with a mill and tailings site bordering its mining lease, and also spanning both sides of the alluvial Pipeline Arroyo streambed.

Uranium Mining and Mill Impacts at Churchrock

With only seven inches of rain per year, the Churchrock area is arid, desert-like terrain. The Rio Puerco is an ephemeral stream, naturally flowing only in response to rainfall and runoff conditions. In contrast, the ore body is found within a very productive groundwater-producing zone, or aquifer, called the Morrison Formation of Jurassic Age. The water found in this aquifer would prevent underground mining without the application of mine dewatering technology. Mine dewatering results in

TABLE 1   Permit Violations by Discharges
from Uranium Mines at Churchrock, New Mexico

Mine/ Mine Operator	Period of Record	Months Out of Compliance	No. of Violations	Parameters Violated
Churchrock/ Kerr-McGee	5/80–3/83	7 of 35	7	total uranium; dissolved radium-226; pH
Northeast Churchrock/UNC	1/80–2/83	13 of 38	19	total uranium; total and dissolved radium-226; chemical oxygen demand
Old Churchrock/ UNC	1/80–2/83	25 of 37	37	total and dissolved radium-226; chemical oxygen demand; total suspended solids

the removal and discharge of water from within the mine. Huge volumes of mine water were removed; dewatering rates reached 5,000 gallons per minute (gpm) — equivalent to 8,000 acre-feet per year—a discharge rate sustained until mine dewatering ceased at the Kerr-McGee and United Nuclear mines in 1986. Neither the Navajo Nation nor the local Churchrock residents were compensated in any way for the removal of this tremendous volume of water from beneath their lands.

At 328,000 gallons per acre-foot, 8,000 acre-feet converts to approximately 2.8 billion gallons per year. This flow was the only perennial flow in the Rio Puerco. This mine water was untreated until 1980, some twenty years after the first uranium was produced in the Churchrock area. Treatment of the water is of concern since it contained radioactive and heavy metal pollutants mixed with the water as it flowed through the mine to in-shaft pumping stations. Few records of the chemical quality of the mine water were retained by the mine operators due to poor operational procedures at the mines and the mine operators' challenges to the jurisdiction of the Federal Water Pollution Control Act over discharges to the Rio Puerco, preventing enforcement of such legislation until jurisdiction was confirmed in 1980. These challenges argue that the Rio Puerco was not "waters of the United States" under the law, and therefore not subject to the water quality protections provided under that Act. During the period between the passage of the Water Pollution Control Act in 1972 and the decision to assert jurisdiction over the stream in 1980, the mines were lawfully permitted to discharge untreated mine water.

To determine the water quality of uranium mine discharges into the Rio Puerco after the Clean Water Act jurisdiction was confirmed, records for the first three years of permitted discharges were reviewed in 1983 by Southwest Research staff to identify permit compliance history. This review showed a consistent pattern of permit violations for hazardous materials such as uranium and radium for all three mines in the area. These frequent permit violations were not the only defilement of the water used by Churchrock area Navajos. On July 16, 1979, the United Nuclear uranium mill tailings dam broke, releasing more than 94,000,000 gallons of tailings liquids, with a pH of 1—similar to battery acid—and 1,100 tons of tailings solids into the Rio Puerco. This flow reached more than 40 miles beyond the tailings facility, into Arizona, and stained the streambed with yellow and green chemical salts. Identified as the largest spill of radioactivity in the history of the U.S. nuclear industry, the Churchrock spill has resulted in impacts on water quality in the Rio Puerco and important changes in the lives of the Navajo communities which have historically used surface and ground water along the Rio Puerco.

The spill precipitated a cleanup effort by United Nuclear Corporation, the owner of the tailings site. To assess potential health effects, human and livestock health studies were conducted by the Center for Disease Control (CDC). During the period after the spill, and continuing to the present, Churchrock Navajos have had severe difficulty trying to sell their livestock to local butchers and meat markets as a result of perceived impacts of the spill contaminants on the animals using the Rio Puerco. The Churchrock tailings site is also listed on the Federal Superfund National Priority List as a result of seepage under the tailings into ground water off site onto allotments, and potentially onto tribal land. The Churchrock site is one of three uranium mill tailings sites on that list of the most hazardous waste disposal sites in the United States.

Uranium Wastewater and Health Risks

Though the spill is among the largest releases of radioactivity in the history of the nuclear industry, it does not appear to have had as devastating an effect on the Rio Puerco as the decades of mine dewatering which preceded the spill. Studies of human and livestock health effects after the spill indicated that the same pollutants found in high concentrations in mine and tailings water had showed up in abnormally high levels in the muscles and organs of cattle, sheep and goats which grazed along the Rio Puerco downstream of the mines and mills. A cow grazing downstream of the mine dewatering flows, but upstream of the tailings spill showed higher levels of radioactive thorium-230, radium-226, lead-210 and polonium-210 than animals grazing elsewhere in the Puerco watershed. CDC studies related these increased levels to the propensity of uranium, thorium and radium to attach to suspended solids in river water, which would distribute contaminants downstream along the Rio Puerco into Arizona.

The CDC report stated that "years of chronic exposure to dewatering effluent may lead to radionuclide levels in the animals that would exceed those expected from the pulse of tailings liquid released in the spill" (CDC, 1980: 22). CDC researchers also determined that federal exposure standards for the general public would be exceeded when livers and kidneys of exposed cattle were eaten over a fifty year period. Liver and kidney meats are regularly eaten by Navajo, particularly the elderly for whom such "choice" meats are provided.

The human health risk assessments which identified this excess cancer risk for resident populations assumed that livestock were the only individuals drinking Rio Puerco water. However, there is a strong record from Navajo residents of the Puerco Valley of direct human ingestion of water from the stream.

Individual interviews with Navajo in the area identified respondents who personally reported drinking from the Rio Puerco prior to and since the spill. "During the summer, when flow would stop," reports one local resident, "we would dig with the shovel and uncover some water, then we drink it ...." After the spill, some local Navajos tried to avoid using the stream in response to signs installed by New Mexico environmental staff "discouraging use of water in the Rio Puerco." However, as no alternative water supplies adequate to meet livestock needs were, or are available, the Rio Puerco continues to be a primary water source for Navajo livestock.

Navajo people along the Rio Puerco filed a lawsuit against United Nuclear for damages, but when the case was settled in 1985 for $550,000 total among 240 plaintiffs (slightly more than $2,000 per plaintiff), many local people thought that the problem had gone away. One resident reported that people "never really knew about the water contamination before the spill" or simply forgot about it after the settlement.

The residents along the stream currently rely on shallow alluvial wells or water from the stream for their livestock and domestic water supplies. This alluvial water supply is directly connected to the surface water so heavily impacted by mine dewater and spill releases. Several of these alluvial wells also show significant contamination from radionuclides and trace elements associated with uranium ore.

Few community water systems exist in the Navajo parts of the Puerco Valley and more than half of the 10,000 Navajo in the Puerco Valley rely on shallow wells for domestic water supplies. This situation continues into the 1990s where water which was contaminated by more than twenty years of uranium mine and mill discharges is still the primary water supply for Navajos and their livestock.

The Navajo Nation has selected land along the Rio Puerco to relocate tribal members being moved off their traditional lands as a result of the Navajo-Hopi Land Partition. Approximately 250,000 acres along the Puerco have been selected and those lands have essentially no surface water available other than the Rio Puerco.

The U.S. Geological Survey has begun a multi-million dollar study to fully document, for the first time, the water quality in the Puerco and its stream bed alluvium. This study is designed to identify water supplies for the "new lands" relocatees and may also benefit the longer term residents of the Puerco who continue to suffer from a lack of reliable, high-quality water supplies.

Recent Community Action for Clean Water

Since 1985, Navajo people in the Puerco Valley, assisted by the Puerco River Education Project of Southwest Research and Information Center, have been actively pursuing the provision of clean water to communities along the Puerco. This program has involved extensive community education to upgrade Navajo tribal recognition, and recognition within New Mexico state government, of the pollution problem in the Puerco. The Project has developed informational material for distribution to Navajo leaders at the Chapter and tribal levels, along with state and federal officials, to inform them and to identify an appropriate solution —local water systems. The Project has also conducted surface and ground water sampling to fill in information gaps and better document the extent of surface water, ground water and soil contamination along the Rio Puerco.

The Puerco River Education Project has also served to link the various Navajo communities along the river to build the cooperation necessary to bring limited funds to bear on the water supply shortage in the valley. This cooperation has lead to the formation of a Puerco Valley Navajo Clean Water Association and a community-planned celebration commemorating the tenth anniversary of the July 16, 1979, spill. This celebration on July 16, 1989 focused on the need for water in the communities, not the horror of the spill itself.

Rather than concentrate on the negative impacts of the accident such as physical and psychological scars and continuing depressed markets for livestock, local residents chose to remember the spill in more positive ways. People came together to run, eat, dance and sing as a community to show the strength of their culture and communities, in spite of the serious problems that have occurred. Involving chapters along the 100 mile reach of the Rio Puerco in both New Mexico and Arizona, the "Celebration for Clean Water" broke new ground by establishing cooperative and non-competitive community relationships. This use of traditional song and dance, Navajo foods, and an uncommon degree of inter-chapter unity resulted in increased community involvement and respect for those individuals organizing to address the need for new water supplies, particularly among elders and elected leaders.

The sponsorship of the "Celebration for Clean Water" by a Navajo-directed organization focused media and government agency attention directly on the people affected by the problems of the Puerco River, and allowed Navajo people themselves to advocate for better water supplies. Beyond the need for new water supplies, the Association has recognized that the community has suffered as a result of the history of irresponsible uranium development in the Puerco Valley (as demonstrated by the history of permit violations and the listing of the Churchrock tailings on the Superfund Priority List) and its continuing legacy for the community. Therefore, the Association has expanded its goals to include the support of community-scale economic development to avoid the kind of long-term environmental consequences associated with uranium production in the region. The Puerco Valley Navajo Clean Water Association (PVNCWA) combines the community leaders' personal recollections of the spill with the understanding that, despite the evidence of contamination from mine dewatering and the spill, little has been done in the past ten years to rectify the Third World water resource and economic conditions which persist in the Rio Puerco Valley section of Navajo land.

Summarizing this point during Inter-Faith Hearings on Toxics in Minority Communities in Albuquerque, New Mexico in September 1989, Kee Joe Benally, PVNCWA leader from Lupton Chapter asserted:

> There's about 14,000 Navajos living in New Mexico and Arizona along the [Puerco]. Many don't have running water in their homes. They don't have enough water for their animals. They don't grow crops because of the water shortage. If we had water, we would have jobs because we could raise more livestock and grow our own food. This is all we ask. Our Association will be learning about how we can help ourselves in our own communities in this way (Benally, 1989: 3).

The Association recognizes that, while $50 to $60 million will be spent on cleanup at the UNC mill (since the spill the site has been included on the Superfund National Priority List), no funds have been allocated to address water needs of the families downstream of the mine and mill. To combat this inequity, the Association has held community meetings, contacted elected leaders and non-profit philanthropic organizations, and hosted national and international delegations to the area concerned about uranium effects on the Native American community. These events have dramatically increased public awareness of the Association's efforts and the poor condition of community water resources, and helped build working relationships among the seven chapters along the Puerco: Mariano Lake, Pinedale, Churchrock, and Manuelito in New Mexico; and Lupton, Houck, and Sanders in Arizona.

In the future, the Association will focus on raising funds and support for community water systems to distribute water to existing Navajo homes. Water is the lifeblood of the people as well as being key to their economic livelihood. In an effort to generate local income opportunities, the Association is investigating small scale economic development programs based on improved water supplies such as community farming, along with its continuing effort to educate local residents and local, tribal, state and federal officials.

While not the first grassroots Navajo group to advocate for social and racial justice around environmental problems, the Association is the first to cover such a wide area and cross state lines. The key to the organization's future is its ability to participate in and control decisions which allocate resources to the chapters and which impact the use—and abuse—of Navajo natural resources.

13

Environmental Racism: Reviewing the Evidence

Paul Mohai and Bunyan Bryant

The United Church of Christ's (1987) report on the distribution of hazardous waste sites in this country has been very influential in raising public awareness about the disproportionate burden of pollution on minorities. This study is important because of its national scope and because of its strong and unequivocal findings regarding the distribution of commercial hazardous waste facilities. It found that the proportion of residents who are minorities in communities that have a commercial hazardous waste facility is about double the proportion of minorities in communities without such facilities. Where two or more such facilities are located, the proportion of residents who are minorities is more than triple. This study further demonstrated that race is the single best predictor of where commercial hazardous waste facilities are located, even when other socioeconomic characteristics of communities, such as average household income and average value of homes, are taken into account.

The United Church of Christ report concluded that it is "virtually impossible" that the nation's commercial hazardous waste facilities are distributed disproportionately in minority communities merely by chance, and that underlying factors related to race, therefore, in all likelihood play a role in the location of these facilities. Among others these factors include: 1) the availability of cheap land, often located in minority communities and neighborhoods (Asch and Seneca, 1978;

Drs. Mohai and Bryant were Co-Principal Investigators of the University of Michigan's 1990 Detroit Area Study. They were also Co-Organizers of the University of Michigan School of Natural Resources' Conference on Race and the Incidence of Environmental Hazards held January 1990 in Ann Arbor, Michigan. Both Drs. Mohai and Bryant served on the National Advisory Committee of the First National People of Color Environmental Leadership Summit held October 1991 in Washington, D.C.

We would like to acknowledge the Detroit Area Study Executive Committee, the Department of Sociology, the School of Natural Resources, the Office of Minority Affairs, and the Office of Minority Research Development of the Rackham School of Graduate Studies at the University of Michigan for their generous support of the 1990 Detroit Area Study. We also wish to thank the Natural Resources and Sociology graduate students at the University of Michigan who contributed to various phases of the project. Special thanks and gratitude are owed to Dr. Karl Landis, former Director of the Detroit Area Study.

Bullard and Wright, 1987; United Church of Christ, 1987); 2) the lack of local opposition to the facility, often resulting from minorities' lack of organization and political resources as well as their need for jobs (Bullard and Wright, 1987; United Church of Christ, 1987); and 3) the lack of mobility of minorities resulting from poverty and housing discrimination that traps them in neighborhoods where hazardous waste facilities are located (Bullard and Wright, 1987; United Church of Christ, 1987). The United Church of Christ report noted that these mechanisms and resulting inequitable outcomes represent institutionalized forms of racism. When the report was released, Dr. Benjamin F. Chavis, Jr., termed the racial biases in the location of commercial hazardous waste facilities as "environmental racism" (Lee, 1992).

The striking findings and the scope of the United Church of Christ study suggest that environmental racism is not confined to hazardous waste alone. A major objective of our investigation was, therefore, to document the existence of other studies which have used systematic data to examine the social distribution of pollution and to determine whether the evidence from these studies, taken together, demonstrates a consistent pattern of environmental racism.

A question that is often raised is whether the racial bias in the distribution of environmental hazards is simply a function of poverty (see, for example, Weisskopf, 1992). That is, rather than race per se, is it not poverty that affects the distribution of environmental hazards? And are not minorities disproportionately impacted simply because they are disproportionately poor?[1] Classical economic theory would predict that poverty plays a role (see Asch and Seneca, 1978, and Freeman, 1972). Because of limited income and wealth, poor people do not have the financial means to buy out of polluted neighborhoods and into environmentally more desirable ones. Also, land values tend to be cheaper in poor neighborhoods and are thus attractive to polluting industries that seek to reduce the costs of doing business (United Church of Christ, 1987). However, housing discrimination further restricts the mobility of minorities (Denton and Massey, 1988; Feagin and Feagin, 1978).[2] Also, because noxious sites are unwanted (the "NIMBY" syndrome) and because industries tend to take the path of least resistance, communities with little political clout are often targeted for such facilities (Bullard and Wright, 1987). These communities tend to be where residents are unaware of the policy decisions affecting them and are unorganized and lack resources for taking political action; such resources include time, money, contacts, knowledge of the political system, and others (Bullard, 1990; Mohai, 1985, 1990). Minority communities are at a disadvantage not only in terms of availability of resources but also because of underrepresentation on governing bodies when location decisions are made (Bullard, 1983). Underrepresentation translates into limited access to policy makers and lack of advocates for minority interests.

Taken together, these factors suggest that race has an additional impact on the distribution of environmental hazards, independent of income. A second major objective of our study, therefore, was to assess the relative influence of income and race on the distribution of pollution. We did so by examining the results of those empirical studies which have analyzed the distribution of environmental hazards by both income and race. To our knowledge, this is the first time such a review and assessment has been undertaken. We also provide new evidence from a multivariate analysis of the distribution of commercial hazardous waste facilities in the Detroit metropolitan area.

Environmental Racism:
Evidence from Existing Studies

Table 1 contains a summary of 15 studies which provide systematic information about the social distribution of environmental hazards. In assessing the distribution of these hazards by income, the typical approach has been to correlate the average or median household or family income of the community (usually approximated by U.S. Census tracts or zip code areas) with the degree of exposure to the hazard. In assessing the distribution of environmental hazards by race, the minority percentage of the community has been typically employed. For example, after matching the location of air quality monitoring sites with U.S. Census tracts, Asch and Seneca (1978) correlated the median family incomes and minority percentages of the Census tracts with the mean annual air pollution levels of the tracts. Likewise, the United Church of Christ (1987) matched the location of commercial hazardous waste facilities with zip code areas, and correlated the mean household income, minority percentage, and other characteristics of these areas with the presence of one or more commercial hazardous waste facilities.

A number of interesting and important facts emerge from an examination of Table 1. First, an inspection of the publication dates of these studies reveals that information about environmental inequity has been available for some time. Rather than being a recent discovery, documentation of environmental injustices stretches back two decades, almost to Earth Day - an event viewed by many as a major turning point in public awareness about environmental issues (Davies and Davies, 1975; Fessler, 1990). Evidently, it has taken some time for public awareness to catch up to the issues of environmental injustice.

It is also interesting to note that most of the studies that have been conducted in this period have focused on the distribution of air pollution. Clearly, systematic studies of the social distribution of other types of environmental hazards, such as water pollution, pesticide exposure, aesbestos exposure, and other hazards are needed. Also worth noting is that these studies vary considerably in terms of their scope—i.e., some studies have focused on single urban areas, such as Washington, DC, or Houston, others have focused on a collection of urban areas, while still others have been national in scope. This observation is important in that it reveals that the pattern of findings is not simply an artifact of the samples used. Irregardless of the scope of the analyses, the findings point to a consistent pattern.

TABLE 1   Studies Providing Systematic Empirical Evidence
Regarding the Burden of Environmental Hazards by Income and Race

Study	Hazard	Focus of Study	Distribution Inequitable by Income?	Distribution Inequitable by Race?	Income or Race More Important?
CEQ (1971)	Air Poll.	Urban Area	Yes	NA*	NA
Freeman (1972)	Air Poll.	Urban Areas	Yes	Yes	Race
Harrison (1975)	Air Poll.	Urban Areas	Yes	NA	NA
	Air Poll.	Nation	No	NA	NA
Kruvant (1975)	Air Poll.	Urban Area	Yes	Yes	Income
Zupan (1975)	Air Poll.	Urban Area	Yes	NA	NA
Burch (1976)	Air Poll.	Urban Area	Yes	No	Income
Berry et al. (1977)	Air Poll.	Urban Areas	Yes	Yes	NA
	Solid Waste	Urban Areas	Yes	Yes	NA
	Noise	Urban Areas	Yes	Yes	NA
	Pesticide Poisoning	Urban Areas	Yes	Yes	NA
	Rat Bite Risk	Urban Areas	Yes	Yes	NA
Handy (1977)	Air Poll.	Urban Area	Yes	NA	NA
Asch & Seneca (1978)	Air Poll.	Urban Areas	Yes	Yes	Income
Gianessi et al. (1979)	Air Poll.	Nation	No	Yes	Race
Bullard (1983)	Solid Waste	Urban Area	NA	Yes	NA
U.S. GAO (1983)	Haz. Waste	Southern Region	Yes	Yes	NA
United Church of Christ (1987)	Haz. Waste	Nation	Yes	Yes	Race
Gelobter (1987; 1992)	Air Poll.	Urban Areas	Yes	Yes	Race
	Air Poll.	Nation	No	Yes	Race
West et al. (1992)	Toxic Fish Consumption	State	No	Yes	Race

* NA = not applicable.

It is clear from examining the results in Table 1 that, regardless of the environmental hazard and regardless of the scope of the study, in nearly every case the distribution of pollution has been found to be inequitable by income. And with only one exception, the distribution of pollution has been found to be inequitable by race. Where the distribution of pollution has been analyzed by both income and race (and where it was possible to weigh the relative importance of each), in most cases race has been found to be more strongly related to the incidence of pollution.

The United Church of Christ (1987), Freeman (1972), Gelobter (1987, 1992), Gianessi, Peskin, and Wolff (1979), and West, Fly, Larkin, and Marans (1992) all found that race was more strongly related than class to the distribution of the environmental hazard under investigation. As mentioned previously, from a multivariate statistical analysis of nation-wide data, the United Church of Christ found that the percentage of minority residents within a community (defined by zip code areas) was the single best predictor of where commercial hazardous waste facilities are located in the country—more so than other socioeconomic variables such as mean household income and mean value of owner-occupied homes.

Using an air pollution exposure index, Freeman (1972) found that low-income groups in three urban areas (Kansas City, St. Louis, and Washington, DC) were more greatly exposed to total suspended particulates and sulfates than upper-income groups. However, racial differences were found to be even more pronounced as minorities in each of the cities were found to be exposed to higher levels of both pollutants than the lowest income group examined (the "under $3,000" group).

Likewise using pollution exposure indices (one for total suspended particulates and another for combined concentrations of total suspended particulates, sulfates, sulfur dioxide, nitrogen oxides, ozone, and carbon monoxide), Gelobter (1987, 1992) found similar results. However, unlike Freeman's study Gelobter's was national in scope. He conducted his analyses in two parts, one focused on the U.S. as a whole, incorporating both rural and urban areas, and a second focused on just urban areas. He found that over a 15 year period (from 1970 to 1984) minorities were consistently exposed to significantly more air pollution than whites. This finding was the same whether the analysis was focused on just the urban areas or on the country as a whole. Inequities in the distribution of air pollution by income were less clear. At the national level, exposure to total suspended particulates was found to be somewhat greater for upper income groups than for lower income groups (a probable result of the fact that both income and pollution tend to be simultaneously higher in urban areas than in rural ones). Within urban areas, however, exposure was found to be greater for those in the lower income categories, although differences by income categories tended to be small. When exposure to combined concentrations of air pollutants was examined, similar patterns were found, although this time lower income groups were found to be more greatly exposed at both national and urban levels of analyses. Nevertheless, as in Freeman's study, racial biases in exposure to pollution tended to be more stark; as in the earlier study, in all cases minorities were found to be more greatly exposed to pollution than the lowest income group examined ("under $3,000").

Gianessi, Peskin, and Wolff's (1979) study is the only other to have attempted a national level analysis of the distribution of air pollution by income and race. However, unlike Gelobter's study, rather than measuring exposure to physical concentrations of air pollution directly, they estimated dollar damage suffered from exposure to air pollution. Also, their estimates were based on EPA data taken for a single time period. Nevertheless, their results are very similar to Gelobter's. Like Gelobter, they found that air pollution damage is distributed progressively (i.e., upper rather than lower income groups suffer more damage) when the analysis is conducted at the national level (as before, this outcome is the probable result of incomes and pollution tending to be simultaneously higher in the more urbanized rather than rural areas of the country). However, when racial differences were examined, the inequities were found to be clear and striking: minorities were much more likely to suffer greater damage from air pollution than whites at all income levels.

Finally, West, Fly, Larkin, and Marans (1992) found from a state-wide survey of licensed fishermen in Michigan that on average minority fishermen and their families are likely to consume more fish (21.7 grams/person/day) than white fishermen and their families (17.9 grams/person/day). The purpose of their study was to assess the potential risk to these groups of ingesting toxic fish. Michigan's Rule 1057, which is designed to regulate the amount of discharge of toxic chemicals into state waters, is based on the assumption that the average consumption of fish in the state is 6.5 grams/person/day (West et al., 1992). Although minority fishermen and their families were found to consume more fish than white fishermen and their families, clearly both groups appear to be at risk based on this standard. Interestingly, West et al. did not find a significant relationship between income and the amount of fish consumed in either their bivariate analysis of income with consumption nor in their multivariate analysis where the simultaneous relationship of income and race with consumption was examined.

Only in three of the eight studies where it was possible to weigh the relative importance of both race and income was income found to be more strongly related to the distribution of environmental hazards. In one of these studies, Kruvant (1975) superimposed Census tract data in the Washington, DC, area with air pollution zones. Using this method, he found that there tended to be a tighter fit between areas of high air pollution and high concentrations of the poor than there were between areas of high air pollution concentrations and blacks. Using a similar technique, Burch (1976) found that while there was a significant relationship between areas of high air pollution and high concentrations of the poor in the New Haven, CT, area, there was no significant relationship between concentrations of air pollution and blacks. Finally, Asch and Seneca (1978) found that the correlations of the "nonwhite" percentages of Census tracts in Chicago, Cleveland, and Nashville with the mean annual levels of various air pollutants tended to be weaker than the correlations of the median family incomes of the Census tracts with pollutant levels; using cities within 23 states (rather than Census tracts within the 3 cities mentioned above) as the units of analysis, Asch and Seneca obtained similar results.

Although two additional studies found the distribution of environmental hazards to be inequitable by both income and race, it was not possible to assess conclusively which, if either, variable was more strongly related because of the methodological approaches employed in these studies. These include Berry et al.'s study (1977) of the distribution of air pollution, pesticide poisoning, noise, solid waste, and rat bite risks in 13 of the nation's major urban areas, and the U.S. General Accounting Office's study (1983) of the distribution of four major hazardous waste landfills located in the South.

In summary, review of the 15 studies which have examined the distribution of environmental hazards by income and race indicates both a class and racial bias. Furthermore, that the racial bias is not simply a function of poverty alone also appears to be born out by the data. All but one of the 11 studies which have examined the distribution of environmental hazards by race have found a significant bias. In addition, in five of the eight studies where it was possible to assess the relative importance of race with income, racial biases have been found to be more significant. Noteworthy also is the fact that all three studies which have been national in scope and which have provided both income and race information have found race to be more importantly related to the distribution of environmental hazards than income. Taken together, these findings thus appear to support the assertion of those who have argued that race has an additional effect on the distribution of environmental hazards that is independent of class.

Environmental Racism:
Evidence from the Detroit Area Study

In order to provide greater clarity to the issue of environmental equity, we provide additional evidence from an analysis of the distribution of commercial hazardous waste facilities in the Detroit area. In so doing, special attention is given to the effects of race. A detailed multivariate statistical analysis is conducted in order to determine whether race has a relationship with the location of commercial hazardous waste facilities that is independent of income. The multivariate analysis is also used to weigh the relative strength of the relationship of race and income with the distribution of sites. There are only two other studies which have applied multivariate statistical techniques to assess the relative effects of race and income on exposure to environmental hazards: the United Church of Christ (1987) and West et al. (1992) studies. Both found race not only to have an independent relationship with the hazard but also found it to be more strongly related to the hazard than income.

Data used for this study are taken from the University of Michigan's 1990 Detroit Area Study (Mohai and Bryant, 1989). Information was obtained from face-to-face interviews of residents 18 years or older in Macomb, Oakland, and Wayne Counties, Michigan (the 3 counties surrounding the city of Detroit). Respondents were identified from households which were selected with equal probability using a stratified two-stage area probability sampling design. Because of the objectives of the study, an additional oversample was drawn of households within 1.5 miles of an existing or proposed commercial hazardous waste treatment or storage facility. Information about the location of the facilities in the Detroit area was obtained from the Michigan Department of Natural Resources. These included 14 existing facilities and two proposed.[3]

Kish (1949) selection tables were used to randomly select one respondent from the eligible persons in each of the households in the base (households not within 1.5 miles of a facility) and supplemental studies. Five hundred four and 289 interviews, respectively, in the two samples were conducted resulting in an overall study response rate of 69%.

For all analyses, cases were weighted by the number of eligible persons in the household. In those analyses where the oversample and base samples were pooled, cases were additionally weighted by a household sampling weight which compensates for the unequal probability of selection between the two samples.

Information about race and household income was obtained for all 793 respondents. The unweighted numbers of whites, blacks, and other nonwhites in the sample were 575, 180, and 38, respectively. For purposes of the analyses the 218 blacks and other nonwhites were combined into the category "minority."

The precise locations of the commercial hazardous waste facilities and the 289 respondents in the oversample were mapped. The distances between these respondents and one of the 16 facilities was measured to the nearest 0.1 mile.

Although our main objective was to assess racial biases in the distribution of commercial hazardous waste facilities within the three counties surrounding the city of Detroit, from a cursory analysis we observed a rather striking racial bias in the distribution of these facilities at the state level as well. Although there are 21 commercial hazardous waste facilities in the state of Michigan, 16 (76 percent) of them are located in the three-county area. And of these 16, half (the two facilities that are proposed are included here) are located in the city of Detroit, proper. This is significant as U.S. Census Bureau data for the state of Michigan and demographic data collected from our Detroit area study indicate that the minority percentages for the state, three-county area, and city are 16 percent, 21 percent, and 76 percent, respectively. Thus, commercial hazardous waste facilities in the state are clearly located disproportionately where minorities are most heavily concentrated.

Our next step was to conduct a detailed analysis of the distribution of

FIGURE 1 Percent of Detroit Area Residents Living Near
a Commercial Hazardous Waste Facility Who Are Members of a
Minority Group or Who Live Below the Poverty Line

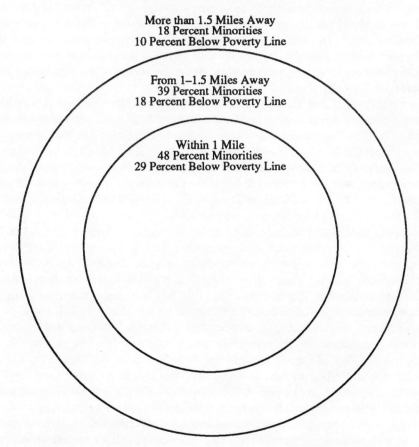

More than 1.5 Miles Away
18 Percent Minorities
10 Percent Below Poverty Line

From 1–1.5 Miles Away
39 Percent Minorities
18 Percent Below Poverty Line

Within 1 Mile
48 Percent Minorities
29 Percent Below Poverty Line

commercial hazardous waste facilities within the three-county metropolitan area, giving special attention to the relative effects of income and race. Using the demographic and socioeconomic information from the 504 residents in our base sample (those in the Detroit area who live more than 1.5 miles away from a commercial hazardous waste facility), we computed the percent who are minority residents as well as the percent who are living below the poverty line.[4] We did likewise with the oversample of 289 residents living within 1.5 miles of a facility. However, we further divided this latter sample into those living strictly within 1 mile and those living between 1 mile and 1.5 miles of a facility.

The diagram in Figure 1 indicates the percent of minorities and the percent of people living below the poverty line within fixed distances of a commercial hazardous waste facility. The percentages indicate a clear bias. Of those people living more than 1.5 miles from a commercial hazardous waste facility only 18 percent are minority residents. Of those people living within 1.5 miles but more than 1 mile away, 39 percent are minority. And of those residents living within 1 mile from the center of a facility, 48 percent are minority. A similar pattern exists when the percentage of people living below the poverty line are examined (see Figure 1). Chi-square tests indicate that these patterns are statistically significant at the .0000 level (see Table 2).

Analysis of our data indicates that only about four percent of the total population in the three-county area lives within one mile of a commercial hazardous waste facility. Broken down by racial groups, three percent of all whites and 11 percent of all minorities live within a mile of such a facility. Although these are small proportions for both groups, the biases are nevertheless clear. As the ratio of the two percentages indicate, if you are living in the three-county area of Detroit and are a minority resident, your chance of living within a mile of a hazardous waste facility is about four times greater than if you are white.

We wanted to determine whether the above results were a function of the disproportionate number of hazardous waste facilities in the city of Detroit (the city contains 50 percent of the 16 commercial hazardous waste facilities in the three-county area but only about 20 percent of its population), or whether the same patterns exist both inside and outside the city. Thus, we repeated the above analysis: 1) once for the city of Detroit alone and 2) again for the suburban area (i.e., the three-county area outside Detroit). The percentages in Table 2 indicate that the biases persist whether the city or the suburban area is examined by itself, although in the case of the City of Detroit the differences do not attain statistical significance. Although the suburban area contains very few minorities (the percentages of minority residents for Macomb, Oakland, and suburban Wayne Counties are seven percent, nine percent, and five percent, respectively, and eight percent as a whole), it is there where the racial biases in the distribution of facilities are most pronounced (Table 2). Although generally the hazardous waste facilities are also disproportionately located in areas with high concentrations of people living below the poverty line, patterns are less clear when suburban areas and the city of Detroit are examined separately. In both the city and the suburban areas, the proportion of people who live below the poverty line is higher among people residing within a mile of a commercial hazardous waste facility than it is among those residing more than 1.5 miles away. However, in Detroit, the smallest concentrations of people living below the poverty line are in the neighborhoods that are between one and 1.5 miles from a facility; in the suburbs, neighborhoods that are between 1 and 1.5 miles from a facility have the highest concentrations (Table 2).

A major objective of our study was to examine the relative strength of the relationship of race and income on the distribution of commercial hazardous waste

TABLE 2   Percent of Detroit Area Residents Living
Within Fixed Distances of a Commercial Hazardous Waste Facility
Who Are Members of a Minority Group or Living Below the Poverty Line

All Three-County Area Residents			Above Poverty Line	Below Poverty Line
	White	Minority		
> 1.5 miles away	82	18	90	10
1–1.5 miles away	61	39	82	18
< 1 mile away	52	48	71	29

Chi-square=26.6328   Chi-square=56.6610
d.f.=2   d.f.=2
P=.0000   P=.0000

City of Detroit Residents			Above Poverty Line	Below Poverty Line
	White	Minority		
> 1.5 miles away	25	76	66	34
1–1.5 miles away	21	79	85	15
< 1 mile away	20	80	48	52

Chi-square=0.4651   Chi-square=11.3457
d.f.=2   d.f.=2
P=.7925   P=.0034

Suburban Residents			Above Poverty Line	Below Poverty Line
	White	Minority		
> 1.5 miles away	93	7	95	5
1–1.5 miles away	88	12	80	20
< 1 mile away	82	18	89	11

Chi-square=7.3690   Chi-square=16.8079
d.f.=2   d.f.=2
P=.0251   P=.0002

facilities in the Detroit area. In order to accomplish this objective, we used multiple linear regression analysis. We tested to see whether race (coded as 1=white and 0=minority) and income (measured in dollars) each had an independent relationship with the distance of residents to a commercial hazardous waste facility. And if so, which had the stronger relationship. We conducted the analysis in two ways. In the first analysis, the dependent variable used to measure distance to a site was an ordinal number which indicated the general proximity of the respondent to the site. Here, 1=within 1 mile, 2=between 1 mile and 1.5 miles, and 3=more than 1.5 miles away. In this analysis, all 793 respondents were included (and appropriately weighted to correct for the varying probability of selection into the study). In the second analysis, the precise distance of the respondent to the center of a facility (measured to the nearest 0.1 mile) was used as the dependent variable. In this latter analysis, only data from the 289 respondents in the oversample were used since precise distances to the commercial hazardous waste facilities were measured only for this group. As Table 3 indicates, either approach yields similar results. The relationship between race and the location of commercial hazardous waste facilities in the Detroit area is independent of income in each of the analyses. And, important to the thesis of this paper, it is race which is the best predictor. In fact, in the second analysis, the relationship between the location of sites and income is no longer statistically significant.

Conclusions

Review of 15 existing studies plus results of our Detroit area study provide clear and unequivocal evidence that income and racial biases in the distribution of environmental hazards exist. Our findings also appear to support the claims of those who have argued that race is more importantly related to the distribution of these hazards than income. Ultimately, knowing which is more important may be less relevant, however, than understanding the conditions associated with race and class that appear to consistently, if not inevitably, lead to inequitable exposure to environmental hazards and in understanding how these conditions can be addressed and how inequities in the distribution of environmental quality can be remedied.

Currently, there are no public policies in place which require monitoring equity in the distribution of environmental quality. Hence, policy makers have little knowledge about what the equity consequences are of the programs designed to control pollution in this country. Are some groups receiving fewer environmental and health remedies than others from existing programs? Have the risks to some actually increased as a result? If the social, economic, and political disadvantages faced by the poor and minorities that lead to environmental inequities are unlikely to be compensated any time soon, then it is clear that proactive government policies will be needed to address this issue. In the future, inequities in the distribution of environmental hazards will need to be monitored; existing policies and programs

TABLE 3   Results of Multiple Linear Regression Analyses of Race
and Income with Distance to a Commercial Hazardous Waste Facility

Where dependent variable (distance of
resident to facility) is 1=within 1 mile,
2=between 1 and 1.5 miles, and 3=more
than 1.5 miles away (includes entire
sample of 793 respondents).

	Beta
Race	.22***
Income	.08*
R^2	.07
Adj. R^2	.06
F	23.5760***

Where dependent variable (distance
of resident to facility) is measured to
nearest 0.1 mile (includes oversample
only of 289 respondents).

	Beta
Race	.22**
Income	−.10
R^2	.04
Adj. R^2	.04
F	5.1133**

* P<.05   ** P<.01   ***P<.001

adjusted; and new programs designed in which enhancing environmental equity is
a criterion for adoption.

   A quarter of a century ago, the Kerner Commission (United States Government,
1968) warned that: "To continue present policies is to make permanent the division
of our country into two societies: one largely Negro and poor, located in the central
cities, the other predominantly white and affluent, located in the suburbs and in
outlying areas." At the time that that warning was made, the EPA had not yet been
created nor the nation's major environmental legislation yet passed. The terms

"environmental racism" and "environmental justice" were unheard of. Results of our study and those of others indicate current environmental policies have allowed for separate societies differing in the quality of their respective environments. To know that these inequities exist but to do nothing about them is to perpetuate separate societies and will continue to leave the poor, blacks, and other minorities vulnerable to current and future environmental policy decisions.

Notes

1.   One has to ask why minorities are disproportionately poor in the first place, however. Obviously, the answer is related to job and educational discrimination which contributes to the low pay and hence poor living conditions of minorities. Thus, the factor of race ultimately cannot be avoided.

2.   That housing discrimination is no insignificant influence on mobility was demonstrated in an ambitious national study by Denton and Massey (1988). Using U.S. Census Bureau data, they found that the degree of segregation found in black communities was not appreciably reduced by controlling for the income, education, and occupational status levels of the communities. This finding led Denton and Massey to conclude that race rather than income was the limiting factor on the mobility of blacks. "Clearly, black segregation in U.S. metropolitan areas cannot easily be attributed to socioeconomic differences from whites" (p. 805).

3.   The survey population for this special supplemental study includes all households who live within a 1.5 mile radial zone of the 16 designated commercial hazardous waste facilities (14 existing and two proposed). From this survey population a two-stage equal probability sample of households was selected. The distribution of sampled households in the 16 zones which comprise the survey population is proportional to the total number of households which reside in each zone. Zones surrounding commercial hazardous waste facilities which have low population densities are expected to have smaller numbers of sampled households than zones with higher household densities. Although all households in the survey population had an equal chance of selection for the study, densities in several of the 16 commercial hazardous waste facility zones are sufficiently low that no sample observations were in fact selected. However, as inference from the sample is to the entire population of people living in all 16 zones, the sample selected is representative of the entire population of residents living within 1.5 miles of these 16 commercial hazardous waste facility zones.

4.   The U.S. Census Bureau definition was used here.

14

Pesticide Exposure of Farm Workers and the International Connection

Ivette Perfecto

The interaction of the environment and race raises a variety of interesting conceptual questions, to say nothing of important practical and moral ones. As James O'Connor (1989) recently pointed out, there is little in the way of formal social theory which relates questions of the environment to the productive process in any way shape or form. The sorts of epistemological questions so common in the class/race/gender debate have not even been raised regarding questions of the environment. While it is not my intent to elaborate a theoretical formulation concerning the interaction between race and environment, some comments are in order if only to put the observations of this paper in some sort of context.

In the modern capitalist world system, firms, regions, and eventually nation-states compete with one another. Competition requires individual capitalists to maintain wages at the lowest possible level. Empirically, we know that their ability to do so is influenced by the race or gender of the workers, allowing greater levels of exploitation through the ideology of biological determinism. While the differentiation of race and/or gender along biological determinist lines does not create exploitation, it permits a greater "efficiency" of exploitation for firms, regions and nation states in the competitive arena. Effectively, the firm, region, or nation-state that exploits most efficiently develops an edge in competition with others.

Race and class, thus, interact with one another—racism allows differentiation of the labor process and labor markets, and reduces overall labor cost via greater efficiency of exploitation. Racism provides the ideological justification that allows that greater efficiency. The proletariat is exploited through the hidden expropriation of labor power, a remarkably efficient form of exploitation because it effectively appropriates the aid of the exploited in the process of exploitation. The exploitation

Ivette Perfecto has a Ph.D. in Ecology and is an Assistant Professor in the School of Natural Resources at the University of Michigan. Her general research interest is in agroecology, particularly integrated pest management in Central America. She has done extensive research in Nicaragua on alternatives to pesticides in the corn agroecosystem. She now teaches Agroforestry and Tropical Natural Resource Conservation in the School of Natural Resources at the University of Michigan.

of people of other "races" is aided by the ideology of biological determinism, sometimes a subtle one, but nevertheless a fundamental process. While the details of the exploitation, with and without racism, are very distinct, the underlying purpose is similar: retaining the competitive edge in a capitalist market.

The environment can be viewed as a similar, although not completely analogous, category. While most theory emphasizes factors, forces, and relations of production, the environment is effectively what Marx saw as the "conditions of production" (O'Connor, 1989). Considering the environment as a category in the framework of the exploitation theory described above, a first approximation is simply that those firms, regions, and nation-states that most effectively "exploit" the environment will be able to gain that critical competitive edge, thus making environmental deterioration a factor on the same level with race and class. But the incorporation of the environment in this manner creates a false identity between an abstraction—the environment—and a material fact—the working class, or the people belonging to an exploited "race," effectively a reification of "the environment."

Martínez-Alier (1989) provides a conceptual framework that allows the incorporation of the environment in a non-reified way by examining the mode of appropriation of the conditions of production from future generations. The efficiency of production (not necessarily the expropriation of current workers) is enhanced by the effective appropriation of the conditions of production from future generations. When the cotton fields of northern Nicaragua were poisoned with pesticides in the 1950s, what was expropriated from whom? Today we see the answer. Nicaraguan agronomists are trying to grow soybeans in the fields where cotton used to be grown, but the beet armyworm (a caterpillar pest of soybean) makes it almost impossible to do so. The beet armyworm is not a "natural" pest, but rather was created as a consequence of the spraying of pesticides in the cotton fields in the 1950s. If it did not exist, contemporary Nicaraguans could benefit from the production of soybeans. Exactly how much are they losing by not being able to produce soybeans? That quantity of loss represents a quantity that had been expropriated from them by the cotton farmers of the 1950s. Many other examples could be cited. The point is simply that environmental degradation can be represented, so as to be parallel with class exploitation and the exploitation of people of other "races," as the expropriation of someone else's potential, and that someone else can be thought of as people in future generations (Martínez-Alier, 1989). One obvious problem with this analysis is that it assumes that the "exploitation" of the environment now will always have negative consequences for future generations. As Martínez-Alier (1989) pointed out when considering the application of externality analysis to the environment, we do not know what the externalities are, and whether these are negative or positive. Nevertheless, the analysis is still useful as an initial attempt to integrate the environment with the race, class and gender analysis.

Expropriation is allowed to occur either (1) because it is hidden from view from those expropriated (the marvel of the capitalist system of class exploitation), or (2) because those expropriated have no right or political power to resist the expropriation. Race and the environment thus can be formulated as two sides of the same coin in that people belonging to a "race" that is considered lower, have no right to resist, nor do unborn generations have the political power to resist.

But there is one structural form in which the people from whom value is expropriated through environmental degradation are people of color. The capability of accomplishing this form of expropriation can become very important when environmental advocates (or advocates of generations yet unborn) become politically active and powerful. The popular claim that "we do not inherit the earth from our parents, we borrow it from our children," while true enough in the abstract, carries a threat for capitalist accumulation in that this one form of "expropriation" (from future generations via environmental degradation) will soon be denied or drastically curtailed. It is at this point that racism and environmental degradation become organically linked, in that environmental degradation may be accomplished through the expropriation from people of color, thus satisfying the rallying cry of the exploiting "race" (whites), that the environment must be preserved for their children.

It is this particular dimension of the race/environment issue that I wish to explore in this paper. The application of pesticides, while undeniably increasing agricultural production in the short term, has also generated significant environmental degradation, and thus it has been argued well and often that future generations will suffer. But there has also been important political organizing against this environmental degradation. The above theoretical framework suggests that such conditions would spawn a closer connection between environmental degradation and race. People of color will become an outlet for activities that are no longer permitted to expropriate value from the future. In what follows I examine how the mainstream environmental movement in the United States, a predominantly white middle class movement, by putting constraints to environmental degradation (therefore reducing the efficiency of exploitation) has resulted in further exploitation of people of color. This paper presents some of the published data associated with this phenomenon, and the interconnection of pesticide abuse and racism, first as it relates to conditions within the developed world, concentrating on the United States, and second as it relates to the Third World.

Pesticides and Minorities in the United States

The United States is the largest single user of pesticides in the world. Each year U.S. farmers use 1.2 billion pounds of pesticides at an expenditure of $4.6 billion, most of which comes from federal subsidies (U.S. Environmental Protection Agency, 1986). More than 600 active ingredients are combined with other inert ingredients to form approximately 35,000 different commercial formulations designed to kill plants, insects, fungi, bacteria, nematodes and rodents (U.S. Environmental Protection Agency, 1986). Nobody really knows the full extent of the hazards pesticides pose to humans, wildlife and the environment. Less than 10 percent of the products in current use have been tested for potential health effects, and of the 600 registered pesticides' active ingredients, the U.S. Environmental Protection Agency (EPA) can provide full safety assurance for only six (Alternative Policy Institute, 1986).

Those who suffer the most from the chemical dependency of U.S. agriculture are the farm workers. It is estimated that perhaps as many as 313,000 farm workers in the U.S. may suffer from pesticide related illnesses each year (Wasserstrom and Wiles, 1985). Ninety percent of the approximately two million hired farm workers in the U.S. are ethnic minorities. Latinos of Mexican origin comprise the largest group (75 percent of the agricultural workforce), followed by black North Americans, black Caribbeans, Puerto Ricans, and a small number of Laotians, Filipinos, Koreans, Vietnamese, and others (Martín et al., 1985; U.S. Department of Agriculture, 1986).

These mostly minority farm workers have among the most dangerous and least protected jobs of all workers. Agriculture is the third most dangerous occupation in the U.S. (Goldsmith, 1989), and the National Safety Council has calculated that the death rate in agriculture is 66 per 10,000, while the industrial average is 18 per 10,000 (Pollack and Grozuczak, 1984). Except for accidents, pesticide poisoning is probably the single largest occupational health problem for farm workers. Although few statistics are available, it is estimated that 800 to 1,000 farm workers die each year as a direct consequence of pesticide exposure (Pollack and Grozuczak, 1984).

Pesticides, Health, and the Environment

Documenting the link between pesticides and health is difficult because most pesticide illnesses go untreated. In 1976, farm worker surveys in California led state officials to estimate that only a small fraction, perhaps only one or two percent, of pesticide-induced illnesses of field workers was being reported (Kahn, 1976), leading state legislators to enact legislation requiring physicians to report pesticide illness to local authorities. Today, California is the state with the most comprehensive methods to monitor pesticide poisoning. Nevertheless, pesticide illnesses still go underreported, and many workers do not seek medical care until several days, even weeks, after being exposed to pesticides, for fear of losing their jobs.

The detrimental effects of pesticides on farm workers, the rural community and the general population can be broadly divided into acute and chronic effects.

Acute health effects range from dizziness, vomiting, eye and upper respiratory tract irritation, and skin irritation, to systemic poisoning that can lead to death (Mosses, 1989). For obvious reasons, farm workers are the ones who suffer the most from these acute effects. They are usually the ones who apply the pesticides and come into direct contact with the crop foliage after application. Although there are laws in the U.S. that prohibit application of pesticides while farm workers are in the field, the laws are not always enforced and, even when they are, the residues of pesticides can remain in the vegetation, primarily on leafy surfaces ("dislodgeable residues") for long periods of time (Mosses, 1989).

In the early 1960s, 94 farm workers suddenly became ill after picking peaches on a California plantation. Similar episodes occurred on neighboring farms. After a long investigation it was discovered that the farms where the incidents occurred had been using parathion, a supposedly non-persistent, but acutely toxic pesticide. Further investigation found that parathion degrades into a compound called paraoxon, which is 55 times more toxic than parathion and which remains on the foliage as a dislodgeable residue. They also found that none of the peaches sampled on the farms exceeded the allowable standards for parathion residues. In other words, the standards succeeded in protecting consumers, but failed to protect farm workers (Wasserstrom and Wiles, 1985).

Chronic health effects related to pesticide exposure are largely unknown due to the lack of attention from the research community, the lack of a record keeping method that would provide the necessary information to document pesticide exposure, and the long period of clinical latency for some of the effects. A recent review (Mosses, 1989) indicates that chronic effects of pesticide exposure include: cancer (e.g., malignant lymphoma, leukemia, multiple myeloma, testicular); reproductive malfunctions (e.g., infertility, sterility, chromosomal abnormality, spontaneous abortion, death of the fetus in utero); a broad range of developmental and behavioral growth problems, and birth defects. It is also well documented that farm workers are affected by these diseases at a significantly higher rate than the population at large (Mosses, 1989).

Pesticides that are carcinogens and/or teratogens are generally persistent in the environment and make their way into the soil, the ground water and the air. The first evidence of ground water contamination emerged in 1978 when DBCP, a pesticide linked to cancer, birth defects and male sterility, was found in ground water wells in the Central Valley of California. Further investigation revealed that over 2,500 wells contained some amounts of DBCP (Litwin, Hantzsche, and George, 1983). A recent study even shows pesticide residues concentrated in fog (Glotfelty, Seiber, and Liljedahl, 1987). These residues tend to accumulate in animal fatty tissue and reach extremely dangerous levels. Breast milk, which has a high concentration of fat, has been found contaminated with a variety of pesticides in women of the rural South (Barnett and Müller, 1979).

In general, pesticides that persist in the environment tend to have low acute toxicity, while those that degrade rapidly are more acutely toxic. Parathion, originally developed in Nazi Germany as a by-product of chemical weapons research, belongs to the family of the organophosphates, acutely toxic pesticides that degrade rapidly, and thus do not persist in the environment. The use of less persistent but more acutely toxic pesticides, such as N-methyl carbamates and organophosphates, like parathion, increased with the banning or restriction of the less toxic but highly persistent organochlorines, like DDT, aldrine, chlordane and others (Mosses, 1989; Wright, 1986). Unfortunately, for farm workers this switch meant that they would be exposed more to the acutely toxic pesticides, as opposed to the ones that produce only chronic effects. Furthermore, organophosphates have also been associated with neuropathological and neurobehavioral delayed or chronic effects, including insomnia, nightmares, night sweats, chronic headaches, chronic fatigue, memory loss and difficulty in maintaining attention (Barnett, 1989; Mosses, 1989).

This switch came as a consequence of the environmental awareness in the U.S., instigated largely as a response to the book by Rachel Carson, *Silent Spring* (1962). The main concern of environmentalists was that future generations and wildlife were being affected by a degradation of the environment. Although unconsciously, a decision was made to protect the environment (and pretty animals) at the expense of the health of farm workers. The fact that most farm workers are people of color made the implementation of this decision seemingly more justifiable. This analysis at first may appear simplistic. But persistent pesticides, like DDT and Aldrin, are very dangerous to farm workers, not to mention the negative effects they have on the environment. They should have been banned. As a matter of fact, the first ban of DDT was the result of a contract negotiated by the United Farm Workers of America. But the general point is that pesticides are dangerous to the health of people, be it now or in the future.

The structure of capitalism promotes whatever expropriation will provide that "all-important" competitive edge necessary for capital accumulation. The same structure has not allowed space for the development of an agriculture that protects both the environment and farm workers. For example, the prevailing force of capitalist agribusiness, including the pesticide industry, has displaced and prevented the development of non-chemical pest control. The industry has therefore opposed alternatives which aim to minimize hazards to workers. Given these characteristics, the decision was effectively made by those in power to protect the environment (for the enjoyment of the future white generations), even if it meant the further exploitation of farm workers (in other words, people of color).

Pesticide Poisoning and the Law

The role played by the state in preserving the existing economic structures, by allowing the exploitation of someone, in this case the people of color that do most of the field work, is evident when the relevant legal structure is examined. Although the U.S. Environmental Protection Agency (1986) asserts that since 1974 federal regulations have provided basic protection to those engaged in field and hand-labor tasks, the reality is that the extant legislation leaves farm workers virtually unprotected against pesticide hazards. The prohibition of direct spraying of workers, although enforced most of the time, does not protect farm workers from the drifting that results from aerial spraying in nearby fields (Monterey County Pesticide Coalition, 1984; Mosses, 1989). The law which requires farmers or applicator companies to provide protective clothing to the workers, applies only to applicators or those who handle the pesticides directly. This is frequently violated (Monterey County Pesticide Coalition, 1984). Farmworkers are not protected from pesticide residues in the field (Barnett, 1989).

In addition, there are several loopholes in the Federal Insecticide and Rodenticide Act (FIFRA) (U.S. Environmental Protection Agency, 1988) that encourage farmers to put economic benefits over the health of farm workers. For example, Sections 18 and 24c, permit state officials to register pesticides within their own jurisdiction to deal with unforeseen pest outbreaks and other emergencies, and to provide registration for additional uses of federally registered pesticides. Furthermore, Section 5 allows the application of unregistered and untested pesticides with an experimental use permit, effectively using farm workers as guinea pigs.

Finally, post-application field re-entry levels, or the time that is considered safe for people to enter a field after it has been sprayed, are set only for a few pesticides, and empirical evidence suggests that at least in several instances such intervals are ineffective or inadequate (Wasserstrom and Wiles, 1985). More research is needed to determine re-entry levels for all pesticides commonly used in agriculture and whether or not current re-entry standards are adequate. Currently re-entry standards are based only on the acute toxicity of pesticides, with no consideration given to the carcinogenic, teratogenic and other chronic health effects (Barnett, 1989).

In addition, studies by the manufacturer have been the basis of some worker safety standards. In 1987 the California Department of Food and Agriculture proposed a reduction of re-entry levels for encapsulated methyl parathion based on a study submitted by the manufacturer. A summary of the study revealed that of the thirteen references used to set the new levels, only five studies had been published; and three levels were based on "confidential" information submitted by the chemical manufacturer (Maddy, 1986).

According to FIFRA's Section 26, states have the primary responsibility for the enforcement of these laws. This is frequently done through the county agricultural commission or a similar local government agency. These local agencies are often so closely identified with the interests of agricultural producers that they have been unwilling to vigorously prosecute pesticide users who break the law (Barnett, 1989).

The Role of Poverty

The impact of minority farm workers' exposure to toxic chemicals is exacerbated by other problems. Poverty is the most obvious one. Although they are responsible for the food we put on our table every day, farm workers seldomly have enough food to put on their own tables, and frequently have health statistics typical of the Third World.

The life expectancy of migrant farm workers is only 49 years, more than 20 years less than the national average. Their average annual income is less than $6,000. Their work is typically temporary, with no unemployment compensation (Goldsmith, 1989). They live and work under some of the worst conditions in the country, and consequently suffer from many diseases that are more common in the Third World than in a developed country. Farmworkers are six times more likely to develop tuberculosis than the general population of employed adults (Goldsmith, 1989). Malnutrition makes children especially vulnerable to such diseases as dysentery, hepatitis B, typhoid fever and other intestinal and respiratory ailments. It was only two years ago that the federal government decreed that farm workers had the right to have toilet facilities in the fields.

The health situation is aggravated due to the fact that most rural counties in the U.S. lack primary care physicians. Many have closed their county hospitals and provide few, if any health care benefits to the poor. Farmworkers are frequently unaware of the fact that the cost of treating occupational illness is supposed to be borne by workers' compensation insurance, and some fear employer discrimination or retaliation if they seek these benefits.

Discrimination Against Farm Workers

One of the reasons that agricultural field work is such a dangerous occupation is because farm workers are specifically excluded, completely or partially, from federal laws that protect other workers. For example, they are excluded from the Occupational Safety and Health Act, which governs standards of health and safety in the workplace, from the Fair Labor Standards Act, which governs minimum wage and child labor, and most importantly, from the National Labor Relations Act, which guarantees the right to join a union and bargain collectively (Coye, 1985; Mosses, 1989).

Why would the government deny farm workers the rights that other workers enjoy? Is the ethnic or racial composition of that labor force relevant? These are actually very difficult questions to which there are no straightforward answers. The historical discrimination against people of color is well entrenched within the institutions of this country, but additionally, the economic structure of capitalism encourages the expropriation of surplus value from someone to maintain competitive advantage. Increasingly that "someone" is likely to be a person of color.

Pesticide Export to the Third World

The international dimensions of the pesticide problem are at least as troubling as the domestic ones. In a practical sense, they are of more concern because they affect many more human beings, and the situation regarding human health is far worse. As in the domestic case, much of the pattern can be seen as a response to the needs of capital accumulation, specifically with regard to the assumption that people of color can be legitimately exploited.

It is not as though the ethical dimensions of the problem are unknown. As Weir noted some time ago:

> [t]he hypocrisy, the duplicity of saying that what we have found out in this country is too dangerous for us but it's okay to dump it on Third World people, is startling. And furthermore, it seems to me that it is hypocritical in turn to say that we can export our advanced technological products on unsuspecting people, but not export our knowledge and our environmental concerns to those same people (Norris, 1982: 102).

This double standard has shaped not only the international trade of pesticides but also the production process and certain legal processes related to liabilities. The most evident of these is the exportation to developing countries of pesticides that have been banned in industrialized countries.

In the 1960s, Rachel Carson's book, *Silent Spring*, raised public awareness of pesticides' impact on wildlife and the environment. In the early 1970s, that awareness took the form of environmental activism, putting enormous pressure on the government to move more aggressively towards the prohibition or restriction of pesticides that were found to present significant environmental and health risks. In the United States, an elaborate system of regulations and controls has evolved since that time. But the situation is different in the international arena. The agrochemical industry has aggressively marketed pesticides to Third World countries, where the environmental movement has not yet created barriers to exploitation of future generations.

Before 1978, it was possible to initiate manufacturing activities, and even distribute pesticides outside of the U.S., without so much as informing the Environmental Protection Agency, since existent regulations covering pesticides did not apply to products shipped outside the U.S. In 1975, over 85 million pounds of such unregistered pesticides were shipped to other countries (Norris, 1982). Furthermore, pesticides that had been banned or severely restricted by the EPA could be exported without any warnings to foreign purchasers or importing governments, a practice described as "dumping."

In 1978 the U.S. Congress moved to establish some controls on pesticide exports under the FIFRA. Although the 1978 and more recent (1988) amendments of FIFRA may seem like a genuine effort to provide importing countries with what they need to make informed decisions about pesticide importations, a critical review of the monitoring process reveals the duplicity and double standards that permeate this legislation.

Section 17 of the FIFRA requires EPA to notify foreign governments of any regulatory changes and of pesticides not registered for use in the US (including pesticides cancelled, suspended, voluntarily withdrawn, or never registered) (U.S. Environmental Protection Agency, 1988). Since FIFRA does not allow EPA to prohibit pesticide exports, this is the only required means of alerting foreign governments to hazardous pesticides. However, EPA has no way of verifying that export notification procedures are followed by companies, or even of knowing if a company is exporting pesticides, unless the company volunteers that information (Marquardt, 1989). Responding to agribusiness interests, the EPA initiated a policy which actually hinders its own monitoring responsibilities. This policy exempts exporters from notification requirements when an unregistered pesticide is similar in composition and use to a registered one. The loophole created by this policy has resulted in the export of approximately 90 percent (by weight or by volume) of unregistered pesticides without notice being given to the EPA or to importing countries (Marquardt, 1989). In May, 1989, the House Subcommittee on the Environment and Natural Resources, upon examining a U.S. General Accounting Office (GAO) report (1979) on the EPA's role in monitoring exports of unregistered pesticides, concluded that the EPA was not fulfilling its responsibilities to monitor pesticide exports and that very little had changed since a previous GAO report in 1979. The lack of enforcement throughout the years suggests that there is little commitment to rein in these unethical practices. It has even been suggested that less developed countries could have served as final testing grounds before these products are released in the more developed countries (U.S. Environmental Protection Agency, 1977).

Patterns of Pesticide Events in the Third World

Of the four billion pounds of pesticides manufactured annually by multinational corporations, more than one fifth are exported, mainly to Third World countries (Weir and Shapiro, 1981). U.S. manufacturers alone export more than 500 million pounds of pesticides annually, an estimated 30 percent of which consist of banned, severely restricted or unregistered products. A report from the World Health Organization conservatively estimated that more than one million people are poisoned by pesticides every year. However, in a 1983 United Nations report, it was suggested that total world pesticide poisoning could be as high as two million people per year, with 40,000 deaths (ESCAP, 1983). A more recent study showed that, if figures from Sri Lanka were applied globally, the figures for pesticide poisoning in the Third World would be far worse: 2.5 million people hospitalized for acute poisoning and 220,000 deaths (Wasilewski, 1987). It is evident that developing countries are disproportionately affected by pesticide poisoning, with rates thirteen times higher than those found in industrialized nations. The people of the Third World suffer half of the pesticide poisoning cases and nearly three quarters of the deaths (Weir and Shapiro, 1981).

The list of banned, severely restricted or unregistered pesticides exported to developing countries is indeed very extensive. The following two examples serve to generally demonstrate how the problem arises and evolves.

The Problem of DBCP

DBCP (dibromochloropropane), now classified as "extremely toxic" by the WHO, was first manufactured in the late 1950s by Shell Oil and Dow Chemical. Scientists from Shell and Dow initiated toxicity studies to fulfill regulatory requirements for registration, but before the studies were completed, the companies pressured the government to speed up regulatory approval (Thrupp, 1989). By 1964, the license for marketing was granted, and soon after DBCP became a remarkable market success. Among the bigger users of this newly approved nematicide were the U.S.-based multinational banana companies in Central America. Between 1966 and 1978 Costa Rica alone imported more than five million kilograms of DBCP, mainly for banana production.

The first trouble signs with DBCP began to appear in the manufacturing plants in California, where several workers became sterile. By 1977, it was widely accepted that DBCP was what caused the sterility, and soon it was banned in California and restricted in the rest of the U.S., except in Hawaii, where it was used to control nematodes in pineapple and banana plantations (Taylor, 1979). It wasn't until after a law suit was filed against the companies by affected workers in the U.S. that it was revealed that previous toxicological studies had shown DBCP to cause significant damage to laboratory animals at low exposure levels. Internal confidential documents revealed that the studies found reduction of sperm and atrophied testicles of rabbits and monkeys (Thrupp, 1989), information that was concealed from the public and federal agencies. Even after DBCP was restricted in the U.S., the companies failed to inform their customers in Third World countries of the initial findings of their own studies. Meanwhile, cases of sterility were beginning to appear among workers in the Standard Fruit Company, on the Atlantic Coast of Costa Rica. The EPA, following the legal procedures stipulated by FIFRA, informed governments in Third World countries about the dangers of DBCP. However, its report considerably underestimated the severity of DBCP's danger, according to some analysts (Thrupp, 1989).

Two of the three major banana companies in Central America decided to stop using DBCP and switched to less hazardous, but more expensive, alternatives. But the Standard Fruit Company refused to desist, citing economic considerations. By 1979, more than 50 banana workers of the SFC were confirmed sterile, presumably due to DCBP, and the Costa Rican government finally banned the pesticide. As a response to this ban, the SFC exported its stock of approximately 180,000 liters of DBCP from Costa Rica to its plantations in Honduras, where managers continue to direct workers to use it without informing them of the hazards. More than a decade later, approximately 1,000 men from the Standard Fruit Company plantations in the Atlantic coast of Costa Rica have been confirmed sterile as a result of applying

DBCP. It is estimated that an astonishing 20 to 25 percent of the male field workers in these banana plantations have been sterilized for life (Thrupp, 1989).

While this episode is a human tragedy of immense proportions, and is arguably significant criminal behavior, since health hazards were concealed and an aggressive marketing strategy was pursued despite known formidable health hazards, it is my argument that "corporate greed" alone does not explain this behavior. The fact that the affected were not only people of the Third World, but also people of color, is a key factor that interacts in an essential way with the need for accumulation of capital. This hypothesis is not only suggested by the Costa Rican example, nor restricted to U.S. corporations. In 1988, French authorities granted SOFT (Societe Occitane de Fabrication et de Technologie) provisional authorization to build a plant in France to manufacture DBCP, banned in France since 1977, for export to Senegal, where it is now widely used by Senegalese peasant farmers (Dirty Dozen Campaigner, 1989). Significantly, farm workers in Hawaii, the only place in the U.S. where DBCP is still allowed, are also people of color.

Heptachlor and Chlordane

Another well-documented, and probably the most well-known case of double standards, is the exportation of heptachlor and chlordane. Velsicol Chemical Corporation is the world's sole producer of these two organochlorine pesticides. As most organochlorines, they are environmentally persistent nerve toxins, and probably human carcinogens. Neither pesticide has been produced for use in the U.S. since 1978, when an EPA/Velsicol agreement prohibited production for domestic use (Marquardt, 1989). Since then, more than 30 countries have banned or severely restricted their use. However, Velsicol continues with its same production and exportation strategy. Seventeen of the 22 major chlordane/heptachlor importers are Third World countries.

The production of heptachlor and chlordane in the United States also has an insidious domestic dimension. The Velsicol plant in Memphis, Tennessee, as well as its main dumpsite in North Hollywood, Memphis, are located in predominantly African American communities. The widespread presence of uncontrolled toxic waste sites in predominantly African American and Latino communities throughout the United States has been well documented (Commission for Racial Justice, 1987), and reflects yet another form of exploitation of people of color.

Recently, Velsicol's manufacturing plant in Memphis, Tennessee, has been the focus of attention of various environmental groups, including Greenpeace. The Memphis plant has been chosen by environmentalists to exemplify the "circle of poison" argument, which refers to how pesticides that are banned in the United States but exported to Third World countries, can end up on the dining table of North Americans as residues in imported food (Weir and Shapiro, 1981).

The "Circle of Poison" and the "Hot Potato"

That pesticides banned in the U.S. sometimes return to the U.S. as residues in foods imported from Third World countries is now a well-known phenomenon, dubbed the "circle of poison" (Weir and Shapiro, 1981). But attempts to mitigate the effects of the "circle of poison" have occasionally had surprising secondary consequences. According to Wright (1986: 29),

> Whereas Weir and Shapiro carefully pointed to the larger social issues surrounding pesticide use in the Third World, in political practice the 'circle of poison' argument has become a dangerous oversimplification. There are important ways in which a narrow focus based on the 'circle of poison' view may actually contribute to the problem of pesticide abuse in the Third World.

Examining the politics of pesticide poisoning of Mexican farm workers in the Culiacan Valley in Northern Mexico, Wright unravels some of the unexpected complexities related to pesticide issues in the Third World.

The Culiacan Valley provides approximately two thirds of all fresh tomatoes sold in the United States during the winter months, or about two thirds of all the Mexican tomatoes exported to the United States. Agriculture in the valley has followed the industrial model since the 1940s, when the Rockefeller Foundation's Mexican research program directed Mexican agricultural development toward the North American pattern (Owasa and Jennings, 1982; Wright, 1985). Farmers in the Culiacan Valley began using technological packages typical of the "green revolution," including very persistent organochlorine insecticides like DDT, toxaphene, chlordane and BHC.

Today, however, it is hard to find a single farmer in the valley using those pesticides, even though several are less expensive than those currently used. To ensure the entry of vegetables into the U.S. under Food and Drug Administration (FDA) residue standards, Mexican farmers switched from the highly persistent organochlorines, which were banned or restricted in the U.S., to the less persistent organophosphates, like guthion, parathion and methamidophos. Mexican officials asserted that those chemicals had been recommended by the EPA and FDA as the ones most likely to ensure entry in the U.S. (Wright, 1986). Unfortunately this transformation, instead of relieving the health threat to those who lived and worked in the Culiacan Valley, increased their immediate public health risk. Organophosphate insecticides are more acutely toxic than the compounds they have replaced. They were recommended by the EPA because they degraded faster and wouldn't persist in the environment or food. The general philosophy of the EPA seems to be that the organophosphates are preferable to the very persistent organochlorines, under the assumption that they can be efficiently and safely managed by regulations, licensing, etc. But, as discussed above, even in the U.S. where a fairly elaborate regulatory system is in place, resources are abundant and information is accessible, this assumption is seldom met. It would be unreasonable to assume that under the prevailing socio-economic conditions of most developing countries, acutely toxic pesticides will be safely managed.

It is clear, from Wright's (1986: 29) study, that "in responding to concerns of North American consumers regarding the 'circle of poison', pesticide users in Mexico have adopted a new mix of dangerous chemical pesticides, mostly manufactured in Mexico but widely used in agriculture in the developed and underdeveloped countries."

A related phenomenon is the "hot potato." When exporting farmers in the developing countries cannot afford to switch to more expensive pesticides, they run the risk of getting their shipment rejected for entry in the developed nation due to high residue levels. When this happens, the products usually return to the national market and are sold to unsuspecting consumers. Norris (1982) described this process as "the hot potato." In 1981, a meat shipment from Costa Rica was returned from the U.S. because it was contaminated with pesticide residues, apparently resulting from animals grazing on land sprayed with persistent pesticides. The rejected meat was returned to Costa Rica and sold in local markets (Norris, 1982). In 1980, it was discovered that tomatoes in local markets in Mexico were contaminated with celathion (Norris, 1982), a pesticide that had been manufactured in West Germany, exported to the U.S. and rejected at the port of entry. Somehow it made its way to Mexico, where it was used on tomatoes for export. The contaminated tomatoes were rejected for entry in the U.S., ending up in Mexican local markets (Becklund and Taylor, 1980). Again, the economic risk was borne by farmers in the Third World, and the health hazard by farm workers, the rural population and consumers in the Third World.

Manufacturing Pesticides in the Third World

The pesticide manufacturing process is likewise plagued with evident double standards. To reduce cost and avoid the high environmental standards in developed countries, the pesticide industry expanded many of its production operations to the Third World. Thousands of subsidiaries and affiliates have spread and continue spreading throughout the globe, increasing even further the burden carried by people of the Third World. Local formulation plants commonly have lower standards and weaker controls than analogous plants in the developed countries (Weir, 1987). The production of paraquat, a highly toxic herbicide, by Imperial Chemical Industries (ICI), provides an excellent case study.

Paraquat, the major weed-killer in the world, is produced mainly by ICI in the United Kingdom. Sales of paraquat, the main formulation of which is Gramoxone, accounts for 33 percent of ICI annual agrochemical sales. Most of paraquat's production takes place in the UK, where 90 percent of it is exported. However, in an attempt to maintain control over growing markets, ICI strategy has been to invest in highly efficient large-scale manufacturing plants in the U.S., Japan and Brazil, and small end-stage processing units in India, Malaysia and Indonesia (Dinham, 1989; Weir, 1987). Although ICI's health and safety record in its Cheshire plant in Northwestern England is not untarnished, it has improved significantly since production started in 1961, and is now said to have half the accident rates of the UK chemical industry as a whole (Dinham, 1989).

But what of its operations in the Third World? In Malaysia, paraquat is manufactured by the Chemical Company of Malaysia, 50 percent owned by ICI. Since 1981, paraquat production in Malaysia has been surrounded by public concern over the possible effects of atmospheric pollution generated from the plant. A study by the Malaysian Ministries of Environment and Health and the Department of Factories and Machinery concluded that workers in the plant were at risk of being exposed to paraquat aerosols above the Threshold Limit Value. Worker's urine samples were found to have paraquat concentrations greater than the acceptable level (Dinham, 1989). To date, the company has done nothing to ensure the health and safety of the workers and the people that live within the proximity of the plant, in contrast to its behavior in the developed world.

These practices saw the most tragic consequences in the 1984 accident of the Union Carbide plant in Bhopal, India. The accident has been reported as the world's worst industrial disaster, with a toll of over 3,400 killed and at least 50,000 permanently injured (Dembo, 1989). Union Carbide's operations in India go back to colonial times, when the first plant opened in 1905. In an attempt to promote development and economic growth through industrialization, the Indian government provided incentives to corporations like Union Carbide to establish its operations there. Sixty years later, the company was allowed to build a plant in Bhopal, on government land at an annual rent of less than $40 per acre. By 1984, when the accident occurred, the initial $1 million investment had developed into a $25 million manufacturing facility (Weir, 1987).

Only four years earlier, in response to the growing demand for Sevin, the company's most important pesticide, the Bhopal plant began the production of methyl isocyanate (MIC). MIC, the toxic gas that eventually asphyxiated the citizens of Bhopal, is an intermediate chemical used in the production of some pesticides, and is especially dangerous because it is heavier than air and thus remains close to the ground (Worthy, 1985). One of its components is phosgene, a nerve gas first used as a chemical weapon during World War I. According to Worthy (1985), Union Carbide was well aware of the hazards of MIC, yet, based on the anticipated doubling of the demand for Sevin, it went ahead with the design of the Bhopal plant.

Union Carbide's grandiose plans were halted when the demand for Sevin levelled off after a drought in 1980. This sunk Indian farmers into a financial crisis, and they began buying less expensive pesticides. Furthermore, in 1981 the Indian government granted licensing for Union Carbide's competitors to sell pyrethroids, a new class of pesticides which are less toxic and can be used in smaller quantities.

The Sevin market shrank and Union Carbide was left with a $25 million "white elephant" that did not meet the standards of analogous plants in the U.S., and it was equipped with three 15,000 gallon storage tanks for the deadly MIC. Within a couple of years, the price was paid by the people of Bhopal.

In this case we also see how the double standard extends all the way through the liability process. On February 14, 1989, the Indian Supreme Court approved an out-of-court settlement between the Indian government and Union Carbide. In the settlement, Union Carbide agreed to pay a total of $470 million in exchange for release from any further legal liability for the disaster (Dembo, 1989). This was supposed to compensate for more than 3,400 deaths and more than 50,000 permanent injuries and all the environmental damage caused by the disaster. As one would expect, the settlement provoked outrage in India. To put this figure in perspective, it can be compared with the $108 million paid by Monsanto Corporation to the family of a single one of its chemical workers who contracted leukemia due to benzene exposure (Dembo, 1989). It has become evident that in the eyes of the multinational corporations (and the Indian Supreme Court) the life of Indian people is worth much less than that of North Americans.

Due to the magnitude of the Bhopal disaster, some could argue that it was a very special and isolated case. However, a look at other law suits for pesticide poisoning reveals the same pattern. Of the 1,000 Costa Rican banana workers confirmed sterile, 400 were "compensated" by the Costa Rican National Insurance Agency for amounts ranging from $300 to $4,000. Many were not satisfied with that and contacted a U.S. law firm to represent them on a liability suit against Shell and Dow and the United Fruit Company. The multinational corporations are fighting against having the hearings in the U.S., arguing that jurisdiction lies within the Costa Rican government (Thrupp, 1989). In the U.S., sterilized workers were awarded over $1 million each in some cases, a figure obtainable only, apparently, by North Americans.

The Politico-Economic Structure
and Pesticides in the Third World

In the 1960s and 1970s large scale Western agricultural technology was introduced to many traditional farming societies in the Third World. Propelled by the so called "green revolution," chemical-intensive practices became the standard. This approach failed to recognize the fact that many tropical agroecosystems are fundamentally different from temperate agroecosystems in that, in particular, the chemical approach so frequently used in temperate zone agriculture is far less effective in tropical zone agriculture (Hansen, 1988). A new foci of "pesticide junkies" began to appear throughout the Third World, significantly boosting the international pesticide market, perhaps saving it from a downfall generated by "environmentalism" at home. Pesticide use in developing countries has virtually exploded in recent decades. From 1974 to 1978 Third World imports of pesticides increased from $641 million to almost $1 billion (Food and Agriculture Organization, 1979). In India in 1950, annual pesticide use was 2,000 tons, while in 1986 it was estimated to be more than 80,000 tons (Gupta, 1986). In the African countries, pesticide usage has increased five-fold over the past decade (Weir, 1987), while in the Philippines it recently grew five-fold in a six year period (Norris, 1982).

The pesticide industry and its apologists argue that pesticides are necessary in developing countries to feed rapidly growing populations. There are at least two fundamental flaws in this argument.

First, it assumes that pesticides are necessary to increase food production. After 50 years of use, pesticides have been shown to be as necessary as crack cocaine for a drug addict. Their initial fulminate action against pests gave them a reputation as the "magic bullet" of agriculture (van den Bosch, 1978). But their efficiency at killing pests proved to be a temporary one, since the pests almost invariably evolved resistance. The destruction of natural enemies (predators, parasites and diseases) that once kept pests under control, combined with evolved resistance, forced farmers to apply stronger pesticides in higher and more frequent doses. This phenomena, commonly known as the pesticide treadmill, is well documented in the entomological and ecological literature (DeBach, 1974; Luck, van den Bosch, and Garcia, 1977; Pimentel et al., 1978) and underscores the parallel with drug addiction. The first use gives a high, but also generates conditions for required use in the future.

The most dramatic example of the pesticide treadmill can be found in cotton production in the tropics. In Nicaragua, for example, pesticides were first introduced in 1950 to control the boll weevil (*Anthonomus grandis*) in cotton. Initially, cotton farmers were applying a maximum of four doses per season to control this pest. By 1960 the numbers of applications had increased to five to ten per season, but nonetheless the number of major pests had risen to seven or eight (Falcón, 1971). Finally, in 1980, applications averaged 27 per season and the list of major pests had sky-rocketed to 21. A very similar sequence of events was reported in Peru (van den Bosch, 1978) and Sudan (Hansen, 1989), and in rice in Indonesia (Treackle and Sacko, 1989). Furthermore, Pimentel et al. (1978) showed that as pesticide use increased from 50 million pounds to 600 million pounds (from the mid 1940s to 1970), economic loss due to pest damage almost doubled. The idea that pesticides are necessary to increased food production has finally been recognized as false by the U.S. National Academy of Science (1989). Its report concluded that farmers who apply little or no chemicals to crops are usually as productive as those who use pesticides and synthetic fertilizers, and recommended changing federal subsidy programs that encourage the use of agricultural chemicals.

Second, the argument that pesticides are necessary to feed growing populations is borrowed from the old, discredited Malthusian argument of overpopulation. It assumes that human populations grow at a faster rate than the production of food and, therefore, must outstrip their food supplies. Ironically, the overpopulation argument has been used most frequently in explaining famine in countries of Africa, one of the most underpopulated continents in the world. It should not be forgotten that in the 1920s and 1930s, Malthusianism was enthusiastically embraced by racists in the eugenics movement to restrict entrance of immigrants of what they considered "lower races," mainly Jews and Southern and Eastern Europeans. However, beside the theoretical, philosophical, and political objections to the "feed the growing poor" argument, it is plainly wrong (Lappe and Collins, 1977). A study cited by Weir and Shapiro (1981) found that 70 percent of the pesticides used in the Third World go for the production of luxury crops grown for export to Europe, the U.S. and Japan. In Africa, while pesticide sales multiplied five-fold from 1964 to 1978, during the same time period, food production was reduced by one percent (Malaret, 1985). Traditional agriculture, which is responsible for most of the basic food production of the Third World, used only 30 percent of the pesticides.

It is irresponsibly naive to assume that an increase in pesticide use will lead to an increase in food production and feed more people. Moreover, this trend is not associated with "feeding people" since the increase in pesticides usually accompanies the transformation of agriculture to structures which aggravate inequalities. It also does nothing to improve the nutritional status of the majority, since pesticides are mainly used for export cash crops.

Structural Legacies of Colonialism in the Third World

Most developing countries, because of their economic conditions, do not have the infrastructure to adequately regulate the use and availability of pesticides, nor to monitor pesticide residues in food or in the environment. Some have virtually no laws controlling pesticide imports, registration and handling (Eckholm and Scherr, 1978). For example, one study found 81 developing countries with no detectable pesticide controls in place (Bates, 1981). As of 1988, the Food and Agriculture Organization of the United Nations estimated that some 50 countries have no pesticide regulations, though many of these are now in the process of setting up some form of control (Goldenman and Rengam, 1988). The situation is aggravated by the large number of products and brands that flood the market, many of which are produced by formulation plants that mix hundreds of chemicals to generate many more brands of pesticides. For example, in Thailand, as of 1979, there were more than a thousand brands of pesticides produced by local formulation plants (Norris, 1982), and in Nicaragua, prior to 1979, there were 1,500 different types of pesticides on the market (Swezey, Daxl, and Murray, 1986). In Costa Rica in 1982, there were approximately 463 types of products, for which there were 3,061 formulations (Thrupp, 1988), many of which are repetitious with only very slight chemical differences among them. All this creates confusion among users and constitutes an economic burden on the importer nation (Thrupp, 1988).

The lack of an adequate infrastructure to administer and coordinate pesticide-related activities also takes its toll on the accessibility of information. In many countries, the only information accessible to those that handle pesticides (peasants, farmers and farm workers) comes from the pesticide industry (salespersons, distributors, etc.). This "information" is frequently useless for the adequate assessment of pesticide hazards. Ignorance about pesticides is not limited to those who directly handle them, but also is frequently found among officials in government agencies that deal with them. In Colombia, for example, a government official from the Ministry of Agriculture, when questioned about Mirex, a dangerous pesticide banned in the United States, and readily available to Colombian farmers, admitted that he never heard of it, nor had he ever heard of the EPA's list of banned products; a manager of a government farm in Bangladesh also admitted not knowing of any banned products in any producing country (Norris, 1982).

Concentration of wealth in the cities is more accentuated in developing countries than in developed ones. Malnutrition is generalized, especially amongst farm workers, making them more susceptible to pesticide poisoning. Child labor is the norm and not the exception. Living conditions in many rural communities increase the possibilities of coming into contact with hazardous pesticides. Wright's (1986: 35) description of a camp for migrant laborers in the Culiacan Valley, Mexico, is particularly telling:

> The campamentos in which the 140,000 to 200,000 migrant workers and their families live are open sheds, surrounded on at least two sides and sometimes four by contiguous vegetable fields. The fumigation aircraft and backpack spray crew must spray the edges of the fields, and to the edge of the campamentos, where children play, people cook and eat, and where people sleep. ...In all the campamentos, the irrigation and drainage canals serve as communal bathing and fishing areas. In some of the older campamentos, latrines are built alongside the canals, providing a further source of water contamination. Local doctors say that virtually all of the people reporting for treatment in rural clinics are malnourished, and that virtually all tested positively for anaemia.

Public health facilities are another victim of the typical economical depression of rural areas of the Third World. Rural health clinics are deficient at best and completely absent at worst. Most are not adequately equipped to handle pesticide poisonings. Physicians as well as workers are frequently ignorant about the symptoms and hazards. Because the symptoms of pesticide poisoning are in most cases similar to many common illnesses among malnourished and poor people, they may be recorded as other illnesses. This makes treatment inappropriate and difficult, and contributes to the seriously underdiagnosis of pesticide poisoning in developing countries. If the attending physician or nurse suspects pesticide poisoning, he or she can order a blood test for plasma acetylcholinesterase levels, which is, up to now, the only available test to detect pesticide poisoning. However, this test only detects organophosphate poisoning.

The lack of safety precautions among those who handle pesticides comes not only from the ignorance about the health hazards of pesticides, but also from the lack of resources to adequately manage toxic chemicals. Safety gear is usually too expensive for peasants, and large-scale farming operations often do not provide farm workers with any protective clothing. Furthermore, in many tropical developing countries, protective clothing is usually hard to use because of hot weather.

Illiteracy also encourages pesticide poisoning in the Third World. The people who directly handle pesticides often cannot read the labels, on those occasions when the container is labelled in the correct language. Too frequently the containers have no label, or the label has insufficient provision of information (Hilje, Castillo, and Thrupp, 1987). Assuming that the pesticide container is labelled and that the user can read, there are still possibilities for poisoning because the product has been inadequately labelled or deliberately mislabelled. According to Weir and Shapiro (1981), over half of the pesticides for sale in Mexico are insufficiently or incorrectly labelled. In Colombia, many chemical companies have been fined for mislabelling pesticides or marketing defective or adulterated pesticides (Weir and Shapiro, 1981).

In rural communities in the Third World, it is very common to see children bathing in containers where pesticides had been stored. Containers are frequently recycled and used to store water, milk, food or cooking oil. This practice has resulted in serious poisoning, including fatalities. In Senegal, for example, 19 people from two families died after eating food cooked with oil sold in a bottle that was previously used to store ethyl parathion (Pesticide Action Network, 1987).

Considering the conditions described above, combined with the fact that many Third World countries have repressive or semi-repressive governments that guard the interest of an elite minority not interested in the well-being of the rural majority, it is not surprising that pesticide poisonings are considerably more frequent in the Third World.

The International Code of Conduct

The alarming number of cases of pesticide poisoning in the world, particularly in Third World countries, has generated concern in the international community. As pesticide-related problems in developing countries were documented, concern grew in various international forums, including the United Nations (Pallemaerts, 1985). In November 1985 the Food and Agriculture Organization of the United Nations adopted the "International Code of Conduct on the Distribution and Use of Pesticides."

This is the first time that a minimum international standard for measuring pesticide-related practices of governments and industry has been established. Some have suggested that the idea of a voluntary code of conduct for the pesticide industry was apparently conceived as a means of staving off the threat of export controls (Goldenman and Rengam, 1988). The pesticide industry, represented by the

International Group of National Associations of Manufacturer of Agrochemical Products (GIFAP), did not oppose the concept of a code. On the contrary, GIFAP supported it, putting forward the image of an industry that was both responsible and concerned with public welfare. This behavior indicates its confidence that an FAO-negotiated code would not be opposed to industry's aims.

The fact that some of the fiercest debate concerning the Code has been around the principle of "prior informed concent"(PIC), is very telling. PIC means that a pesticide banned, withdrawn or severely restricted in one country should not be imported to another unless the imported country's government (1) has been fully informed of the reasons for the regulatory action, and (2) has positively consented to the importation of the controlled pesticide. From the beginning, the pesticide industry fought any type of export control, arguing that restricting exports of pesticides banned in their country of origin would infringe on another country's sovereign right to determine which pesticides are used within its borders. Importing countries responded that where there is no regulatory apparatus, only PIC would allow a government to determine if controlled products should enter its borders. In fact, they see PIC as a prerequisite for informed decision making, which will guarantee sovereignty (Goldenman and Rengam, 1988).

The Pesticide Action Network International, a world-wide (developed as well as developing countries) citizen's coalition of environmentalists, consumers' groups, farmers' groups, and others who are opposed to the irrational spread or misuse of pesticides, participated in the drafting of the code, which included PIC. However, last minute backdoor maneuvers succeeded in getting PIC and several other key provisions dropped just before adoption. In 1985 the Code was approved without the PIC provision. However, at the formal review of the Code two years later, in 1987, the FAO General Conference adopted a resolution deciding that PIC should be incorporated into the code by 1989. This accomplishment of the Third World importing countries (as well as PAN International) did not come easily. The pesticide-exporting countries, especially the United States, West Germany, France and the United Kingdom, lobbied intensively against incorporating PIC into the Code, and the FAO Secretariat attempted to stop a full discussion of the Pesticide Code in 1987, arguing that governments had not had sufficient time to implement it (Goldenman and Rengam, 1988). Even after the approval of incorporation of PIC into the Code, the pesticide-exporting countries are trying to block it, arguing that alternatives to PIC should still be considered. The U.S. government is even threatening to mobilize the General Agreement on Tariffs and Trade against PIC.

The PIC is only a part of an extensive code, which provides basic definitions, outlines regulatory processes, and lays down some concrete guidelines for responsible industry practice. It calls for uniform international standards, and contains useful provisions on packing, labelling and advertising. Although the pesticide industry affirms that the code is generally working well and is being implemented, a report from the Nairobi-based Environmental Liason Center (International)

(ELCI) showed that, although some corporations have adopted some of the provisions, the industry is very far from complying with the code (Pesticide Action Network, 1987). ELCI's survey of thirteen developing countries found such irresponsible practices by the pesticide industry, as inadequate labelling, misleading advertising, and sale of pesticides restricted in their country of origin.

In addition to the problems of implementation and compliance with a voluntary code, there are more fundamental problems. For example, the code explicitly incorporates the assumption that pesticides are necessary to increase food production. The FAO resolution that adopted the Code starts with: "Recognizing that increased food production is a high priority need in many parts of the world and that this need cannot be met without the use of indispensable agricultural inputs such as pesticides,...." It also assumes that a "safe use" is possible, and ignores the right of workers to ensure safe working conditions for themselves—there is no workers' protection provision (Goldenman and Rengam, 1988).

In summary, although the Code provided a useful action tool for importing governments and concerned citizens, it will not solve the problem of pesticide proliferation and misuse. The large picture will enable us to see that an FAO-generated and approved code has to be harmonious with FAO's general philosophy. FAO has long promoted pesticide use as part of its mandate to increase agricultural productivity in developing countries. Its technical assistance helped open up the Third World as a major market for agrochemicals, including pesticides, and its Plant Protection Service maintains strong informal links with the pesticide industry through its global trade association, GIFAP (Group of National Associations of Manufacturers of Agrochemical Products).

The Political Economy of Pesticide Export

According to George Ball, former U.S. Under-Secretary of State and current Chairman of Lehman Brothers International, "Working through great corporations that straddle the earth, men are able for the first time to utilize world resources with an efficiency dictated by the objective logic of profit." "[the nation state] is a very old-fashioned idea and badly adapted to our present complex world" (Barnett and Müller, 1974: 16).

Global trade in pesticides is an enormous business controlled by transnational corporations (TNCs). Approximately $13 billion worth of pesticides were sold around the world in 1983 as a result of twenty five years of sustained sales growth averaging 12.5 percent per year (Weir, 1987). About three dozen companies control over 90 percent of the world trade in pesticides, with the top ten accounting for over 50 percent of that total. Approximately twenty five percent of the trade ($4 billion) is controlled by only three companies: Bayer of West Germany, Ciba-Geigy of Switzerland, and Monsanto of the United States (Weir, 1987). Some of these corporations have economies bigger than some of their client countries in the Third World. By 1974, a decade before the Bhopal tragedy occurred, Union Carbide was selling its products in 125 countries, 75 of which had smaller economies than the corporation (Oil, Chemical and Atomic Workers International Union, 1974).

Transnational corporations, whether from the U.S. or Europe, are so strong and powerful that they manage to dominate Departments of Agriculture, not only in the Third World, but also in the developed countries. Ministries of Agriculture throughout the world have effectively turned into mere subsidiaries of the TNCs. The infrastructure developed by these government agencies (plant protection departments, research stations, extension agents, etc.) help to promote chemically intensive agriculture. Agricultural education is also strongly influenced by the corporate sector and, in many countries, depends on this sector for financial support. Together they are capable of dominating agricultural development economically, politically and ideologically. In Mexico, for example, both private and government institutions specify to lenders the kinds and quantities of pesticides they must apply to crops in order to qualify for production loans (Wright, 1986).

The economies of many agrarian Third World countries are characterized by the disarticulation of the two main sectors: the agroexport sector, which generates much of the foreign exchange, and the peasantry, which is engaged in agriculture for subsistence or food production for domestic markets (de Janvry, 1981). Historically peasants have been utilized by the agroexporters as a source of cheap, seasonal labor which can be dismissed when necessary without major social consequences. The economic links of the powerful agroexport sector are with the developed countries, which are the buyers of their products and the suppliers of their agricultural inputs.

This economic structure has resulted in serious economic crises, characterized by high foreign debts, stagnant growth rates, escalating inflation, high unemployment and increased poverty. These crises create pressures on the agroexport producers to increase crop production in the short run, resulting in an increased use of pesticides and other agrochemicals.

The rapid proletarization of the peasantry, which results from the expansion of the agricultural export sector, further increases the incidence of pesticide poisonings in the Third World. Increasingly, peasants who were engaged in traditional farming, with very little contact with or knowledge of hazardous pesticides, find themselves being sprayed with pesticides while working in large commercial fields.

Especially during times of economic crisis, international financial organizations like the World Bank and the International Monetary Fund, and development aid agencies such as USAID, play crucial roles in directing development strategies of Third World nations. In 1988 the World Bank allocated $4.5 billion (approximately 20 percent of total allocations) to 56 agricultural and rural development projects in the Third World (Hansen, 1989). It is clear that this organization can have a profound effect on agricultural policies and practices in the countries to which it grants loans.

Throughout their histories, World Bank and USAID projects have generally reflected the arrogant view that Third World development should be modelled on Northern industrial development, which, in the case of agriculture means capital and chemical intensive. The mission of the World Bank agricultural projects in the Third World was the transformation of traditional agriculture to "modern" agriculture (Hansen, 1989).

The Bank is a business, and as such, it makes loans that need to be repaid. This influences the type of projects that receive funding, and biases the Bank toward encouraging pesticide use by making farmers increase their involvement in the market economy (or commercial agriculture). Food self-sufficiency does not generate the hard currency that is needed for loan repayment. On the other hand, producing coffee, miniature gourmet vegetables, macadamia nuts, etc., does, and is therefore promoted by international finance institutions.

Another way in which the World Bank promotes pesticides is by providing loans to Third World governments to provide pesticide subsidies to farmers. One study found that in the nine Third World countries investigated, government subsidies for pesticide use amounted to an average of 44 percent of the retail price of the pesticides and in some cases went over 90 percent (Repetto, 1985).

Pesticide subsidies artificially reduce pesticide cost, making Integrated Pest Management (IPM) more difficult. A pivotal concept in IPM is that of "economic threshold level." This is the "break-even point," the level of a pest just before the economic loss from pest damage exceeds the cost of a control measure (i.e. pesticide). In other words, when the economic threshold level is reached, the farmer should apply pesticides to avoid economic loss. Its calculation is based, among other things, on the price of pesticides at that time. If pesticides are cheap, threshold levels will be very low, which means that the farmer would spray at very low levels of the pest, even when employing a rational IPM program.

In 1985, pressured by criticisms from environmentalist and citizens groups in the Third World, the World Bank released a set of guidelines for the selection and use of pesticides in projects financed by the Bank. In these guidelines it explicitly recognized that the chemical approach does not work and proclaimed that Integrated Pest Management, a pest control approach which seeks to minimize chemical pesticide use, would be the Bank's objective in its strategy for agricultural development (World Bank, 1985). However, a recent study from the Institute for Consumers Policy Research found few signs that the Bank is actually trying to implement its pesticide guidelines (Hansen, 1989). Of the 24 projects examined in the study, only one even mentioned IPM.

Conclusion
The pesticide issue is like any other environmental issue in that, at first glance, it appears to be a problem shared equally by all people. The president of Union

Carbide is just as likely to be rendered paralyzed by a dose of methyl bromide as the Indian peasants who live next to his plant in Bhopal. Rich, white males will be rendered just as sterile from exposure to DBCP as poor Latino banana workers. "We are all in this together" has become the popular battle cry of the environmental movement generally, and the popularization of "the circle of poison" has reinforced this general perception. But an examination of the pesticide issue as it relates to the Third World and to people of color in the U.S., suggests a very different situation. While the toxicology of pesticides is egalitarian, the way they are used within the constraints of capitalist economic structures is not. I have argued that people of color in the U.S. and people of the Third World are disproportionally affected by pesticides, and that this disproportionality is a direct consequence of underlying structures of capitalism, as they relate to class, race, and the environment.

The case of pesticides is particularly interesting in that the historical record generally reflects the dynamic political environment that shaped the issue as scientific knowledge accumulated.   Furthermore, the pesticide issue offers evidence in support of the general thesis that expropriation will incorporate race, when possible, as much as class, and that the environmental issue is generally not independent of race and class, but rather only appears to be so at the initial stage of evolution, when scientific knowledge is scant.

As a metaphor for the multitude of class and race-based contradictions that arise in the pesticide issue, the way in which the chemical nature of pesticides interacted with class interests is instructive. The issue arose from the chemical fact that high acute toxicity correlates with rapid degradation and low acute toxicity correlates with persistence. This fact set up a natural confrontation between those who work directly with pesticides (minority farm workers), and those who experience residues and secondary effects only (the general population as consumers and as future generations). In a class-free, racism-free society, concern would have been voiced over both long-term and short-term effects. But what actually happened was that the short-term effects were shunted off to people of color. Less acutely poisonous chemicals were eliminated because they poisoned everyone, including the people with political power. More acutely poisonous chemicals were substituted because they only poisoned people of color. The workers in the Culiacan valley are now worse off than they had been before, and their worsening environmental situation is partially due to the biased actions of the environmental movement acting in a capitalist economy. Effectively, the problem is formulated (albeit not openly) as: "we must decide whether we wish to poison ourselves and our children, or the Mexican field workers and their children." Given that those are the only two options, seemingly fixed by the realities of chemistry (acute poisoning is associated with small after effects, less acute poisoning is associated with large after effects), someone could appear as simply a realist in accepting the poisoning of Mexicans ("it is the unfortunate price we have to pay for progress"). What is not allowed on the agenda, is the argument that it is wrong for there to be class and race distinctions that allow us to frame the question in this way. And it is here that the conservatism of the environmental movement in the U.S. has played such an important role.

The history of the pesticide/race/class relationship can be thought of in three periods. First was the age of innocence, characterized by a lack of knowledge about the harmful effects of pesticides to the environment, people and wildlife. During this period pesticides in fact did more or less affect everyone the same. Pesticides formulated during this period were generally persistent, and affected consumers, the environment, farm workers and the rural community, with very little discrimination regarding class or race. Second came the age of concern, probably marked by the publication of Rachel Carson's book. Scientific knowledge concerning the harmful effects of pesticides began to accumulate and concern emerged among those affected, including farm workers. The idea that "pesticides kill without regard to race or class and we are all in this together" emerged as a potent ideology during this age. Finally, the age of contradictions emerged upon realizing that the white upper/middle class was being affected, that not only were the members of this class and "race" group being affected currently, but it was their children from whom advantage was being expropriated through environmental degradation. With these realizations, the rules changed. Legislation protecting consumers began to appear, highly persistent pesticides were banned and substituted by less persistent ones, exportation of banned pesticides to the Third World sky-rocketed, and manufacturing and waste disposal site locations were decided with an eye to political repercussions.

It is during the age of contradictions, in which we still live, that the race and class-biased political goals of the mainstream environmental movement come in conflict with those of other, more progressive, movements. These other movements include, for example, the labor movement in the U.S., including farm worker movements, movements for national liberation and grassroots development movements in the Third World. The mainstream environmental movement has focused on improving the quality of life of the white upper-middle class of today and the future. By doing so, it has neglected the occupational health hazards of people of color and especially farm workers in the U.S., and contributed to the deterioration of the quality of life in the Third World.

But also during the age of contradictions, a progressive sector within the environmental movement has begun to emerge, providing a critique of the unnecessary dualism of analyzing the environment separately from the more traditional progressive concerns of class and race. This new sector has begun to form alliances with the labor movement, including farm workers, and the civil rights movement in the U.S. as well as with progressive movements in the Third World. Although these new progressive sectors do not yet represent the main line of environmentalism in the U.S., nevertheless they are growing and getting stronger. This represents a challenge to the capitalist class' construction of a social reality that had convinced the majority of society to accept the notion that the working class and people of color (or ethnic minorities) are poisonable. It should also be acknowledged that much of this growing awareness probably has come from a fruitful cross-fertilization of ideas of the environmental movement of the Developed World, a remarkably conservative movement, with the ideas of the environmental movements in the Third World, which are more progressive.

Finally, we can hope for a fourth period in the evolution of the pesticide/race issue, the era of resolution. This will happen when strong alliances are formed between environmentalists and farm worker movements, national liberation struggles, and a multitude of other progressive movements, to put a stop to the irrational use of pesticides and to put forward a new agenda for the development of an ecologically rational agriculture that protects the health of all people, today or in the future, in the developed or developing countries, and of all races and ethnic backgrounds.

15

The Dumping of Toxic Waste in African Countries: A Case of Poverty and Racism

Mutombo Mpanya

The Western world is expressing increased concern about the environmental consequences of industry. Initially, this was a concern of the middle class, an issue of natural beauty and scenic preservation. With greater awareness of the negative impact of industries on human and nonhuman health, this concern is deepening and becoming an issue of life itself. The ozone layer has been affected in Antarctica. Increases in temperatures worldwide have been documented. During the last decade, it has become evident that the effects of Western industries are not localized regional problems but issues of global significance.

Despite this broadening awareness, the myth has persisted that some industrial waste can be redirected—that there are specific areas or parts of the world where it can be disposed of harmlessly. Some people recommend burying waste underground—others favor incineration. What no one recommends is disposal in their own backyards. For those who believe that Africans' desire for money and progress outweighs environmental concerns, Africa has become the ultimate vacant lot. A perception of Africa as naive, incompetent, corrupt and needy, leads these people to conclude they have found the ideal solution to the disposal of industrial waste.

This attitude, in part, is encouraged by some African nations themselves. Several countries look to development and industrialization to provide the necessary capital for the survival of their citizens. In this prioritization of values, less emphasis is placed on protecting the environment.

In the last two years, several instances of toxic waste dumping on the African continent have come to light. Many African countries have reacted strongly by levying heavy penalties on the importers of these wastes—up to and including threats of death before firing squads.

This paper describes selected cases of toxic waste dumping in Africa and

Mutombo Mpanya received his Ph.D. from the Urban and Regional Planning Program at the University of Michigan. He is presently Director of International Environmental Studies at World College West, Petaluma, California, as well as an international consultant.

explores some of the background variables behind these incidents. It also compares the dumping of wastes in Africa with that in African American communities as a way of exploring the relationship between race and disposal policies.

Interrupted Life Cycles

On June 8th, 1988, Guinean newspapers reported that vegetation on Kassa Island, just off the coast, was dying. After investigation, the government discovered that the destruction of indigenous life on the island was directly associated with the dumping of 15,000 tons of toxic incinerator ash from the city of Philadelphia. The ash was dumped by a Norwegian company, Bulkhandling Inc., with the collaboration of Alco Guinea, the complicity of four Guinean government officials in the Ministry of Trade and some involvement from the Norwegian Consul in Conakry. The guilty parties were punished—the government officials from the Ministry of Trade each receiving a four year jail term. The Guinean government ordered the ash to be removed. On July 2nd, 1988, the Bulkhandling Inc. vessel Banja picked up the ash from Kassa Island and returned it to Philadelphia.

That same June, the Nigerian government discovered about 4,000 tons of toxic waste from Italy in the little delta port of Koko. An Italian businessman, Gianfranco Raffaelli, imported the waste—storing it on the property of a Nigerian citizen, Sunday Nana. Sunday Nana was paid $100 per month as rental for the storage of 8,000 drums of hazardous waste including highly toxic PCBs.

At least 54 people associated with the scandal were jailed. Only after an Italian ship and several Italian citizens were seized by the Nigerian authorities did the Italian government agree to remove the waste and return it to Italy.

A substantial number of the 150 Nigerian workers employed in the cleanup effort were hospitalized with severe chemical burns, nausea, vomiting blood, partial paralysis and coma. Additionally, the rate of premature birth in Koko increased dramatically. It is estimated that the Nigerian government spent $1 million on the cleanup, including the peripheral costs of hospitalizations, imported medications, blood and ambulances.

During the last two years there have been many incidences of toxic waste dumping in Africa. Each is tainted with the suspicion of clandestine criminal activities. Each poses a serious threat to life, both human and nonhuman. Fundamental moral values seem to be completely lacking; the worlds of politics and business strive only to make money, even at the expense of human life.

Why do Western companies target African countries instead of storing their waste in their own lands? Is the situation so bad that the West must use Africa as a dumping ground, a continental landfill? Can Western materialist development be termed "progress" if it means that Africans will have to die in the garbage this progress leaves behind?

Increasing Risks

The dumping of toxic waste in African countries is extremely dangerous not only because of the threat it poses to all life forms but also in terms of its poisonous effect on global relationships in a shrinking world. It is essential to understand that the dangers of toxic waste have become extremely high. Between 1980 and 1986 there were three known cases of dumping on the African continent. South Africa imported between twenty and thirty tons of mercury waste per year from the United States. Sierra Leone imported waste from an American company and stored it in old mine galleries. Zimbabwe also imported hazardous waste from the United States; a local firm, Chempex, arranged to receive 12,485 gallons of dangerous toxins through a fraudulent deal with Colbert, Inc.

In the last two years, toxic waste dumping in Africa has increased more than tenfold; from three cases in three separate countries in 1987 to forty cases involving twenty-five African nations in 1989. Almost half of Africa's countries have been approached by Western interests to determine their willingness to serve as dump sites. West Africa has been particularly favored, due to its more easily accessible coast. As many of the Western countries (Guinea, Bissau, Benin) are geographically small and densely populated, the risk of local inhabitants coming in contact with toxic substances is greatly increased. Such was the case in Koko.

Unsafe dumping sites are another problem. In Guinea Bissau, the bedrock selected was porous, meaning water could both enter and leave the dump site, carrying with it the toxic wastes. In Senegal, the site was situated perilously close to the water table that provides the capital city Dakar with drinking water. According to Nigeria's Ministry of Health, an epidemic of cholera in that nation was caused by waste leaking into drinking water. The waste killed some types of bacteria while allowing other, more dangerous varieties to explode in population.

The deals by which these toxic wastes get moved and dumped are significant in and of themselves. An average shipment is around 5 million tons. The offers that tempt nations to accept this size load for storage on or in their soil range from $10 to $25 million. In some countries this may be a monthly figure. The Western nations most inundated with toxic wastes (the United States, the United Kingdom, West Germany, Italy and the Netherlands) are also the most politically powerful and, therefore, the most likely to get their way in Africa.

The risks Africans face from the rest of the world's toxic wastes increase daily. It is crucial to identify and examine the major forces that lie behind this dangerous situation.

Secrecy and Complicity

It could be argued that reports of toxic waste dumping in Africa are exaggerated. Not all of Africa is caught up in the mad scramble for dump sites. Out of the more than fifty countries on the continent, only twenty-five have been approached by Western nations as potential dumping grounds. Though some nations are currently storing toxic wastes for the West, the cumulative amount is no more than 1 percent of the world's total waste.

This type of argument does not take into account a number of factors. First, there is a great deal of secrecy surrounding the business of toxic waste trading. Of the agreements that are known to have been made, almost all have been conducted as clandestine operations. The fear of public knowledge of transactions seems to be extreme; everything is done to keep the public ignorant. When plans are uncovered, the official response is usually categorical denial. A Lisbon newspaper article on a toxic waste trade between the government of Angola and Arnold Kuenzler, the Swiss arms dealer implicated in the Iran-Contra scandal, was followed by a denial by Angolan President Dos Santos. The public was unconvinced. In Benin, rumors of negotiations to receive toxic waste were at first partially confirmed by the President. Later, Benin's Ambassador to Nigeria flatly contradicted these rumors, claiming that Benin had not considered importing hazardous materials.

Denial is just one form of deception common to the toxic waste trade. In Guinea Conakry, waste was imported under the guise of "raw materials for bricks." In Zimbabwe, thousands of toxic chemicals were brought into the country as "dry cleaning solvent." In Sierra Leone, waste was imported, in part, as "road construction materials." Finally, there is the case of Rodell Development, a British waste firm that attempted to set up a covert operation to send toxic wastes into Liberia. Journalists posing as representatives of other chemical companies were told by Rodell officials that the waste would be shipped as "liquid fertilizer," accompanied by falsified customs declarations and invoices.

Such deliberately deceptive efforts to hide the nature and extent of the waste trade from the public make it impossible to estimate the volume of toxic chemicals on the African continent, the level of risk, or the true dangers. In the United States, the Environmental Protection Agency (EPA) is required to disclose information only about waste defined as hazardous. No EPA restrictions are likely to be applied if materials are shipped under false labels.

Despite the difficulties in gathering accurate statistical data, it is plain that the incidence of toxic waste trading and dumping is increasing at an alarming rate. In the United States, notices to the EPA informing them of intent to export hazardous waste have soared from twelve in 1980 to 522 in 1988. Contrary to the assumption that things may not be as bad as they seem, when the veils of secrecy that surround the toxic waste trade are lifted, things may be found to be far worse than previously believed.

More Jobs and More Money

To countries experiencing severe economic difficulties, the promise of more money and new jobs is sore temptation against the risk of increased danger from imported toxic wastes. In most of the deals that have been uncovered, the financial factor is of primary importance. Nedlog Technology in Colorado offered the government of Sierra Leone $25 million per year to receive toxic wastes. In a developing country, a figure like this is quite impressive. The country of Benin received a package deal—direct income from the waste trade and an additional $0.50 per ton to be invested in agriculture and tourism. The economic needs of the nation placed enormous pressure on its decisionmakers to accept the toxic waste deal. Similarly, when Liberia sat down to negotiate, it was offered not only the regular income for accepting the waste, but additional benefits, such as the construction of a hospital and up to $1 million worth of imported medicine. Guinea Bissau received a proposal worth $600 million—four times the country's GNP and double its foreign debt. Namibia was offered investment projects of about $2 billion, the construction of a deep water port, a railway and a township. When the deal fell through, the same offer was made to Angola with the addition of 15,000 jobs to be created.

Clearly, those that buy and sell toxic wastes on this level view the trade as a possible route to Third World economic development. Perhaps it is important to note at this point that many African countries are experiencing economic difficulties. A significant percentage of export earnings, as high as 50 percent in some countries, goes toward reducing their foreign debt. The balance of payment has been deteriorating for the last five or six years. Investments in productive sectors have been declining. Indeed, Africa's economic future appears quite bleak. Under these circumstances, it is hardly surprising that the huge amounts of money offered for their complicity, fees that represent sizable increases in their national incomes, seduce African nations into storing toxic wastes. Christian Gilbert-Bembet, a minister in the Congolese government, best described the link between poverty and the dumping of toxic waste in his comments upon the cancellation of a waste deal by his government. "Congo," he said, "prefers to stay poor with honor" (Vallette, 1989: 22).

Lack of Knowledge, Lack of Policy
With the exception of a few countries that conduct their own tests on imported waste, such as Sierra Leone and Nigeria, most African nations lack the technical knowledge to manage the toxic wastes they are being asked to store. Ironically, it is the exporting companies that are most often asked to do the necessary studies and determine the potential impact of the waste disposal. Senegal asked a group of French authorities to conduct a geological survey for them as the exporting company's study was inadequate. Namibia was also forced to consult outside experts, Angola sought the aid of the Swiss in a feasibility study, and Gabon requested French technical assistance to determine the impact of proposed waste treatment plants on its country.

Africa is turning to third parties for technological studies because it is unable to trust the exporting companies. When Kuenzler stated that his company would build a waste treatment facility as good as Ciba-Geigy's in Switzerland, Angola had no means of verifying his promise. African governments are dependent on foreign aid to deal with the problems toxic wastes present. Zanzibar, for example, called upon industrialized nations to help it dispose of expired chemicals that had been imported as pesticides. Recently, the International Dump Watch, an organization that African countries depend on to monitor the toxic waste situation, has stated that it will need a lot of foreign aid if it is to do its job.

When Africa must rely on the international community, it must also accept the codes and standards of developed nations. Lack of knowledge may be responsible for reducing levels of confidence in African countries, for making it doubt its abilities to deal with the problems of toxic waste. This, in turn, may be what is leading it into taking the strong position of asking for a complete ban on toxic waste trading. One of the most compelling reasons evoked by Equatorial Guinea for not accepting toxic waste was the government's inability to determine the risks involved.

Associated with this lack of technical knowledge is the general lack of public awareness and education regarding environmental issues. Few African countries have environmental legislation strong enough to force industries to control and manage wastes safely. This absence of regulation is taken by some companies as an incentive to pollute. Most countries are also lacking a tax system that would penalize polluters and generate revenue to abate the pollution problems. Without serious environmental regulation, the African countries have little chance of containing the problems of toxic waste disposal.

Even where policies and regulations exist, they may not be strong enough to produce significant effects on the behavior of the toxic waste industry. Until recently, African governments themselves perceived environmental concerns as coming from the developed nations' middle class and inapplicable to their own circumstances. Some officials have suggested that their countries are too poor to worry about the environment. Where a young, environmentally-aware cadre has evolved, their efforts are easily over-ruled by higher authorities. Officials in several African countries have been told specifically by their superiors not to show over-sensitivity to environmental issues, as this may discourage foreign investors. Environmental pollution, it was added, may very well be the price of development. Within this context, it is difficult to expect citizens' organizations and government officials to seriously monitor the activities of industries located in their countries.

In spite of this policy environment, public opinion, both national and international, has been instrumental in inspiring strong declarations from African nations. These statements of position could provide reference points from which to orient future policies on these issues. In May of 1988, the Organizations of African Unity (OAU) passed a resolution declaring the dumping of toxic waste in Africa "a crime against Africa and the African people" (Vir, 1988: 26). In June of the same year, the

Economic Community of West African States (ECOWAS) also passed a resolution calling for stiff penalties for those that dump toxic wastes. Following these resolutions, individual countries have begun to take more drastic legal measures. July 1988 saw the Ivory Coast adopting a law that specifies fines up to $1.6 million and jail sentences as long as 20 years. In Gambia, the law sets the prison terms at 5 to 20 years.

Overall, however, what is needed is not merely penalties, but preventive measures. These will come about only when a broader and more coherent legal and educational framework and viable financial and personnel structures are in place to make them work.

Landfills and Lifestyles

In addition to the internal (African) factors, there are external (international) factors that influence the dynamics of the toxic waste trade. Two of these are the increasing costs of waste disposal due to decreased landfill capacities and the belief, held in Western countries, that excessive consumption of goods is the key to happiness.

A ton of waste costs over $200 to store in the United States, 1000 F in Europe, but only $40 in Benin. A ton of PCBs would cost 1800 FS to dispose of in Switzerland. The cost of disposal becomes critical when the amount of toxic waste is examined. The European Community has the capacity to dispose of only 10 million tons of waste while it generates between 30 and 40 million tons per year. The United States has lost about 70 percent of all its designated landfills due to a lack of space and tighter regulations.

Costs are expected to increase and the available landfill areas to diminish. The United States Department of Energy has 3,000 toxic sites (17 of them aging), 6,000 hazardous dumps spread out over 600 military installations, and 200 billion gallons of hazardous wastes poured into unlined pits and lagoons. Some 45 million gallons of high level radioactive effluent are stored in giant underground tanks. The military alone generates about 750,000 tons of hazardous waste annually. At U.S. military sites, carcinogen levels in ground water have been tested and shown to be between 5,000 and 20,000 times higher than EPA safety standards. If government facilities are valid indicators of what is happening in America, then the ability of the United States to dispose of its toxic waste is seriously compromised.

In Western Europe things are little better. Some countries, strongly influenced by the Green Party, can boast tougher regulations. As of 1990, Europeans will no longer use the North Sea as a dumping ground for toxic waste. Yet, many of their remaining sites are nearly filled to capacity. Switzerland produces 300,000 tons of waste a year but can treat only 115,000. In Italy, of the 4.5 million tons produced annually, only 1 million is legally processed. In Germany, 35,000 sites are considered dangerous and in the Netherlands 4,300 sites are contaminated. The situation is marginally better in England, but is not likely to remain so. Other, poorer regions of the United Kingdom are being considered as possible dump sites. Even should some old Scottish mine be selected to store a portion of the hazardous waste, finding new sites is only a temporary solution at best. Western Europe, like the rest of the industrialized world, is simply running out of room to store its toxic waste.

Perhaps the most important aspect of this issue is the pattern of consumption which support the materialistic lifestyle of the West. According to the Organization for Economic Cooperation and Development (OECD), industrialized countries produce about 320 million tons of toxic waste each year. In the United States alone, there are are over 3,000 new chemical products released onto the market annually. In Europe, the number may be slightly smaller but is still staggering.

Each product, no matter how tiny, is associated with its own brand of waste problems. Each year car owners in Switzerland rid themselves of 12,000 tons of batteries. These batteries are full of lead, arsenic and sulfuric acid. The manufacture of the car itself poses a serious waste disposal problem. For every 500 kg of automobile, there are 320 kg of metal waste to dispose of, 100 kg of toxic sand, 40 kg of packaging, 20 kg of chemicals, 10 kg of grease and 10 kg of paint. Considering the volume of goods produced by the Western world to meet its needs, it is evident that were the whole earth available for a dumping ground, there would not be room enough for all the waste. Clearly the problem is not where to put the waste, or even how best to treat it, but what can be done to change the lifestyles that create it.

Callous Policies

Western patterns of consumption create a favorable climate for the development of laissez faire policies towards toxic waste. In the United States, the export of toxic wastes is authorized by the government. The only two stipulations are that the country of destination be notified and that there be written documentation of this notification or prior informed consent. The exporter is further required to disclose to authorities in both countries the nature of the waste to be shipped.

The problems with this policy are that monitoring is impossible and that countries through which the shipments must travel need not be notified as to the nature of the cargo. Some export companies have intentionally provided inaccurate descriptions of their waste. The mislabelling of its toxic waste from Colbert Brothers, Inc., as dry cleaning solvent and its subsequent sale to a US AID sponsored company in Zimbabwe is one example. The 15,000 tons of incinerator ash imported to Guinea under the label of "raw materials for bricks" is another. The country of destination is not always adequately informed as to the nature of the waste that it is to store, and/or may not have the technical expertise to deal with the waste safely. Some of the liability provisions established in the United States are not easily invoked when dealing with extraterritorial situations. A citizen of another country cannot depend on American laws to solve its local hazardous waste disposal problems.

The European Community (EC) also has a notice and authorization system to handle the transport of toxic waste involving EC member and non-member states. Notice is required to describe the nature of the waste and to include proof of insurance against the affected third parties. The EC directives are not without problems. Member states have different definitions of hazardous waste, liability and insurance. The directives themselves are often simply ignored by disinterested countries; in fact, very few nations take the time and trouble to implement them.

Both U.S. and EC export policies do not make enough provisions for liability to third parties. Both rely on already overburdened customs officials for enforcement. More fundamental to the problem is that the directives do not try to discourage, let alone bar, the export of toxic waste. Basically, the policies of industrial countries are designed to turn the lands of Africa and other Third World nations into landfills — the garbage dumps of the prosperous industrial powers — in order to keep the Western world beautiful.

On March 22, 1989, thirty-three countries signed a treaty in Basel, Switzerland. This global agreement provides directives for the export of toxic wastes. Essentially, the treaty reiterates already established policies of the U.S. and EC. The issue of banning toxic waste dumping, an action many African and other lesser-developed countries supported, was not considered. In a sense, the convention legitimized toxic waste trading by furthering the illusion that the toxic waste trade is under control. Many African nations declined to sign the agreement on the grounds that the treaty did not offer any protection to countries that refuse to accept toxic wastes.

The Race Connection

In examining reports on toxic waste disposal, the suggestion continues to arise that some form of racism is behind the choice of Africa as a dumping ground. CETIM reports underline the fact that there is a low level of appreciation for Africa and African people among Western business-people (CETIM, 1989). Africa is perceived of as a continent of immense jungles, populated by naive people who are guided by a corrupt and unintelligent leadership.

Arthur Kuenzler, discussing his waste incineration project in Angola, remarked that he intended to build the same type of installation in Switzerland. He added, "If it is good for the Swiss, it is good for the Blacks!" An official from Rodell Development, Inc., asked to comment on the possible health hazards its toxic waste shipment, bound for Liberia, might pose to the indigenous population responded, "If anything happens to the Africans because of the waste, that's too bad. It's not our problem."

Perhaps the most revealing insights into the relationship between race and toxic waste disposal can be gleaned from three American studies. In the first, a report on four landfill sites in the southeastern part of the nation conducted by the United States General Accounting Office, it was found that blacks comprised the majority of the population in three of the four communities surrounding the sites. More to the point, two studies were commissioned in 1987 by the United Church of Christ to look into the relationship between race and the location of commercial hazardous waste facilities. In these studies, race was found to be the most significant factor among all variables tested. Three out of the five largest commercial hazardous waste landfills in the United States are located in predominantly black or Hispanic communities. Three out of every five black and Hispanic Americans live in communities with uncontrolled toxic waste sites. It is virtually impossible that these patterns resulted by chance.

In the light of this research, the connection between racism and the dumping of toxic waste in Africa should not be lightly dismissed. Rather, it should be seriously considered by the international community. Aggressive and responsible action must be taken to create a policy environment that will protect the African people against destructive racist attitudes.

Conclusion

The toxic waste situation forces a re-examination of the future of development in Africa. To what extent does the money offered for the storage of toxic waste justify the trade as a potential contributor to the development of African nations? Compared to investments African countries have made in their own lands during the last two decades, the total monies raised by toxic waste trading is quite small. If the last two decades of investment have not resulted in substantial development, why think that revenues derived from toxic waste will make a difference? Furthermore, what kind of development will it be if the health and well-being of the people of Africa are destroyed by the toxic substances they are storing?

Ultimately, to deal with the problem of toxic waste in Africa a number of actions must be taken.

1. A massive environmental education program should be enstated to inform people about the volume and locations of toxic waste in their country and its immediate and long-term effects on their lives. This campaign should not only reach the masses but also the local cadre of environmental activists, journalists, and top officials;
2. grassroots organizations are needed to monitor the production and disposal of toxic wastes in their countries. If these grassroots organizations network with one another, their knowledge and political power are increased. These organizations can make connections with major international associations. They should have the power to act against violations of environmental standards and to take the violators to courts of law, even if they are government agencies; and

3. countries must design appropriate environmental policies for themselves, policies that not only take advantage of but strengthen international toxic waste handling and transport regulations.

To date, African nations have done little to achieve these ends. Some have banned waste imports and instituted criminal penalties against importers of hazardous materials. Pan-African organizations, such as OAU and ECOWAS, have issued statements against the importation of toxic waste. These statements have been reinforced by strong words from noted African statesmen like Robert Mugabe, the President of Zimbabwe.

> [w]e indignantly protest the callousness shown by the industrialized nations in dumping their nuclear and toxic waste in Africa. Africa already has enough problems of her own, without becoming the garbage bin of the wealthy northern nations. It is not fair that the poorest nations should be the ones to suffer the worst effects of a progress in which they do not share (Vir, 1988: 27).

Or as Major General I.O.S. Nwachuku, Minister of Foreign Affairs in Nigeria puts it: "The international community must accept, as my government has actively canvassed, that dumping of toxic and radioactive waste is a moral equivalent to war" (Vir, 1988: 27).

The dumping of toxic and nuclear waste in African countries is not simply a reflection of corruption on the continent. It is also a reflection of the interconnections of the global community. The waste products of Western consumption have dramatic consequences for the peoples of Africa; the pressure is on all interdependent nations to broaden their concepts of democracy and to open their hearts and minds to global levels of understanding. Divided, with inequitable rights and powers, the human race will not survive. The issue of toxic wastes in Africa presents a challenge to the world, a challenge of equality, reciprocity, and a truly global perception of humanity.

16

Summary

Bunyan Bryant and Paul Mohai

Since the 1990 Michigan Conference on Race and the Incidence of Environmental Hazards was held, several events have occurred to help bring currency to the health- and often life-threatening environmental issues facing the poor and people of color. As mentioned earlier, in January of 1991 workshops on environmental racism were held as part of the Martin Luther King Day Celebration at the University of Michigan. In September of 1991, the Southwest Network for Environmental and Economic Justice organized a conference to strengthen their collective effort to resist polluters and to fight for economic justice in an eight state region in the Southwest. In October of the same year, the First National People of Color Environmental Leadership Summit was held in Washington, D.C. The Summit signaled a new avenue for renewed social activism. This was the first time that over five hundred participants came together from a variety of traditions and cultural and economic backgrounds to engage each other for the purpose of building unity and an effective agenda for environmental justice and action. During the three day Summit there were more than 50 workshops, panels, presentations, introductions, ceremonies, plenary sessions, actions, and caucuses. An atmosphere of mutual respect, hard work, and excitement prevailed throughout. The Summit helped to focus attention of the general public, policy makers, and social scientists to the environmental concerns of minority groups and added credence to recent studies and various conferences that show minorities are disproportionately impacted by a range of environmental hazards. The outcome of the three day Summit was 17 agreed-upon principles to empower people in their regions to challenge decision makers regarding the safety and the siting of hazardous waste facilities and polluting industries. The preamble and the 17 principles are as follows:

> We, the People of Color, gathered together at this multinational People of Color Environmental Leadership Summit, to begin to build a national and international movement of all peoples of color to fight the destruction and taking of our lands, and communities, do hereby re-establish our spiritual interdependence to the sacredness of our Mother Earth; to respect and celebrate each of our cultures, languages and beliefs about the natural world and our roles in healing ourselves; to ensure environmental justice; to promote economic alternatives

which would contribute to the development of environmentally safe livelihoods; and, to secure our political, economic and cultural liberation that has been denied for over 500 years of colonization and oppression, resulting in the poisoning of our communities and land and the genocide of our peoples, do affirm and adopt these Principles of Environmental Justice:

1.   Environmental justice affirms the sacredness of Mother Earth, ecological unity and the interdependence of all species, and the right to be free from ecological destruction.

2.   Environmental justice demands that public policy be based on mutual respect and justice for all peoples, free from any form of discrimination or bias.

3.   Environmental justice mandates the right to ethical, balanced and responsible uses of land and renewable resources in the interest of a sustainable planet for humans and other living things.

4.   Environmental justice calls for universal protection from nuclear testing, extraction, and the production and disposal of toxic/hazardous waste and poisons that threaten the fundamental right to clean air, land, water, and food.

5.   Environmental justice affirms the fundamental right to political, economic, cultural and environmental self-determination of all peoples.

6.   Environmental justice demands the cessation of the production of all toxins, hazardous waste, and radioactive materials, and that all past and current producers be held strictly accountable to the people for detoxification and the containment at the point of production.

7.   Environmental justice demands the right of all to participate as equal partners at every level of decision-making including needs assessment, planning, implementation, and enforcement and evaluation.

8.   Environmental justice affirms the right of all workers to a safe and healthy work environment, without being forced to choose between an unsafe livelihood and unemployment. It also affirms the right of those who work at home to be free from environmental hazards.

9.   Environmental justice protects the right of victims of environmental injustices to receive full compensation and reparations for damages as well as quality health care.

10.   Environmental justice considers governmental acts of environmental injustice a violation of international law, the Universal Declaration on Human Rights, and the United Nations convention on Genocide.

11.   Environmental justice must recognize a special legal and natural relationship of Native Peoples to the U.S. government through treaties, agreements, compacts, and covenants which impose upon the U.S. government a paramount obligation and responsibility to affirm the sovereignty and self-determination of the indigenous peoples whose lands it occupies and holds in trusts.

12.   Environmental justice affirms the need for urban and rural ecological

policies to clean up and rebuild our cities and rural areas in balance with nature, honoring the cultural integrity of all our communities, and providing fair access for all to the full range of resources.

13. Environmental justice calls for the strict enforcement of
principles of informed consent, and a halt to the testing of experimental reproductive and medical procedures and vaccinations on people of color.

14. Environmental justice opposes the destructive operations of multinational corporations.

15. Environmental justice opposes military occupation, repression and the exploitation of lands, peoples and cultures, and other life forms.

16. Environmental justice calls for the education of present and future generations which emphasizes social and environmental issues, based on our experience and an appreciation of our diverse cultural perspectives.

17. Environmental justice requires that we, as individuals, make personal and consumer choices to consume as little of Mother Earth's resources and to produce as little waste as possible; and make the conscious decisions to challenge and reprioritize our lifestyles to ensure the health of the natural world for present and future generations.

Clearly, the above principles, adopted on October 27, 1991, in Washington, are comprehensive. They are the result of hours of discourse and redrafting. In the course of the debate, participants of the Summit were both teachers and learners, as people from different parts of the country discussed multiple issues that were important to them and their communities at home. The 17 principles developed at the Summit made participants aware of problems other than their own. We hope these principles will be disseminated in communities across the country to be used for teaching, learning, and organizing. We encourage people to ask questions about their meaning and their relevance in order to stimulate dialogue, planning, action, and reflection. While the document is not conclusive, it will undoubtedly change over time to fit the needs of local communities. Truth comes from struggle. Truth is always evolving. And what may be true today may not be true tomorrow.

Instead of building a national organization, Summit participants were encouraged to return to their respective regions to build strong regional organizations. As regional organizations are built, based upon these seventeen principles of agreement, this will require new ways of people working together. Environmentalists need to find new ways of working with people of color on urban environmental issues; new power relationships will have to be forged in order for meaningful coalitions to be built across racial and intergenerational lines. Public health and other governmental officials need to change their assumptions about the intellectual abilities of low-income people and minorities to understand complex information and include them as partners in solving community environmental problems as opposed to dysfunctional adversaries lacking the capacity to understand complex scientific information. Freudenburg (1984) shows that activist groups can understand complex information and shows that most of such groups' information comes from professional people. If the old assumptions continue, it will only aggravate the conflict between professional bureaucrats and community activists, and, thus, exacerbate social conflict.

The struggle for environmental equity will not be easy, particularly as we gear up as a nation to create, develop, and manufacture more chemicals and products to regain our world economic status. As more and more products come to market, so will the need to dispose of them. Even now cities are running out of land space and methods of dealing with millions of tons of hazardous waste. The struggle will not be easy as corporations put together attractive economic packages in an attempt to locate their polluting industries or waste facilities in minority and low-income neighborhoods. The struggle will not be easy as mayors of cities attempt to sacrifice long-term health needs for short-term gainful employment. We need to ask the question: Is short-term gainful employment worth the risk to health and our very lives? Or should one's health (including medical bills) or even death be used to subsidize economic growth for the more affluent?

Decent paying jobs are not the issue but decent paying jobs that are safe and benign to environmental surroundings. We need clean and safe streets, quality schools, and communities that do not turn the young into enemies of the people. As we continue to struggle for what is just and humane, we also will have to ask pointed questions: Is it right that we should transport hazardous waste to third world countries? Is it right to exploit their need for foreign exchange? Is it right for people of Third World countries to subsidize their health for economic gain? Will industries be unable to compete internationally if they are constrained by strict environmental standards, as they so often claim? No doubt the solutions to problems posed by environmental hazards and polluting industries create a serious problem. A failure to deal with the question of environmental equity may send reverberations throughout society that will surpass both the peace and civil rights movements of the 1960s.

Even though such problems may seem insurmountable, we feel there is hope for a brighter future. We should feel optimistic for the future and view environmental inequity as a challenge that brings meaning to our lives. Environmental equity should not only be viewed as challenges to be met, but it should be viewed as opportunities to build long-term sustainable, socially just, and diverse communities. Environmental inequity should not be viewed just as deteriorating cities filled with crime, urban blight, and unhealthy people—costing billions of dollars, but should be viewed as a challenge to overcome, just as we so aptly did in the space program, particularly since the Cold War is over and there is thus less perceived need to spend a lion's share of our tax dollars on weapons of destruction. We feel that both the government and foundations should take on this challenge to provide resources to grassroots environmental organizations to help them participate in the development of their own communities and to build their own training institutions to become environmentally effective citizens. All too often the staff of such organizations are underpaid and overworked, even though they provide critical insights, services, and a means for people to participate in local democratic processes. Along with this there should be regional and university-based environmental equity centers to help with technical assistance, research, retrieval dissemination, policy, and a mechanism for students to provide much needed resources to community groups. Regulatory agencies should be challenged to collect and monitor data by social class and race in order to ascertain the differential impacts of environmental pollutant on certain population groups; they should be challenged to make environmental equity their highest priority and challenged to make policy decisions in the face of inconclusive data, particularly when dealing with the lives of people; they should be challenged to spend more money on research to isolate those contaminants or combination of contaminants that are injurious to our health; they should be challenged to encourage industry to use non-toxic materials at the front end of production so there will be less pollution at the back end of production; they should be challenged to get communities and local governments and corporations across the country to engage in reducing, reusing, recovering, and recycling at decent paying wages for those who are seeking jobs; they should be challenged to improve upon inter- and intra-agency coordination so that contradictory and fragmented policies will no longer exist. The challenge has to go beyond regulatory agencies too. We have to challenge ourselves, all levels of government, and all corporate power to alleviate poverty by providing decent paying jobs, by cleaning up our neighborhoods, by providing affordable insurance for all and by, as James Boggs once said, recivilizing our cities so they will become safe and sustainable places to grow and develop, where people can act with confidence without feeling threatened by pollutants, and where people feel at peace with themselves and their neighborhoods.[1] The challenge is basically ours. The time is now. If not now, when?

Notes

1.   In 1992 we had conversations with James and Grace Boggs, and with David Hahn-Baker, regarding "Detroit Summer '92." In the spirit of the 1960s when students went South to work in the Civil Rights Movement, both James and Grace Boggs are a part of the National Green Movement that is attempting to get students from all over the country to come to Detroit during the summer of 1992 to help rebuild it. In the course of the discussion, on February 10, the concept of "recivilizing" our cities came up.

References

Chapter 1:
Introduction
by Bunyan Bryant and Paul Mohai

Asch, P. and J. J. Seneca. 1978. "Some Evidence on the Distribution of Air Quality." *Land Economics* 54(3): 278-97.

Berry, B. J. L. 1977. *The Social Burdens of Environmental Pollution: A Comparative Metropolitan Data Source:* Cambridge, MA: Ballinger Publishing Company.

Blackwelder, B. 1987-88. "Message from the Chairman." *The National Environmental Scorecard.* Washington, DC: League of Conservation Voters.

Bullard, R. 1983. "Solid Waste Sites and the Houston Black Community." *Sociological Inquiry* 53(Spring): 273-88.

Bullard, R. and B. Wright. 1987. "Environmentalism and the Politics of Equity: Emergent Trends in the Black Community." *Mid-American Review of Sociology* 12: 21-38.

Commission for Racial Justice. 1987. *Toxic Wastes and Race in the United States: A National Report on Racial and Socio-Economic Characteristics of Communities with Hazardous Waste Sites.* New York: United Church of Christ Commission for Racial Justice.

Council on Environmental Quality. 1971. *The Second Annual Report of the Council on Environmental Quality.* Washington, DC: U.S. Government Printing Office.

Freeman, M. A. 1972. "The Distribution of Environmental Quality." In A. Kneese and B. T. Bower, eds., *Environmental Quality Analysis.* Baltimore, MD: Johns Hopkins University Press for Resources for the Future.

Gelobter, M. 1988. "The Distribution of Air Pollution by Income and Race." Paper presented at the Second Symposium on Social Science in Resource Management, Urbana, IL.

Gianessi, L., H. M. Peskin, and E. Wolff. 1979. "The Distributional Effects of Uniform Air Pollution Policy in the U.S." *Quarterly Journal of Economics* (May): 281-301.

Gregory, R. and H. Kunreuther. 1990. "Successful Siting Incentives." *Civil Engineering* 60(April): 73-5.

Hare, N. 1970. "Black Ecology." *The Black Scholar* 6: 2-8.

Harrison, D., Jr. 1975. *Who Pays for Clean Air: The Cost and Benefit Distribution of Automobile Emission Standards.* Cambridge, MA: Ballinger.

Jordan, V. 1978. "Energy Policy and Black People". *Vital Speeches of the Day* 46: 341-44.

Kruvant, W. J. 1975. "People, Energy, and Pollution." In D. K. Newman and D. Day, eds., *The American Energy Consumer*. Cambridge, MA: Ballinger.

McCaull, J. 1977. "Discriminatory Air Pollution." In W. R. Burch, ed., *Readings in Sociology, Energy, and Human Society: Contemporary Perspectives*. New York: Harper and Row.

Miller, G. T., Jr. 1988. *Living in the Environment/Fifth Edition*. Belmont, CA: Wadsworth Publishing Company.

_____. 1982. *Living in the Environment/Third Edition*. Belmont, CA: Wadsworth Publishing Company.

Mohai, P. 1990. "Black Environmentalism." *Social Science Quarterly* 71(4): 744-65.

Mohai, P. and B. Bryant. 1992. "Environmental Racism: Reviewing the Evidence." In B. Bryant and P. Mohai, eds. *Race and the Incidence of Environmental Hazards: A Time for Discourse*. Boulder, CO: Westview Press.

Moyer, W. and P. Heines. 1975. "How We Cause World Hunger." *Win* Vol. XI(3).

O'Hare, M. 1977. "'Not on My Block You Don't'—Facilities Siting and the Importance of Compensation." *Public Policy* 25: 407-58.

Portney, K. E. 1985. "The Potential of the Theory of Compensation from Mitigating Public Opposition to Hazardous Waste Treatment Facility Siting: Some Evidence from Five Massachusetts Communities." *Policy Studies Journal* 14(1): 81-9.

Rifkin, J. 1981. *Entropy*. New York: Bantam.

Russell, D. 1989. "Environmental Racism." *The Amicus Journal* 11(2): 12-8.

Taylor, D. 1989. "Blacks and the Environment: Toward an Explanation of the Concern and Action Gap Between Blacks and Whites." *Environment and Behavior* 21(2): 175-205.

Truax, H. 1990. "Minorities at Risk." *Environmental Action* (January/February): 19.

United Nations. 1986. *1986 Demographic Yearbook*. New York: United Nations/Nations Unies.

U.S. General Accounting Office. 1983. *Siting of Hazardous Waste Landfills and Their Correlation with Racial and Economic Status of Surrounding Communities*. Washington, DC: U.S. General Accounting Office.

Zupan, J. M. 1973. *The Distribution of Air Quality in the New York Region*. Baltimore, MD: Johns Hopkins University Press for Resources for the Future, Inc.

Chapter 2:
Toxic Waste and Race in the United States
by Charles Lee

Allen, M. 1986. "Asbestos in Chicago Housing Authority Apartments Poses Possible Health Hazards." *Chicago Reporter* 15: 1-4.

Asher, J. 1984. "A Warning to Employers: Unique Charge of Murder." *Philadelphia Inquirer*, February 26.

Bullard, R. D. 1984. "Unplanned Environs: The Price of Unplanned Growth in Boomtown Houston." *California Sociologist* 7: 85–101.

_____. 1987a. "Environmentalism, Economic Blackmail, and Civil Rights: Competing Agendas Within the Black Community." Paper presented at the Annual Meeting of the Society for the Study of Social Problems, August 14–16.

_____. 1987b. "Implications of Toxics in Minority Communities." *Proceedings of Conference on Community Toxic Pollution Awareness for Historically Black Colleges and Universities*. Tallahassee, FL: Legal Environmental Assistance Foundation.

_____. 1988. *Environmentalism and HBCU's: Forging An Agenda for Change*. Unpublished paper. New York: United Church of Christ.

Bullard, R. D. and B. H. Wright. 1986. "The Politics of Pollution: Implications for the Black Community." *Phylon* 47: 71–8.

Center for the Biology of Natural Systems. 1987a. *Prospectus*. Flushing, NY: Queens College.

_____. 1987b. *Research and Educational Activities, 1986-1987*. Flushing, NY: Queens College.

Conyers, J. 1987. Personal Communication. Member, U.S. House of Representatives, Washington, DC, May 2, 1987.

Debro, T. 1987. "Federal Government Funding Opportunities." *Proceedings of Conference on Community Toxic Pollution Awareness for Historically Black Colleges and Universities*. Tallahassee, FL: Legal Environmental Assistance Foundation.

Editorial. 1987. "Dumping on Black America." *Atlanta Constitution*, April 27.

_____. 1989. "A Walk for Toxic Justice." *Environmental Action* January/February.

Freudenberg, N. 1984a. "Citizen Action for Environmental Health: Report on a Survey of Community Organizations." *American Public Health Journal* 74: 444–48.

_____. 1984b. "Not In Our Backyards: Community Action for Health and the Environment." *Monthly Review Press* 22: 34-9.

Greenhouse, S. 1985. "Business and the Law: Responsibility for Job Safety." *New York Times*, June 25.

Gunter, B. and Williams, M. 1984. "Alabama: The Nation's Dumping Ground—A Special Report on Hazardous Wastes and Toxic Chemicals in Alabama."*Montgomery Advertiser* (June and December): Two-part special supplement.

Hoagland, D. 1987. "Church Persists as Farmworker Advocate." *Fresno Bee,* August 16.

Hopkins, D. R. 1987. Correspondence to Benjamin F. Chavis, Jr., July 31.

Human Environment Center. 1981a. *Minority Education for Environmental and Natural Resource Professions: Before College.* Washington, DC: Human Environment Center.

_____. 1981b. *Minority Education for Environmental and Natural Resource Professions: Higher Education.* Washington, DC: Human Environment Center.

Lee, C. 1987a. "Toxic Wastes and Race: Developing A National Agenda." Keynote Speech at the Center for Third World Organizing Toxics and Minorities Conference, August 5.

_____. 1987b. Toxic Wastes and Race: Its Significance for Historically Black Colleges and Universities." *Proceedings of Conference on Community Toxic Pollution Awareness for Historically Black Colleges and Universities.* Tallahassee, FL: Legal Environmental Assistance Foundation.

Murray, L. R. 1987. Personal Communication. Former Director of Occupational and Environmental Medicine, Meharry Medical College, Nashville, TN, May 12, 1987.

National Council of Churches. 1987/88. "The Lumbee River, Lumbee Indians and GSX, Inc." *The Egg: National Journal of Eco-Justice* (Winter): 10–1.

Nelson, D. 1987. "Our Toxic Trap: Crisis on Far South Side." *Chicago Sun-Times,* May 31-June 5. Six-part series.

Porter, J. W. 1987. Correspondence to Benjamin F. Chavis, Jr., July 1.

Puerto Rico Industrial Mission. 1986. *General Proposal.* San Juan, PR: Puerto Rico Industrial Mission.

Ruffins, P. 1989. "Blacks Suffer Health Hazards Yet Remain Inactive on Environment." *Los Angeles Times*, August 27.

Russell, D. 1989. "Environmental Racism: Minority Communities and Their Battle Against Toxics." *Amicus Journal* (Spring): 22–32.

Shuey, C. 1984. "Uranium Mill Tailings: Toxic Waste in the West." *Engage/Social Action* (October): 40–5.

Sidel, V. W. 1987. Personal Communication. Former President, American Public Health Association, New York, NY, May 18, 1987.

Southern Organizing Committee for Economic and Social Justice. 1989. "New Anti-Toxics Drive Taking Root." *Southern Fight Back* 14: 22.

Southwest Organizing Committee. 1989. *The Southwest Organizing Project Community Environmental Program.* Albuquerque, NM: Southwest Organizing Committee.

Student Environmental Health Project. 1987. *1987 Summer Internship Sites.* Personal correspondence with Maria Shutt, November 20.

_____. 1985. *Annual Report: 1984–1985.* Nashville, TN: Vanderbilt University Center for Health Services.

_____. 1986. *Annual Report: 1985–1986.* Nashville, TN: Vanderbilt University Center for Health Services.

Stults, K. 1988. "Roulette, Southern Style." In *Everyone's Backyard.* Arlington, VA: Citizen's Clearinghouse for Hazardous Wastes.

Taylor, R. A. 1984. "Do Environmentalists Care about the Poor?" *U.S. News & World Report* 96: 51-2.

United Church of Christ Commission for Racial Justice. 1987. *Toxic Wastes and Race in the United States: A National Report on the Racial and Socio-Economic Characteristics of Communities Surrounding Hazardous Waste Sites.* New York: United Church of Christ.

United Farm Workers Union. 1985. *Vineyard Pesticides More Dangerous than Watermelon Poison; Check Grape Pesticides Before Placing on Market, Chavez Demands.* Press Release, July 17.

_____. 1986. "The Wrath of Grapes: The Tragedy of Pesticide Poisoning." *Food and Justice* (February/March): 4–7.

U.S. Department of Health and Human Services. 1985. *Report of the Secretary's Task Force on Black and Minority Health.* Washington, DC: U.S. Department of Health and Human Services.

U.S. General Accounting Office. 1983. *Siting of Hazardous Waste Landfills and Their Correlation with the Racial and Socio-Economic Status of Surrounding Communities.* Washington, DC: U.S. General Accounting Office.

Vanderbilt University Center for Health Services. 1987. *Mission Statement.* Personal correspondence with Maria Shutt, November 20.

Wasserstrom, R. F. and R. Wiles. 1985. *Field Duty: US Farmworkers and Pesticide Safety.* Washington, DC: World Resources Institute.

Weisskopf, M. 1987. "Rights Group Finds Racism in Dump Siting." *Washington Post*, April 16.

Chapter 3:
Can the Environmental Movement Attract
and Maintain the Support of Minorities?
by Dorceta Taylor

American Land Resource Association and the Natural Resources Council of America. 1988. *A Guide to Minority Natural Resource Issues and Organizations.* Washington, DC: American Land Resource Association.

Berry, J. M. 1977. *Lobbying for the People.* Princeton, NJ: Princeton University Press.

Boas, G. 1948. *Essays on Primitivism and Related Ideas in the Middle Ages.* Baltimore, MD: Johns Hopkins Press.

Bullard, R. 1983. "Solid Waste Sites and the Black Houston Community." *Sociological Inquiry* 53: 273–88.

Bullard, R. and B. H. Wright. 1987. "Environmentalism and the Politics of Equity: Emergent Trends in the Black Community." *Mid-American Review of Sociology* 12: 21–38.

Buttel, F. H. 1987. "New Directions in Environmental Sociology." *Annual Review of Sociology* 13: 465–88.

Buttel, F. H. and W. L. Flinn. 1974. "The Structure and Support for the Environmental Movement, 1968-70." *Rural Sociology* 39: 56–69.

_____. 1978. "Social Class and Mass Environmental Beliefs: A Reconsideration." *Environment and Behavior* 10: 443–50.

Carson, R. 1962. *Silent Spring.* Boston: Houghton Mifflin Co. (Previously published in the *New Yorker* in 1960.)

Citizens Clearinghouse for Hazardous Wastes. 1986. *Five Years of Progress 1981–86.* Arlington, VA: Citizens Clearinghouse for Hazardous Wastes.

_____. 1989. *Action Bulletin #23.* Arlington, VA: Citizens Clearing House for Hazardous Wastes.

Clark, P. B. and J. Q. Wilson. 1961. "Incentive Systems: A Theory of Organizations." *Administrative Science Quarterly* 6: 129–66.

Clean Air Act of 1970. Pub. L. 91-604, 15(c), 84 Stat. 1713.

Collette, W. 1987. "Citizens Clearinghouse for Hazardous Wastes." *Environment* 29: 44–5.

Commission for Racial Justice. 1987. *Toxic Wastes and Race in the United States: A National Report on the Racial and Socio-Economic Characteristics of Communities with Hazardous Waste Sites.* New York: The United Church of Christ.

Commoner, B. B. 1971. *Closing Circle—Nature, Man and Technology.* New York: Alfred Knopf.

Conservation Leadership Project. 1989. *Conservation Staff Survey.* Missoula, MT: Conservation Leadership Project.

Conservation Leadership Project Minorities Round Table. 1989. Held in Seattle, Washington, August 25–26.

Coombs, D. 1972. "The Club Looks at Itself." *Sierra Club Bulletin* 57: 35–9.

Cotgrove, S. 1982. *Catastrophe or Cornucopia: The Environmentalists, Politics, and the Future.* New York: Wiley.

Cotgrove, S. and A. Duff. 1980. "Environmentalism, Middle Class Radicalism, and Politics." *Sociological Review* 28: 333–51.

Curti, M. 1951. *The Growth of American Thought.* New York: Harper.

Dennis, S. and E. H. Zube. 1988. "Voluntary Association Membership of Outdoor Recreationists: An Exploratory Study." *Leisure Sciences* 10: 229-45.

Desert Land Act of 1877. Ch. 107, 19 Stat. 377.

Devall, W. B. 1970. "Conservation: An Upper-Middle Class Social Movement: A Replication." *Journal of Leisure Research* 2: 123–26.

Devall, W. B. and G. Sessions. 1985. *Deep Ecology, Living as if Nature Mattered*. Salt Lake City, UT: Gibbs Smith.

Douglas, M. and A. Wildavsky. 1983. *Risk and Culture: An Essay on the Selection of Technological and Environmental Dangers*. Berkeley: University of California Press.

Drake, St. Clair and H. Clayton. 1945. *Black Metropolis, A Study of Negro Life in a Northern City*. New York: Harcourt, Brace and Co.

Eisenger, P. 1972. "The Pattern of Citizen Contacts with Urban Officials." In Harlan Hahn, ed., *People and Politics in Urban Society*. Beverly Hills, CA: Sage.

Endangered Species Act of 1973. Pub. L. 93–205, 87 Stat. 884.

Faich, R. G. and R. P. Gale. 1971. "The Environmental Movement: From Recreation to Politics." *Pacific Sociological Review* 14: 270–87.

Fairchild, H. N. 1931. *The Romantic Quest*. Philadelphia, PA: A. Saifer.

Federal Pesticide Act of 1978. Pub. L. 95–396, 92 Stat. 841.

Federal Water Pollution Control Act of 1972. 33 U.S.C.A., 1251, 1387.

FitzSimmons, M. and R. Gottlieb. 1988. "A New Environmental Politics." In M. Davis and M. Sprinkler, eds., *Reshaping the U.S. Left: Popular Struggles in the 1980s*. London: Verso.

Fleming, B. F. 1972. "Roots of the New Conservation Movement." *Perspectives in American History* 6: 7–94.

Forest Management Act of 1897. U.S. Statutes at Large, 30, p. 35.

Fox, S. 1985. *The American Conservation Movement, John Muir and His Legacy*. Madison, WI: University of Wisconsin Press.

Frazier, E. F. 1957. *The Negro in the United States*. New York: MacMillan.

Gale, R. P. 1972. "From Sit-In to Hike-In: A Comparison of the Civil Rights and the Environmental Movements." In W. Burch Jr., N. Cheek, Jr., and L. Taylor, eds., *Social Behavior, Natural Resources, and the Environment*. New York: Harper & Row.

General Mining Law of 1872. 30 U.S.C. 22 *et. seq.*

Gerth, H. H. and C. W. Mills. 1946. *From Max Weber: Essays in Sociology*. New York: Oxford University Press.

Goodwin, K. and R. C. Mitchell. 1982. "Rational Models, Collective Goods and Nonelectoral Political Behavior." *Western Political Quarterly* 35: 161–81.

Gordon, C.W. and N. Babchuk. 1959. "A Typology of Voluntary Associations." *American Sociological Review* 24: 22–9.

Hall, B. 1988. *Environmental Politics: Lessons from the Grassroots*. Baton Rouge, LA: Institute for Southern Studies.

Harry, J., Gale, R., and J. Hendee. 1969. "Conservation: An Upper-Middle Class Social Movement." *Journal of Leisure Research* 1: 246–54.

Hays, S. 1959. *Conservation and the Gospel of Efficiency: The Progressive Conservation Movement.* Cambridge, MA: Harvard University Press.

Hendee, J.C., W. R. Catton, L. D. Marlow, and C. F. Brockman. 1968. *Wilderness Users in the Pacific Northwest—Their Characteristics, Values, and Management Preferences.* USDA Forest Service Research Paper PNW-61. Portland, OR: USDA Forest and Range Experiment Station.

Hershey, M. R. and D. B. Hill. 1977–78. "Is Pollution 'a White Thing'? Racial Differences in Pre-adults' Attitudes." *Public Opinion Quarterly* 41: 439–58.

Homestead Act of 1862. 43 U.S.C. 161–302.

Jacoby, A.P. and N. Babchuk. 1963. "Instrumental and Expressive Voluntary Associations." *Sociology and Social Research* 47: 461–71.

Jenkins, J. C. 1983. "Resource Mobilization Theory and the Study of Social Movements." *Annual Review of Sociology* 9: 527–53.

Kreger, J. 1973. "Ecology and Black Student Opinion." *The Journal of Environmental Education* 4: 30-4.

LaBalme, J. 1987. *A Road to Walk, A Struggle for Environmental Justice.* Durham, NC: The Regulator Press.

Lester, S. V. 1989. Personal Communication. Citizens Clearinghouse for Hazardous Wastes, Arlington, VA, September 25, 1989.

Lovejoy, A. O. 1941. "The Meaning of Romanticism for the Historian of Ideas." *Journal of the History of Ideas* 2: 257–78.

_____. 1955. "On the Discrimination of Romanticisms." In *Essays in the History of Ideas.* New York: G. Braziller.

Lovejoy, A. O., and G. Boas. 1935. *Primitivism and Related Ideas in Antiquity.* Baltimore, MD: Octagon Books.

Lowe, G. D. and T. K. Pinhey. 1982. "Rural-Urban Differences in Support for Environmental Protection." *Rural Sociology* 47: 114–28.

Lowe, G. D., T. K. Pinhey, and M. D. Grimes. 1980. "Public Support for Environmental Protection: New Evidence from National Surveys." *Pacific Sociological Review* 23: 423-45.

Maslow, A. H. 1954. *Motivation and Personality, 2nd. ed.* New York: Viking Press.

McCarthy, J. D. and M. N. Zald. 1973. *The Trend of Social Movements.* Morristown, NJ: General Learning Press.

_____. 1977. "Resource Mobilization and Social Movements." *American Journal of Sociology* 82: 1212–41.

Meeker, J. W ., W. K. Woods, and W. Lucas. 1973. "Red, White and Black in the National Parks." *North American Review* 258: 6–10.

McFarland, A. S. 1976. *Public Interest Lobbies: Decision Making on Energy.* Washington, DC: American Enterprise Institute of Public Policy Research.

Mitchell, R. C. 1979a. "Silent Springs/Solid Majorities." *Public Opinion* 2: 16–20.

_____. 1979b. "National Environmental Lobbies and the Apparent Illogic of Collective Action." In C. Russell, ed., *Collective Decision Making*. Baltimore, MD: Johns Hopkins University Press.

Moe, T. 1980. *The Organization of Interests*. Chicago, IL: University of Chicago Press.

Mohai, P. 1985. "Public Concern and Elite Involvement in Environmental-Conservation Issues." *Social Science Quarterly* 66: 820–38.

Morrison, D. E. and R.E. Dunlap. 1986. "Environmentalism and Elitism: A Conceptual and Empirical Analysis." *Environmental Management* 10: 581-9.

Morrison, D. E., K. E. Hornback, and W. K. Warner. 1972. "The Environmental Movement: Some Preliminary Observations and Predictions." In W. Burch, Jr., N. Cheek, Jr., and L. Taylor, eds., *Social Behavior, Natural Resources, and the Environment*. New York: Harper & Row.

Mueller, E. and G. Gurin. 1962. "Participation in Outdoor Recreation: Factors Affecting Demand Among American Adults." In *ORRRC Study Report #20*. Washington, DC: U.S. Government Printing Office.

Nash, R. 1982. *Wilderness and the American Mind, 3rd edition*. New Haven, CT: Yale University Press.

National Environmental Policy Act of 1969. 42 U.S.C.A. 4321 to 4370a.

National Toxics Campaign. 1989. *Toxic Times* (2), Spring 1989.

Noise Control Act of 1972. 42 U.S.C.A. 49010 to 4918.

Olson, M. 1965. *The Logic of Collective Action, Public Goods and the Theory of Groups*. Cambridge, MA: Harvard University Press.

Orum, A. M. 1974. "On Participation in Political Protest Movements." *Journal of Applied Behavioral Science* 10: 181–207.

Paehlke, T. 1989. *Environmentalism and the Future of Progressive Politics*. New Haven, CT: Yale University Press.

Pepper, D. 1986. *The Roots of Modern Environmentalism*. London: Croom Helm Ltd.

Pollack, S., J. Grozuczak, and P. Taylor. 1984. *Reagan, Toxics and Minorities*. Washington, DC: Urban Environment Conference, Inc.

Rawls, J. 1985. "Justice as Fairness: Political not Metaphysical." *Philosophy and Public Affairs* 14: 50–83.

Reed, A. L., Jr. 1989. *The Jesse Jackson Phenomenon*. New Haven, CT: Yale University Press.

Resource Conservation and Recovery Act of 1976. 42 U.S.C.A., 6901–6987 Pub. L. 94–580.

Russell, D. 1989. "Environmental Racism, Minority Communities and their Battle against Toxics." *The Amicus Journal* 11: 22–32.

Russell, F. 1968. "The Vermont Prophet: George Perkins Marsh." *Horizon* 10: 3–5.

Salisbury, R. H. 1969. "An Exchange Theory of Interest Groups." *Midwest Journal of Political Science* 13: 1–32.

Sharp, E. B. 1980. "Citizen Perceptions of Channels of Urban Service Advocacy." *Public Opinion Quarterly* 44: 362–76.

Sills, D. L. 1975. "The Environmental Movement and its Critics." *Human Ecology* 3: 1–41.

Silver, K. 1984. "Minorities and Toxics." *Exposure* (January/February): 36-7.

Smith, D. H., J. Macaulay, and Associates. 1980. *Participation in Social and Political Activities.* San Francisco, CA: Jossey-Bass Publishers.

Stein, M. 1989. Personal Communication. National Toxics Campaign, Boston, MA, September 25, 1989.

Suro, R. 1989. "Grass Roots Groups Show Power Battling Pollution Close to Home." *New York Times*, July 2; Section A1.

Taylor, D. E. 1989. "Blacks and the Environment: Toward an Explanation of the Concern and Action Gap Between Blacks and Whites." *Environment and Behavior* 21: 175–205.

Taylor, R. A. 1984. "Do Environmentalists Care about the Poor?" *U.S. News and World Report* 96: 51-2.

Tilly, C. 1978. *From Mobilization to Revolution.* Reading, PA: Addison-Wesley.

Timber Culture Acts. Ch. 277, 17 Stat. 605 (1873) ch. 55. 18 Stat. 21 (1874).

Toxic Substances Control Act of 1976. 15 U.S.C.A. 2601 to 2654.

Truman, D. B. 1971. *The Governmental Process, 2nd edition.* New York: Knopf.

United States General Accounting Office. 1983. *Siting of Hazardous Waste Landfills and Their Correlation with Racial and Economic Status of Surrounding Communities.* Washington, DC: U.S. Government Printing Office.

Urban Environment Conference, Inc. 1980. *Environmental Cancer, Causes, Victims and Solutions.* Washington, DC: Urban Environment Conference, Inc.

_____. 1985. *Taking Back Our Health, An Institute on Surviving the Toxics Threat to Minority Communities.* Washington, DC: Urban Environment Conference, Inc.

Van Ardsol, M. D., Jr., G. Sabagh, and F. Alexander. 1965. "Reality and the Perception of Environmental Hazards." *Journal of Health and Human Behavior* 5: 144–53.

Van Liere, K. D. and R. E. Dunlap. 1980. "The Social Bases of Environmental Concern: A Review of Hypotheses, Explanations and Empirical Evidence." *Public Opinion Quarterly* 44: 181–97.

Verba, S. and N. Nie. 1972. *Participation in America: Political Democracy and Social Equity.* New York: Harper & Row.

Walsh, H. J. and R. H. Warland. 1983. "Social Movement Involvement in the Wake of a Nuclear Accident: Activists and Free Riders in the TMI Area." *American Sociological Review* 48: 764-80.

Whitney, L. 1934. *Primitivism and the Idea of Progress in English Popular Literature of the Eighteenth Century.* Baltimore, MD: Johns Hopkins Press.

Wilderness Act of 1964. 16 U.S.C., 1131-1136.

Wilson, J. Q. 1973. *Political Organizations*. New York: Basic Books.
Zwerdling, D. 1973. "Poverty and Pollution." *The Progressive* 37: 25–9.

Chapter 4:
The Environmental Voting Record of the Congressional Black Caucus
by Henry Vance Davis

Bailes, J. C. 1985. *Environmental History: Critical Issues in Comparative Perspective*. Lanham, MD: University Press of America.
Blackwelder, B. 1987–88. "Message from the Chairman." *The National Environmental Scorecard*. Washington, DC: League of Conservation Voters.
Carson, R. 1962. *Silent Spring*. Boston, MA: Houghton Mifflin.
Casten, L. C. 1988. "A Town Is Being Poisoned." *The Nation* (March 19): 370–72.
Castleman, B. I. 1986. *Asbestos: Medical and Legal Aspects, 2nd ed.* Clifton, NJ: Law and Business; [s.i.]: Harcourt Brace Jovanovich.
Cooley, R. A. and G. Wandesforde, eds. 1970. *Congress and the Environment*. Seattle, WA: University of Washington Press.
Editorial. 1988. "Toxic Terrorism Invades Third World Nations." *Black Enterprise* (November): 31.
Grieves, R. T. 1988. "Poverty as Pollution." *Forbes* 14 (November): 14-7.
Marsh, G. P. 1864. *Man and Nature*. New York: Charles Scribner and Company.
Matlock J., M.D. 1986. Personal Communication. Former aide to Reps. John Conyers (D-MI) and Harold Ford (D-TN), Washington, DC.
McConnell, G. 1970. "Prologue: Environment and the Quality of Political Life." In R. A. Cooley and G. Wandesforde, eds., *Congress and the Environment*. Seattle, WA: University of Washington Press.
McEntee, G. W. 1989. "President's Column." *Public Employee* 9(August): 1.
Nash, R. 1989. *The Rights of Nature: A History of Environmental Ethics*. Madison, WI: University of Wisconsin Press.
Nicholson, M. 1987. *The New Environmental Age*. New York: Cambridge University Press.
Osborn, F. 1953. *The Limits of the Earth*. Boston, MA: Little, Brown.
Petulla, J. M. 1977. *American Environmental History: The Exploitation and Conservation of Natural Resources*. San Francisco, CA: Boyd & Fraser Pub. Co.
_____. 1980. *American Environmentalism: Values, Tactics, Priorities, 1st ed.* College Station, TX: Texas A&M University Press.
Robbins, W. G. 1982. *Lumberjacks and Legislators: Political Economy of the United States Lumber Industry, 1890-1941*. College Station, TX: Texas A&M University Press.
Schrepfer, S. R. 1983. *Fight to Save the Red Woods: A History of Environmental Reform*. Madison, WI: University of Wisconsin Press.

Schuyler, D. 1986. *The New Urban Landscape: The Redefinition of City Form in Nineteenth Century America*. Baltimore, MD: Johns Hopkins University Press.

Sears, P. B. 1935. *Deserts on the March*. Norman, OK: University of Oklahoma Press.

Short, C. B. 1989. *Ronald Reagan and the Public Lands: America's Conservation Debate, 1979-1984, 1st ed*. College Station, TX: Texas A&M University Press.

Udall, S. L. 1988. *The Quiet Crisis and the Next Generation, 1st ed*. Salt Lake City, UT: Peregrine Smith Books.

Vogt, W. 1948. *Road to Survival*. New York: W. Sloane Associates.

Chapter 5:
Toward a Model of "Environmental Discrimination"
by Michel Gelobter

Albrecht, S. 1972. "Environmental Social Movements and Countermovements: An Overview and an Illustration." *Journal of Voluntary Social Action* 1: 2–11.

Anderson, J. E. 1986. "U.S. Population Distribution and the Location of Hazardous Waste Sites." Paper presented at the Population Association of America Annual Meetings, April 1986.

Asch, P. and J. J. Seneca. 1978. "Some Evidence on the Distribution of Air Quality." *Land Economics* 54: 278–97.

Baumol, W. J. 1974. "Environmental Protection and Income Distribution." In H. H. Hochman and G. E. Peterson, eds., *Redistribution Through Public Choice*. New York/London: Columbia.

Baumol, W. J. and W. E. Oates. 1975. *The Theory of Environmental Policy: Externalities, Public Outlays, and the Quality of Life*. Englewood Cliffs, NJ: Prentice-Hall, Inc.

Berry, B. J. 1977. *The Social Burdens of Environmental Pollution*. Cambridge, MA: Ballinger Publishing Co.

Bish, R. L. 1971. *The Public Economy of Metropolitan Areas*. Chicago, IL: Markham.

Bittner, E. 1965. "The Concept of Organisation." *Social Research* 32: 239–55.

Block, F. 1977. "The Ruling Class Does Not Rule." *Socialist Revolution* 7: 6–28.

Bullard, R. D. 1983. "Solid Waste Sites and the Black Houston Community." *Sociological Inquiry* 53: 273–88.

Bullard, R. D. and B. H. Wright. 1985. "Endangered Environs: Dumping Grounds in a Sunbelt City." *Urban Resources* 2: 5–10.

Buttel, F. H. 1985. "Environmental Quality and the State: Some Political Sociological Observations on Environmental Regulation." *Research in Political Sociology* 1: 167–88.

Buttel, F. H. and W. L. Flinn. 1978. "Social Class and Mass Environmental Beliefs: A Reconsideration." *Environment and Behavior* 10: 443-50.

Clark, G. L. and M. Dear. 1984. *State Apparatus: Structures and Language of Legitimacy*. Boston, MA: Allen and Unwin.

Crenson, M. 1971. *The Unpolitics of Pollution: A Study of Non-decisionmaking in the Cities*. Baltimore, MD: Johns Hopkins University Press.

Farley, R. 1984. *Blacks and Whites: Narrowing the Gap?* Cambridge, MA: Harvard University Press.

Feagin, J. R. 1977. "Indirect Institutionalized Racism." *American Politics Quarterly* 5: 177-200.

Feagin, J. R. and D. L. Eckberg. 1980. "Discrimination: Motivation, Action, Effects, and Context." *Annual Review of Sociology* 6: 1-20.

Feagin, J. R. and C. B. Feagin. 1986. *Discrimination American Style: Institutional Racism and Sexism, 2nd augmented edition*. Malabar, FL: R.E. Krieger Pub. Co.

Freeman, A.M. 1972. "The Distribution of Environmental Quality." In A. V. Kneese and R. M. Bower, eds., *Environmental Quality Analysis*. Baltimore, MD: Resources For the Future.

_____. 1977. "The Incidence of the Costs of Controlling Automotive Air Pollution." In F. T. Juster, ed., *The Distribution of Economic Well-Being*. Cambridge, MA: Ballinger Publishing Co.

Gelobter, M. 1986. *The Distribution of Outdoor Air Pollution by Income and Race: 1970-1986*. Master's Thesis, Energy and Resource Group. Berkeley, CA: University of California.

Gianessi, L.P. and H. M. Peskin. 1980. "The Distribution of Federal Water Pollution Control Policy." *Land Economics* 56: 85-102.

Gianessi, L. P., H. M. Peskin, and E. Wolff. 1977. "The Distributional Implications of National Air Pollution Damage Estimates." In F. T. Juster, ed., *The Distribution of Economic Well-Being*. Cambridge, MA: Ballinger Publishing Co.

_____. 1979. "The Distributional Effects of Uniform Air Pollution Policy in the U.S." *Quarterly Journal of Economics* (May): 281-301.

Handy, F. 1977. "Income and Air Quality in Hamilton, Ontario." *Alternatives* 6(3): 18-24.

Hare, N. 1970. "Black Ecology." *Black Scholar* 1: 2-8.

Harrison, D. and D. L. Rubinfeld. 1977. *The Distribution of Benefits from Improvements in Urban Air Quality. Discussion Paper D77-15*. Cambridge, MA: Department of City and Regional Planning, Harvard University.

_____. 1978. "The Distribution of Benefits from Improvements in Urban Air Quality." *Journal of Environmental Economics and Management* 5: 313-32.

Hawkins, K. O. 1984. *Environment and Enforcement: Regulation and the Social Definition of Pollution*. Oxford, UK: Clarendon Press.

Henderson, J. and V. Karn. 1987. *Race, Class and State Housing: Inequality and the Allocation of Public Housing in Britain*. Brookfield, VT: Gower Publishing Co.

Knoepfel, P. 1986. "Distributional Issues in Regulatory Policy Implementation—The Case of Air Quality Control Policies." In A. Schnaiberg, K. Zimmerman and N. Watts, eds., *Distributional Conflicts in Environmental-Resource Policy*. New York: St. Martin's Press.

Kruvant, W. J. 1976. "People, Energy, and Pollution." In D. K. Newman and D. Day, eds., *The American Energy Consumer*. Cambridge, MA: Ballinger.

Logan, J. R. and H. L. Molotch. 1987. *Urban Fortunes: The Political Economy of Place*. Berkeley, CA: University of California Press.

Meidinger, E. 1986. "The Politics of 'Market Mechanisms' in US Air Pollution Regulation: Social Structure and Regulatory Culture." In A. Schnaiberg, K. Zimmerman and N. Watts, eds., *Distributional Conflicts in Environmental-Resource Policy*. New York: St. Martin's Press.

Morrison, D. E. 1973. "The Environmental Movement: Conflict Dynamics." *Journal of Voluntary Social Action* 2: 74–85.

_____. 1986. "How and Why Environmental Consciousness Has Trickled Down." In A. Schnaiberg, K. Zimmerman and N. Watts, eds., *Distributional Conflicts in Environmental-Resource Policy*. New York: St. Martin's Press.

Morrison, D. E. and R. Dunlap. 1980. "Environmentalism, Equity, and Elitism." Paper presented at the Annual Meeting of the American Sociological Association, New York, August 1980.

Newton, K. 1975. "American Urban Politics: Social Class, Political Structure, and Public Goods." *Urban Affairs Quarterly* 11: 241–64.

Noyelle, T. J. and T. Stanback, Jr. 1983. *The Economic Transformation of American Cities*. Totowa, NJ: Rowman and Allanheld.

Pellizzari, E. D. et al. 1984. *Total Exposure Assessment Methodology: Team Study. First Season Interim Report*. Washington, DC: U.S. Environmental Protection Agency.

Rex, J. 1986. *Race and Ethnicity*. Philadelphia, PA: Open University Press.

Skocpol, T. 1981. "Political Response to Capitalist Crisis: Neo-Marxist Theories of the State and the Case of the New Deal." *Politics and Society* 10: 155–201.

Speizer, F. E. 1990. "Asthma and Persistent Weaze in Harvard's Six Cities Study." *Chest* 98(5): Suppl. 191S–195S.

Tiebout, C. 1956. "A Pure Theory of Local Expenditures." *Journal of Political Economy* 64: 416–24.

United Church of Christ, Commission for Racial Justice. 1987. *Toxic Wastes and Race in the United States: A National Report on the Racial and Socio-Economic Characteristics of Communities with Hazardous Waste Sites*. New York: United Church of Christ, Commission for Racial Justice.

U.S. General Accounting Office. 1983. *Siting of Hazardous Waste Landfills and Their Correlation with Racial and Economic Status of Surrounding Communities.* Washington, DC: U.S. General Accounting Office.

Van Liere, K. D. and R. E. Dunlap. 1980. "The Social Bases of Environmental Concern: A Review of Hypotheses, Explanations, and Empirical Evidence." *Public Opinion Quarterly* 44: 181–97.

Williams, J. 1985. "Redefining Institutional Racism." *Ethnic and Racial Studies* 8: 323-48.

Zimmerman, K. 1984. "Die Inzidenz der Umweltpolitik in theoretischer und empirischer Sicht (The Incidence of Environmental Policy: Theoretical Aspects and Empirical Evidence)." *Jahrbücher für Nationalökonomie und Staatlicher Politik* 199: 502–21.

_____. 1986. "Distributional Considerations and the Environmental Policy Process." In A. Schnaiberg, K. Zimmerman and N. Watts, eds., *Distributional Conflicts in Environmental-Resource Policy.* New York: St. Martin's Press.

Zupan, J. M. 1973. *The Distribution of Air Quality in the New York Region.* Baltimore, MD: Resources For the Future/Johns Hopkins Press.

Chapter 6:
Environmental Blackmail in Minority Communities
by Robert Bullard

Babcock, R. 1982. "Houston: Unzoned, Unfettered, and Mostly Unrepentant." *Planning* 48: 21–3.

Bloom, J. 1987. *Class, Race and the Civil Rights Movement.* Bloomington, IN: Indiana University Press.

Bluestone, B. and B. Harrison. 1982. *The Deindustrialization of America.* New York: Basic Books.

Brown, M. H. 1987. *The Toxic Cloud: The Poisoning of America's Air.* New York: Harper and Row.

Bullard, R. D. 1983. "Solid Waste Sites and the Black Houston Community." *Sociological Inquiry* 53: 273–88.

_____. 1984. "Endangered Environs: The Price of Unplanned Growth in Boomtown Houston." *California Sociologist* 7: 84–102.

Bullard, R. D. and B. H. Wright. 1986. "The Politics of Pollution: Implications for the Black Community." *Phylon* 47: 71–8.

_____. 1987a. "Blacks and the Environment." *Humboldt Journal of Social Relations* 14: 165–84.

_____. 1987b. "Environmentalism and the Politics of Equity: Emergent Trends in the Black Community." *Mid-American Review of Sociology* 12: 21–37.

Commission for Racial Justice. 1987. *Toxic Wastes and Race: A National Report on the Racial and Socioeconomic Characteristics of Communities with Hazardous Wastes Sites.* New York: United Church of Christ.

Dunlap, R. E. 1987. "Public Opinion on the Environment in the Reagan Era: Polls, Pollution, and Politics Revisited." *Environment* 29: 6–11, 31–7.

Edelstein, M. R. 1987. *Contaminated Communities: The Social and Psychological Impacts of Residential Toxic Exposure.* Boulder, CO: Westview Press.

Epstein, S. S., L. O. Brown, and C. Pope. 1982. *Hazardous Waste in America.* San Francisco, CA: Sierra Club Books.

Fisher, R. 1984. *Let the People Decide: Organizing in America.* Boston, MA: Twayne Publishers.

Franklin, B. A. 1986. "In the Shadow of the Valley." *Sierra* 71: 38–43.

Gale, R. P. 1983. "The Environmental Movement and the Left: Antagonists or Allies." *Sociological Inquiry* 53: 179–99.

Geiser, K. and G. Waneck. 1983. "PCB and Warren County." *Science for the People* 15: 13–7.

Goldfield, D. R. 1987. *Promised Land: The South Since 1945.* Arlington Heights, VA: Harlan Davidson.

Gottlieb, R. and H. Ingram. 1988. "The New Environmentalists." *The Progressive* 52: 14–5.

Hamilton, L. 1985. "Concern about Toxic Waste: Three Demographic Predictors." *Sociological Perspectives* 28: 463–86.

Hays, S. P. 1987. *Beauty, Health, and Permanence: Environmental Politics in the United States, 1955–1985.* Cambridge, UK: Cambridge University Press.

Human Environment Center. 1981. *Minority Education for Environmental and Natural Resources Professions: Higher Education.* Washington, DC: Human Environment Center.

Humphrey, C. R. and F. R. Buttel. 1982. *Environment, Energy and Society.* Belmont, CA: Wadsworth.

Jordon, V. 1980. "Sins of Omission." *Environmental Action* 11: 26–30.

Kazis, R. and R. Grossman. 1982. *Fear at Work: Job Blackmail, Labor, and the Environment.* New York: The Pilgrim Press.

Kruvant, W. J. 1975. "People, Energy and Pollution." In D. Newman and D. Day, eds., *The American Energy Consumer.* Cambridge, MA: Ballinger.

Kushner, J. A. 1980. *Apartheid in America: An Historical and Legal Analysis of Contemporary Racial Segregation in the United States.* Arlington, VA: Carrolton Press, Inc.

Levine, A. 1982. *Love Canal: Science, Politics, and People.* Lexington, KY: Lexington Books.

Logan, J. R. and H. Molotch. 1987. *Urban Futures: The Political Economy of Place.* Berkeley, CA: University of California Press.

McCaull, J. 1975. "Discriminatory Air Pollution: If Poor Don't Breathe." *Environment* 19: 26–32.

Miller, A. S. 1980. "Toward an Environment/Labor Coalition." *Environment* 22: 32–9.

Mitchell, R. C. 1979. "Silent Spring/Solid Majorities." *Public Opinion* 2: 16–20.

Mohai, P. 1985. "Public Concern and Elite Involvement in Environmental-Conservation Issues." *Social Science Quarterly* 66: 820–38.

Momeni, J. A. 1986. *Race, Ethnicity, and Minority Housing in the United States.* New York: Greenwood Press.

Morell, D. 1987. "Siting and the Politics of Equity." In R. W. Lake, ed., *Resolving Locational Conflict.* New Brunswick, NJ: Rutgers University Center for Urban Policy Research.

Morell, D. and C. Magorian. 1982. "Risk, Fear, and Local Opposition: 'Not in My Back Yard'." In D. Morell and C. Magorian, eds., *Siting Hazardous Waste Facilities: Local Opposition and the Myth of Preemption.* Cambridge, MA: Ballinger.

Morris, A. D. 1984. *The Origins of the Civil Rights Movement: Black Communities Organizing for Change.* New York: The Free Press.

Morrison, D. E. 1980. "The Soft Cutting Edge of Environmentalism: Why and How the Appropriate Technology Notion is Changing the Movement." *Natural Resources Journal* 20: 275–98.

_____. 1986. "How and Why Environmental Consciousness Has Trickled Down." In A. Schnaiberg, N. Watts, and K. Zimmermann, eds., *Distributional Conflict in Environmental Resource Policy.* New York: St. Martin's Press.

Morrison, D. E. and R. E. Dunlap. 1986. "Environmentalism and Elitism: A Conceptual and Empirical Analysis." *Environmental Management* 10: 581-9.

Neiman, M. and R. O. Loveridge. 1981. "Environmentalism and Local Growth Control: A Probe into the Class Bias Thesis." *Environment and Behavior* 13: 759–72.

O'Hare, M., L. Bacow and D. Sanderson. 1983. *Facility Siting and Public Opposition.* New York: Van Nostrand Reinhold.

Pollack, S. and J. Grozuczak. 1984. *Reagan, Toxics and Minorities.* Washington, DC: Urban Environment Conference, Inc.

Porterfield, A. and D. Weir. 1987. "The Export of Hazardous Waste." *The Nation* 245: 340–44.

Portney, K. E. 1985. "The Potential of the Theory of Compensation for Mitigation of Public Opposition to Hazardous Waste Siting: Some Evidence from Five Massachusetts Communities." *Policy Studies Journal* 14: 81–9.

Schnaiberg, A. 1980. *The Environment: From Surplus to Scarcity.* New York: Oxford University Press.

_____. 1983. "Redistributive Goals Versus Distributive Politics: Social Equity Limits in Environmentalism and Appropriate Technology Movements." *Sociological Inquiry* 53: 200–19.

Taylor, D. E. 1989. "Blacks and the Environment: Toward Explanation of the Concern and Action Gap between Blacks and Whites." *Environment and Behavior* 21: 175–205.

Taylor, R. A. 1984. "Do Environmentalists Care about the Poor." *U.S. News and World Report* 96: 51-2.

United States General Accounting Office. 1983. *Siting of Hazardous Waste Landfills and Their Correlation with Racial and Economic Status of Surrounding Communities.* Washington, DC: U.S. General Accounting Office.

Urban Environment Conference, Inc. 1985. *Taking Back Our Health, An Institute on Surviving the Toxics Threat to Minority Communities.* Washington, DC: Urban Environment Conference, Inc.

Vallette, J. 1989. *The International Trade in Wastes: A Greenpeace Inventory.* Washington, DC: Greenpeace.

Van Liere, K. D. and R. E. Dunlap. 1980. "The Social Bases of Environmental Concern: A Review of Hypotheses, Explanations, and Empirical Evidence." *Public Opinion Quarterly* 44: 181–97.

Chapter 8:
Minority Anglers and Toxic Fish Comsumption: Evidence from a State-Wide Survey of Michigan
by Patrick C. West, J. Mark Fly, Frances Larkin and Robert W. Marans

Foran, J. A., M. Cox, and D. Croxton. 1989. "Sport Fish Consumption Advisories and Projected Cancer Risks in the Great Lakes Basin." *American Journal of Public Health* 79: 322–25.

Hays, W. 1963. *Statistics for Psychologists.* New York: Holt, Reinhart and Winston.

Humphrey, H. 1976. *Evaluation of Changes of the Level of Polychlorinated Biphenyls (PCB's) in Human Tissue. Final Report on FDA Contract 223–73–2209.* Lansing, MI: Michigan Dept. of Public Health.

_____. 1983. *Evaluation of Humans Exposed to Waterborne Chemicals in the Great Lakes. Final Report to the EPA Cooperative Agreement CR–807192.* Lansing, MI: Michigan Dept. of Public Health.

Nie, N. H., C. H. Hull, J. G. Jenkins, K. Steinbrenner, and D. H. Bent. 1975. *Statistical Package for the Social Sciences, 2nd edition.* New York: McGraw-Hill.

Norusis, M.J. 1986. *SPSS/PC+ for the IBM PC/XT/AT.* Chicago, IL: SPSS, Inc.

Shorett, J.E. 1986. *Residential Energy Conservation: A Threshold Model.* Ph.D. Dissertation, School of Natural Resources. Ann Arbor, MI: University of Michigan.

West, P.C. 1989. "Urban Region Parks and Black Minorities: Sub-culture, Marginality, and Interracial Relations in Park Use in the Detroit Metropolitan Area." *Leisure Sciences* 11: 11–28.

West, P. C., J. M. Fly, R. Marans, and F. Larkin. 1989a. *Michigan Sport Anglers Fish Consumption Survey. A Report to the Michigan Toxic Substance Control Commission.* Ann Arbor: University of Michigan, School of Natural Resources, Natural Resource Sociology Research Lab. Technical Report #1.

_____. 1989b. *Michigan Sport Anglers Fish Consumption Survey, Supplement I, Non-Response Bias and Consumption Suppression Effect Adjustments.* Ann Arbor: University of Michigan, School of Natural Resources, Natural Resource Sociology Research Lab. Technical Report #2.

Chapter 9:
The Effects of Occupational Injury, Illness, and Disease on the Health Status of Black Americans: *A Review*
by Beverly Hendrix Wright

American Cancer Society. 1986. *Cancer Facts and Figures: 1986.* New York: American Cancer Society.

Ashford, N. A. 1976. *Crisis in the Workplace: Occupational Disease and Injury. Report to the Ford Foundation.* Cambridge, MA: MIT Press.

Blaire, A. 1979. "Causes of Death Among Laundry and Dry-Cleaning Workers." *American Journal of Public Health* 69: 509.

Blot, W. 1978. "Lung Cancer after Employment in Shipyards during World War II." *New England Journal of Medicine* 21.

Bullard, R. D. and B. H. Wright. 1985. "Endangered Environs: Dumping Grounds in a Sunbelt City." *Urban Resources* 2: 37–9.

_____. 1986. "The Politics of Pollution: Implications for the Black Community." *Phylon* 47: 71–8.

Bureau of Labor Statistics. 1989. *Occupational Injury and Illness Incidence by Industry, 1986 and 1987.* Washington, DC: U.S. Department of Labor.

Congressional Quarterly, Inc. 1981. *Environment and Health.* Washington, DC: Congressional Quarterly, Inc.

Creech, J. L. and M. N. Johnson. 1974. "Angiosarcoma of the Liver in Manufacture of Polyvinyl Chloride." *Journal of Occupational Medicine* 16: 150–51.

Davis, M. E. 1977. "Occupational Hazards and Black Workers." *Urban Health* (August): 16–8.

_____. 1981. "The Impact of Workplace Health and Safety on Black Workers: Assessment and Prognosis." *Labor Studies Journal* 4: 29–40.

Davis, M. E. and A. Rowland. 1983. "Problems Faced by Minority Workers." In B. S. Levy and D. H. Wegman, eds., *Occupational Health: Recognizing and Preventing Work Related Disease.* Boston, MA: Little Brown and Company.

Elling, R. 1986. *The Struggle for Workers' Health: A Study of Six Industrialized Countries.* New York: Baywood Publishing Co., Inc.

Epstein, S. S. 1978. *The Politics of Cancer.* San Francisco, CA: Sierra Club Books.

Epstein, S. S., L. O. Brown, and C. Pope. 1982. *Hazardous Waste in America.* San Francisco, CA: Sierra Club Books.

Eyer, J. 1975. "Hypertension as a Disease of Modern Society." *International Journal of Health Services* 5: 547.

Gafafer, W.M. 1970. *Health of Workers in Chromate-Producing Industry: A Study.* Washington, DC: U.S. Health Service.

Hall, E. 1979. *Inner City Health in America.* Washington, DC: Urban Environment Foundation.

Henschke, U.K., K. D. Leffal, and C. H. Mason. 1973. "Alarming Increases of the Cancer Mortality in the U.S. Black Population, 1950–1967." *Cancer* 31: 763–68.

Kazis, R. and R. Grossman. 1982. *Fear at Work: Job Blackmail, Labor and the Environment.* New York: Pilgrim Press.

Kotelchuck, D. 1978. "Occupational Injuries and Illness among Black Workers." *Health PAC Bulletin* 81–82: 33–4.

Kotin, P. 1977. "Address to the American Occupational Medicine Association." Denver, CO.

Lucy, W. 1985. "Keynote Speech." In *Taking Back Our Health, An Institute on Surviving the Toxics Threat to Minority Communities.* Washington, DC: Urban Environment Conference, Inc.

Mason, T. J. 1976. *Altas of Cancer Mortality among U.S. Nonwhites: 1950-1969.* Washington, DC: U.S. Government Printing Office.

McMichael, A. J. 1976. "Mortality Among Rubber Workers: Relationships to Specific Jobs." *Journal of Occupational Medicine* 18: 178–84.

Nelkins, D. and M. S. B. Bown. 1984. *Workers at Risk: Voices from the Workplace.* Chicago, IL: University of Chicago Press.

Robinson, J. 1984. "Racial Inequality and the Probability of Occupation-Related Injury or Illness." *Milbank Memorial Fund Quarterly-Health and Safety* 62: 567–90.

Rockett, H. and C. Redmond. 1976. "Long-Term Mortality Study of Steelworkers, X, Mortality Patterns Among Masons." *Journal of Occupational Medicine* 18: 541–45.

Urban Environment Conference, Inc. 1984. *Reagan, Toxics and Minorities: A Policy Report.* Washington, DC: Urban Environment Conference, Inc.

_____. 1985. *Taking Back Our Health, An Institute on Surviving the Toxics Threat to Minority Communities.* Washington, DC: Urban Environment Conference, Inc.

U.S. Council on Environmental Quality. 1980. *Environmental Quality: The Tenth Annual Report.* Washington, DC: U.S. Government Printing Office.

U.S. Department of Commerce, Bureau of the Census. 1983. *America's Black Population, 1970 to 1982: A Statistical View.* Washington, DC: U.S. Department of Commerce, Bureau of the Census.

U.S. Department of Health and Human Services. 1985. *Report of the Secretary's Task Force on Black and Minority Health.* Washington, DC: U.S. Government Printing Office

Weiss, J. 1976. *Psychological Factors in Stress and Disease.* San Francisco, CA: W. H. Freeman and Co.

Williams, L. 1969. "Long-Term Mortality of Steelworkers, I, Methodology." *Journal of Occupational Medicine* 11: 301.

_____. 1970. "Long-Term Mortality of Steelworkers, IV, Mortality by Work Area." *Journal of Occupational Medicine* 12: 157.

_____. 1971. "Long-Term Mortality of Steelworkers, V, Respiratory Cancer in Coke Plant Workers." *Journal of Occupational Medicine* 13: 55.

Williams, R. 1975. *Textbook of Black-Related Diseases.* New York: McGraw Hill Book Company.

Young, J. Jr., S. Devesa, and S. Cutler. 1975. "Incidence of Cancer in United States Blacks." *Cancer Research* 35: 3523-36.

Chapter 10:
Hazardous Waste Incineration and Minority Communities
by Harvey L. White

Begley, S., M. Hager and H. Hunt, III. 1989. "Is Breathing Hazardous to your Health." *Newsweek*, April 3.

Borysenko, J. 1987. *Minding the Body, Mending the Mind.* Reading, PA: Addison-Wesley.

Brunner, C.R. 1988. "On-Site Incineration: A Look at Items." *Waste Age* (May): 55-60.

Bullard, R.D. 1983. "Solid Waste Sites and the Black Houston Community." *Sociological Inquiry* 53: 273-88.

Bullard, R. D, and B. H. Wright. 1986. "The Politics of Pollution: Implications for the Black Community." *Phylon* 47: 71-8.

Commission for Racial Justice. 1987. *Toxic Waste and Race: A National Report on the Racial and Socioeconomic Characteristics of Communities with Hazardous Wastes Sites.* New York: United Church of Christ.

Craig, J. W. and J. L. Warren. 1988. "EPA's Latest Hazardous Waste Data." *Waste Age* (October): 75-84.

de Castro, B. R. 1989. "A Big Role for Rolling Incinerators." *Waste Age* (January): 98-104.

Edelstein, M. R. 1987. *Contaminated Communities: The Social and Psychological Impacts of Residential Toxic Exposure.* Boulder, CO: Westview Press.

Editorial. 1985. "Plant Fined by Judge Over Odor." *The Times-Picayune*, October 1.

_____. 1986. "Rollins Targeted Over Fumes That May Have Made Kids Ill." *The Times-Picayune*, February 12.

EPA Fact Sheet. 1989. Washington, DC: U.S. Government Printing Office.

Freedman, A. M. 1986. "Rollins Environmental Waste Plant Is Under Investigation in Louisiana." *The Wall Street Journal*, February 18.

Gould, J. M. 1986. *Quality of Life in American Neighborhoods: Levels of Affluence, Toxic Waste, and Cancer Mortality in Residential Zip Code Areas.* Boulder, CO: Westview Press.

Grisham, J. and W. Grisham. 1986. "Health Aspects of Hazardous Waste Disposal." *Environment* (April) 28: 38–45.

Haenszel, W., D. B. Loveland and M. G. Sirken. 1962. "Lung Cancer Mortality as Related to Residence and Smoking Histories I: White Males." *Journal of the National Cancer Institute* 28.

Hagstron, R. M., H. A. Sprague, and E. Landau. 1967. "The Nashville Air Pollution Study VII: Mortality From Cancer in Relation to Air Pollution." *Archives of Environmental Health* 15: 237-47.

Haurwitz, R. 1988. "Incineration Projects Fueling Debate Over Safety, Cost." *The Pittsburgh Press*, September 14.

ICF Inc. 1988. *1986–1987 Survey of Selected Firms in the Commercial Hazardous Waste Management Industry.* Washington, DC: ICF Inc.

Joseph, M. E. and H. White. 1986. *A Study of the Attitudes of the Alsen Community Toward the Effect of Rollins Environmental Services.* Baton Rouge, LA: School of Public Policy, Southern University.

Lave, L. B. and E. P. Seskin. 1977. "Air Pollution and Human Health." In R. Dorfman and N. S. Dorfman, eds., *Economics of the Environment.* New York: W. W. Norton.

Levine, A. 1983. "Psychosocial Impact of Toxic Waste Dumps." *Environmental Health Perspectives* 48: 13–24.

Messing, M. and F. Soloman. 1986. "Environmental Sociology: Perceptions of Nuclear War." *Environment* 28 (September): 44–5.

National Solid Wastes Management Association. 1988a. "Is NIMBYism Here To Stay?" *Waste Age* (March): 35–7.

_____. 1988b. "Editorial." *Waste Alternatives* 1: 4–9.

Ornstein, R. and D. Sobel. 1987. "The Healing Brain." *Psychology Today* (March): 42–52.

Peele, E. 1980. *The Socio-Economic Effects of a Nuclear Waste Storage Site on Rural Areas and Small Communities.* Hearing: U.S. Senate Committee on Agriculture, Nutrition, and Forestry; Subcommittee on Rural Development, August 26.

Pirages, S. 1989. "Incineration's Future: Muddy, But Strong." *Waste Age* (May): 46–54.

Robert, M. 1987. "Moody Immunity." *Psychology Today* (November): 4.

Rollins Environmental Service. 1986. *Summary Overview of PCBs and Their Destruction by Incineration.* Baton Rouge, LA: Rollins Environmental Service.

Shoaf, N. L. 1989. "When Stress Closes In On You". *The Plain Truth* 54: 3–6.

Snyder, D. 1985. "Friendship, Dreams Killed by Fumes." *The Times-Picayune*, September 11.

Stocks, P. and J. M. Campbell. 1955. "A Report on Air Pollution and Lung Cancer". *British Medical Journal* 2: 923.

Swartz, S. 1986. "Rollins Environmental in Fight Over Plant: Regulators Seek to Close Toxic-Waste Facility." *The Wall Street Journal,* March 6.

Tuma, G. 1989. "Accident at TMI Still Touches Lives of Those on the Scene." *The Pittsburgh Post-Gazette,* March 22.

U.S. Environmental Protection Agency. 1989. *Toxins in the Community: National and Local Perspectives.* Washington, DC: U.S. Government Printing Office.

Washington Analysis Corp./County Securities. 1988. *USA Environment Report.* Washington, DC: Washington Analysis Corp.

White, H.L. 1989. "Hazardous Waste Management: A Challenge for Social Scientists." Paper presented at the Annual Meeting of the National Conference of Black Political Scientists in Baton Rouge, LA, March 1989.

Winkelstein, W., Jr. and S. Kantor. 1969. "Respiratory Systems and Air Pollution in an Urban Population of North Eastern U.S." *Archives of Environmental Health* 18: 760-76.

Chapter 11:
Environmentalism and Civil Rights in Sumter County, Alabama
by Conner Bailey and Charles E. Faupel

Alabama Blackbelt Defense Committee. n.d. *The Accused Speak.* Gainesville, AL: Alabama Blackbelt Defense Committee.

Alabama Department of Economic and Community Affairs. 1984. *Alabama County Data Book 1984.* Montgomery, AL: ADECA.

_____. 1989. *Alabama County Data Book 1988.* Montgomery, AL: ADECA.

Bailey, C., C. E. Faupel, S. Holland, and A. Waren. 1989. *Public Opinions and Attitudes Regarding Hazardous Waste in Alabama: Results from Three 1988 Surveys.* Department of Agricultural Economics and Rural Sociology. Auburn, AL: Auburn University.

Bethell, T. N. 1982. *Sumter County Blues; The Ordeal of the Federation of Southern Cooperatives. Report to the National Committee in Support of Community Based Organizations.* Washington, DC: Center for Community Change.

Bittner, E., I. Holston, I., and D. T. King, Jr. 1988. "Prediction and Detection of High-Permeability Zones within the Alabama Coastal Plain Chalky Marls." *Bulletin of the Association of Engineering Geologists* XXV(4): 508–14.

Bittner, E., D. T. King, Jr. and I. Holston. 1988. "Fracturing in the Upper Cretaceous Selma Group Chalky Marls, Inner Coastal Plain of Alabama: Stratigraphic (Facies) Control of Joint Development and Regional Joint-Strike Orientations." *Transactions—Gulf Coast Association of Geological Societies* XXXVIII: 277–82.

Brown, K. W. and J. C. Thomas. 1987. "A Mechanism By Which Organic Liquids Increase the Hydraulic Conductivity of Compacted Clay Materials." *Soil Scientist Society Americus* 51: 1451–59.

Bullard, R. D. and B. H. Wright. 1987. "Blacks and the Environment." *Humboldt Journal of Social Relations* 14: 165–84.

Center for Demographic and Cultural Research. 1987. *Alabama Population Data Sheet.* Montgomery, AL: Auburn University at Montgomery.

Cerrell Associates, Inc. 1984. "Political Difficulties Facing Waste-to-Energy Conversion Plant Siting." *Report prepared for the California Waste Management Board. Technical Information Series, Chapter 3a.* Los Angeles, CA: Cerrell Associates, Inc.

Chemical Waste Management, Inc. 1989. *1988 Annual Report.* Oak Brook, IL: Chemical Waste Management, Inc.

Dorfman, J. H. 1989. "Chemical Waste's Red-Hot Rise This Year Sets Off Widespread Short-Selling Reaction." Heard on the Street (regular column). *Wall Street Journal,* C2, October 27, 1989.

Falk, W. W. and T. A. Lyson. 1988. *High Tech, Low Tech, No Tech: Recent Industrial and Occupational Change in the South.* Albany, NY: State University of New York Press.

Faupel, C. E., C. Bailey, and G. Griffin. 1990. "Not Necessarily the News: A Case Study of Local Media Coverage of Hazardous Wastes." Unpublished manuscript, Department of Agricultural Economics and Rural Sociology. Auburn, AL: Auburn University.

General Accounting Office. 1983. *Siting of Hazardous Waste Landfills and Their Correlation with the Racial and Socio-Economic Status of Surrounding Communities. RCED–83–168.* Washington, DC: U.S. General Accounting Office.

Lewis, P. 1990. "Is the Water Supply Really Safe?" *Montgomery Advertiser-Journal,* February 4: B–1.

Keasler, T. R. 1986. *An Analysis of the Economic Impact of Chemical Waste Management, Inc. and ENRAC, Inc. on the Regional Economy of West Alabama and East Mississippi.* Livingston, AL: Center for Business and Economic Services, Livingston University.

Russell, D. 1989. "Environmental Racism; Minority Communities and Their Battle Against Toxics." *Amicus Journal* (Spring): 22–32.

Sanders, H. 1986. "Defending Voting Rights in the Alabama Black Belt." Interview with Hank Sanders by Frances M. Beal, Associate Editor. *The Black Scholar* (June): 25–34.

United Church of Christ. 1987. *Toxic Wastes and Race in the United States: A National Report on the Racial and Socio-Economic Characteristics of Communities with Hazardous Waste Sites.* New York: Commission for Racial Justice, United Church of Christ.

U.S. Environmental Protection Agency. 1986. *Hazardous Waste Data Management System (HWDMS)*. Washington, DC: U.S. Environmental Protection Agency.

Chapter 12:
Uranium Production and Its Effects on
Navajo Communities Along the Rio Puerco in Western New Mexico
by Wm. Paul Robinson

Arizona Department of Health Services. 1985. *Water Quality Study: Puerco River, Arizona, 1985 (DRAFT REPORT)*. Phoenix, AZ: Ambient Water Quality Unit, Water Assessment Section, Office of Emergency Response and Environmental Analysis.

Begay, K. 1980. "Deposition in Benally v. UNC Resources, Inc." District Court for the District of New Mexico (Albuquerque). No. CIV 80-750-HB. February 22.

Begay, R. and C. Shuey. 1989. "Navajos Fight for Clean Water." In *The Workbook* Vol. XIV, No. 3. Albuquerque, NM: Southwest Research and Information Center.

Benally, K. J. 1989. Notes from Public Meeting: "Inter-Faith Hearing on Toxics in Minority Communities." Albuquerque, NM.

Centers for Disease Control. 1980. *Biological Assessment after Uranium Mill Tailings Spill, Church Rock, New Mexico*. Washington, DC: U.S. Public Health Service, CDC, Chronic Diseases Division, Bureau of Epidemiology. EPA–79–94–2.

Gallaher, B. 1983. "The Puerco River: Muddy Issues Raised by Mine Water Dominated Ephemeral Stream." In *Water Quality in New Mexico—Proceedings of the 28th Annual New Mexico Water Conference. WRRI Report No.169*. Las Cruces, NM: New Mexico Water Resource Research Institute, New Mexico State University.

Hilpert, L. 1969. "Uranium Resources of Northwestern New Mexico." *U.S. Geological Survey Professional Paper 603*. Washington, DC: U.S. Government Printing Office.

Shuey, C. 1986. "The Puerco River—Where Did The Water Go?" In *The Workbook*, Vol. XI, No.1. Albuquerque, NM: Southwest Research and Information Center.

Shuey, C. and R. Morgan. 1987. *Summary of Surface Water and Ground Water Quality Investigations Conducted by Southwest Research and Information Center in the Puerco River Valley, New Mexico and Arizona, 1986–1987*. Albuquerque, NM: Southwest Research and Information Center.

Chapter 13:
Environmental Racism: Reviewing the Evidence
by Paul Mohai and Bunyan Bryant

Asch, P., and J. J. Seneca. 1978. "Some Evidence on the Distribution of Air Quality." *Land Economics* 54(3): 278-97.

Berry, B. J., L. S. Caris, D. Gaskill, C. P. Kaplan, J. Piccinini, N. Planert, J. H. Rendall III, and A. de Ste. Phalle. 1977. *The Social Burdens of Environmental Pollution: A Comparative Metropolitan Data Source.* Cambridge, MA: Ballinger Publishing Co.

Bullard, R. D. 1983. "Solid Waste Sites and the Houston Black Community." *Sociological Inquiry* 53(Spring): 273-88.

_____. 1990. *Dumping in Dixie: Race, Class, and Environmental Quality.* Boulder, CO: Westview Press.

Bullard, R. D., and B. H. Wright. 1987. "Environmentalism and the Politics of Equity: Emergent Trends in the Black Community." *Mid-American Review of Sociology* 12: 21-38.

Burch, W. R. 1976. "The Peregrine Falcon and the Urban Poor: Some Sociological Interrelations." In P. Richerson and J. McEvoy, eds. *Human Ecology, An Environmental Approach.* Belmont, CA: Duxbury Press.

Council on Environmental Quality. 1971. *The Second Annual Report of the Council on Environmental Quality.* Washington, DC: U. S. Government Printing Office.

Davies, J. C., and B. S. Davies. 1975. *The Politics of Pollution, 2nd Edition.* Indianapolis, IN: Pegasus.

Denton, N. A. and D. S. Massey. 1988. "Residential Segregation of Blacks, Hispanics, and Asians by Socioeconomic Status and Generation." *Social Science Quarterly* 69(4): 797-817.

Feagin, J. R., and C. B. Feagin. 1978. *Discrimination American Style: Institutional Racism and Sexism, 2nd Edition.* Malabar, FL: Krieger Publishing Company.

Fessler, P. 1990. "A Quarter-Century of Activism Erected a Bulwark of Laws." *Congressional Quarterly Weekly Report* 48(3): 153-56.

Freeman, A. M. 1972. "The Distribution of Environmental Quality." In A. V. Kneese and B. T. Bower, eds., *Environmental Quality Analysis.* Baltimore, MD: Johns Hopkins University Press for Resources for the Future.

Gelobter, M. 1987. *The Distribution of Outdoor Air Pollution by Income and Race: 1970-1984.* Master's Thesis, Energy and Resource Group. Berkeley, CA: University of California.

_____. 1992. "Toward a Model of Environmental Discrimination." In B. Bryant and P. Mohai, eds., *Race and The Incidence of Environmental Hazards: A Time for Discourse.* Boulder, CO: Westview Press.

Gianessi, L., H. M. Peskin, and E. Wolff. 1979. "The Distributional Effects of Uniform Air Pollution Policy in the U.S." *Quarterly Journal of Economics* (May): 281-301.

Handy, F. 1977. "Income and Air Quality in Hamilton, Ontario." *Alternatives* 6(3): 18-24.

Harrison, D., Jr. 1975. *Who Pays for Clean Air: The Cost and Benefit Distribution of Automobile Emission Standards*. Cambridge, MA: Ballinger.

Kish, L. 1949. "A Procedure for Objective Respondent Selection within the Household." *American Statistical Association Journal* (September): 380-87.

Kruvant, W. J. 1975. "People, Energy, and Pollution." In D. K. Newman and D. Day, eds. *The American Energy Consumer*. Cambridge, MA: Ballinger.

Lee, C. 1992. "Toxic Waste and Race in the United States." In B. Bryant and P. Mohai, eds. *Race and The Incidence of Environmental Hazards: A Time for Discourse*. Boulder, CO: Westview Press.

Mohai, P. 1985. "Public Concern and Elite Involvement in Environmental-Conservation Issues." *Social Science Quarterly* 66(4): 820-38.

_____. 1990. "Black Environmentalism." *Social Science Quarterly* 71 (4): 744-65.

Mohai, P. and B. Bryant. 1989. "Race and the Incidence of Environmental Hazards: A Proposal for the 1990 Detroit Area Study." School of Natural Resources. Ann Arbor, MI: University of Michigan.

United Church of Christ. 1987. *Toxic Wastes and Race in the United States: A National Report on the Racial and Socio-Economic Characteristics of Communities with Hazardous Waste Sites*. New York: Commission for Racial Justice, United Church of Christ.

U. S. General Accounting Office. 1983. *Siting of Hazardous Waste Landfills and Their Correlation with Racial and Economic Status of Surrounding Communities*. Washington, DC: U. S. General Accounting Office.

U. S. Government Printing Office. 1968. *Report of the National Advisory Commission on Civil Disorders*. Washington, DC: U.S. Government Printing Office.

Weisskopf, M. 1992. "Minorities' Pollution Risk Is Debated." *The Washington Post*, January 16.

West, P. C., J. M. Fly, F. Larkin, and R. Marans. 1992. "Minority Anglers and Toxic Fish Consumption: Evidence from a State-Wide Survey of Michigan." In B. Bryant and P. Mohai, eds. *Race and The Incidence of Environmental Hazards: A Time for Discourse*. Boulder, CO: Westview Press.

Zupan, J. M. 1973. *The Distribution of Air Quality in the New York Region*. Baltimore, MD: Johns Hopkins University Press for Resources for the Future, Inc.

Chapter 14:
Pesticide Exposure of Farm Workers and the International Connection
by Ivette Perfecto

Alternative Policy Institute. 1986. *Toxics and Minority Communities.* Oakland, CA: Center for Third World Organizing.

Barnett, P. G. 1989. *Survey of Research on the Impacts of Pesticides on Agricultural Workers and the Rural Environment.* Working Group on Farmlabor and Rural Poverty, Working Paper #2. Davis, CA: California Institute for Rural Studies.

Barnett, R. J. and R. E. Müller. 1979. *Global Reach: The Power of the Multinational Corporations.* New York: Simon and Schuster.

Bates, J. A. R. 1981. "Pesticides—Constraints and Controls in Importing Countries." Paper presented at the International Seminar on Controls of Chemicals in Importing Countries, Dbronik, April 1981.

Becklund, L. and R. B. Taylor. 1980. "Toxic Residues Halt Tomatoes Bound for U.S." *Los Angeles Times,* March 16.

Carson, R. 1962. *Silent Spring.* Boston, MA: Houghton Mifflin Co.

Commission for Racial Justice. 1987. Toxic Wastes and Race in *the United States: A National Report on the Racial and Socio-Economic Characteristics of Communities Surrounding Hazardous Waste Sites.* New York: United Church of Christ.

Coye, M. J. 1985. "The Health Effects of Agricultural Production: 1. The Health of Agricultural Workers." *Journal of Public Health Policy* 6: 349–70.

DeBach, P. 1974. *Biological Control by Natural Enemies.* New York: Cambridge University Press.

De Janvry, A. 1981. *The Agrarian Question and Reformism in Latin America.* Baltimore, MD: Johns Hopkins University Press.

Dembo, D. 1989. "Bhopal: Settlement or Sellout?" *Global Pesticide Monitor* 1.

Dinham, B. 1989. "Where Paraquat Starts: ICI and the United Kingdom." *Journal of Pesticide Reform* 9: 22–3.

Dirty Dozen Campaigner. 1989. "Planned DBCP Plant Meets Resistance at Home and Abroad." *Dirty Dozen Campaigner,* May.

Eckholm, E. and J. Scherr. 1978. "Double Standards and the Pesticide Trade." *New Scientist* 77: 441–43.

ESCAP. 1983. *Development/Environment Trends in Asia and the Pacific; A Regional Overview.* Bangkok: ESCAP, Committee on Industry, Technology and Human Settlements.

Falcón. 1971. "Progreso del Control Integrado de Algodón en Nicaragua." *Revista Peruana de Entomología* 14: 376-78.

Food and Agriculture Organization, United Nations. 1979. *Trade Yearbook, 33.* Rome: FAO, UN.

Glotfelty, D. E., J. N. Seiber, and L. A. Liljedahl. 1987. "Pesticides in Fog." *Nature* 325: 602–05.

Goldenman, G. and S. R. Rengam. 1988. *Problem Pesticides, Pesticide Problems.* Penang, Malaysia: International Organization of Consumers Unions and Pesticide Action Network.

Goldsmith, M. F. 1989. "As Farmworkers Help Keep America Healthy, Illness May Be Their Harvest." *Journal of the American Medical Association* 261: 3207–13.

Gupta, Y. P. 1986. "Pesticide Misuse in India." *The Ecologist* 16: 36-9.

Hansen, M. 1988. *Escape from the Pesticide Treadmill: Alternatives to Pesticides in Developing Countries.* Penang, Malaysia: IOCU.

_____. 1989. "The World Bank and Pesticides: Guidelines and Realities." *Journal of Pesticide Reform* 9: 13–7.

Hilje, L., L. Castillo, and L. A. Thrupp. 1987. *El Uso de los Plaguicidas en Costa Rica.* Editorial. San José, Costa Rica: Universidad Estatal a Distancia.

Kahn, E. 1976. "Pesticide Related Illness in California Farmworkers." *Journal of Occupational Medicine* 18: 693–96.

Lappe, F. M. and J. Collins. 1977. *Food First: Beyond the Myth of Scarcity.* Boston, MA: Houghton Mifflin Co.

Litwin, Y. J., N. N. Hantzsche, and N. A. George. 1983. *Ground Water Contamination by Pesticides: A California Assessment.* Berkeley, CA: Submitted to California State Water Resources Control Board by Ramlit Associates. Publication 83-4 SP.

Luck, R. F., R. van den Bosch, and R. García. 1977. "Chemical Insect Control, a Troubled Management Strategy." *BioScience* 27: 606–11.

Maddy, K. T. 1986. *Estimated Safe Levels of Foliar Pesticide Residues to Allow Unprotected Workers Reentry into Treated Fields in California.* Sacramento, CA: California Department of Food and Agriculture, Workers Health and Safety Branch. HS–1280.

Malaret, L. 1985. *Safe Pest Control: An NGO Action Guide.* Nairobi: Environment Liaison Centre (International).

Marquardt, S. 1989. "Hazardous Pesticide Exports and the EPA." *Global Pesticide Monitor* 1.

Martín, P., R. Mines, and A. Diaz. 1985. "A Profile of California Farmworkers." *California Agriculture* 6: 16–8.

Martínez-Alier, J. 1989. "Ecological Economics and Eco-Socialism." *Capitalism, Nature, Socialism* 2: 109–22.

Monterey County Pesticide Coalition. 1984. *The Health Effects of Pesticides and Enforcement of Pesticide Safety Laws in Monterey County.* Monterey, CA: A report and recommendations to the Council of Monterey County.

Mosses, M. 1989. "Pesticide-Related Health Problems and Farmworkers." *A.A.O.H.N. Journal* 37: 115–30.

Norris, R. 1982. *Pills, Pesticides and Profits: International Trade in Toxic Substances.* With contributions by A. K. Ahmed, S. J. Sherr, and R. Richter. New York: North River Press Inc.

O'Connor, J. 1989. "Socialism and Ecology." *Capitalism ,Nature, Socialism* 2: 5–11.

Oil, Chemical and Atomic Workers International Union. 1974. *Union Carbide: A Study in Corporate Power and the Case for Union Power.* OCAWIU.

Owasa, E. K. and B. J. Jennings. 1982. "Science and Authority in International Agricultural Research." *Bulletin of Concerned Asian Scholars* 14: 12–5.

Pallemaerts, M. 1985. *Diplomacy and Double Standards: The Regulation of International Trade on Pesticides.* Master's Thesis, Harvard Law School. Cambridge, MA: Harvard University.

Pesticide Action Network. 1987. *Informe y Control Sobre la Implementación del Código Internacional de Conducta Sobre el Uso y Distribución de Pesticidas.* Nairobi: Centro de Enlace para el Medio Ambiente.

Pimentel, D., J. Krummel, D. Gallahan, J. Hough, A. Merrill, I. Schreiner, P. Vittum, F. Koziol, E. Baeck, O. Yen, and S. Fiance. 1978. "Benefits and Costs of Pesticide Use in U.S. Food Production." *BioScience* 28: 772, 778–84.

Pollack, S. and J. A. Grozuczak. 1984. *Reagan, Toxics and Minorities.* Washington, DC: Urban Environment Conference, Inc.

Repetto, R. 1985. *Paying the Price: Pesticide Subsidies in Developing Countries.* Washington, DC: World Resources Institute.

Swezey, S., R. Daxl, and D. Murray. 1986. "Nicaragua's Revolution in Pesticide Policy." *Environment* 28: 6–9.

Taylor, R. B. 1979. "DBCP Still Used Despite Dangers." In *The Poisoning of America.* Reprints from the *Los Angeles Times*, June 28.

Thrupp, L. A. 1988. "Pesticides and Policies: Approaches to Pest Control Dilemmas in Nicaragua and Costa Rica." *Latin American Perspectives* 15: 37–70.

_____. 1989. "Direct Damage: DBCP Poisoning in Costa Rica." *Dirty Dozen Campaigner*, May.

Treakle, K. and J. Sacko. 1989. "Where There's a Will There's a Way: Indonesia, Rice, and Alternatives to 57 Pesticides." *Journal of Pesticide Reform* 9: 18–9.

U.S. Department of Agriculture. 1986. *USDA Statistics, 1986.* Washington, DC: U.S. Government Printing Office.

U.S. Environmental Protection Agency. 1977. *Pesticide Protection: A Training Manual for Health Personnel.* Washington, DC: EPA Office of Pesticide Programs.

_____. 1986. *Pesticides Fact Book.* Washington, DC: EPA Office of Public Affairs.

_____. 1988. *The Federal Insecticide, Fungicide, and Rodenticide Act as Amended.* Washington, DC: EPA Office of Pesticide Programs.

U. S. General Accounting Office. 1979. *Better Regulation of Pesticide Exports and Pesticide Residues in Imported Food Is Essential.* Washington, DC: U.S. Government Printing Office.

U.S. National Academy of Science. 1989. *Alternative Agriculture*. Washington, DC: National Research Council, National Academy of Science.

van den Bosch, R. 1978. *The Pesticide Conspiracy*. Garden City, NY: Doubleday.

Vandermeer, J. H. and I. Perfecto. 1989. *The Environment as a Category and Its Relationship to the Class/Race/Gender Debate*. Unpublished Manuscript. School of Natural Resources. Ann Arbor, MI: University of Michigan.

Wasilewski, A. 1987. "The Quiet Epidemic: Pesticide Poisoning in Asia." *IRDC Reports* 16: 1–13.

Wasserstrom, R. F. and R. Wiles. 1985. *Field Duty, U.S. Farmworkers and Pesticide Safety. Study 3*. Washington, DC: World Resources Institute, Center for Policy Research.

Weir, D. 1987. *The Bhopal Syndrome*. San Francisco, CA: Sierra Club Books (Center for Investigative Reporting).

Weir, D. and M. Shapiro. 1981. *The Circle of Poison*. San Francisco, CA: Institute for Food and Development Policy.

World Bank. 1985. *Guidelines for the Selection and Use of Pesticides in Bank Financed Projects and Their Procurement When Financed by the Bank*. OPN 11.01.

Worthy, W. 1985. "Methil Isocyanate: the Chemistry of a Hazard." *Chemical and Engineering News*, February 11

Wright, A. 1985. "Innocents Abroad: American Agricultural Research in Mexico." In W. Jackson, W. Berry and B. Colman, eds. *Meeting the Expectations of the Land*. San Francisco, CA: North Point Press.

———. 1986. "Rethinking the Circle of Poison; the Politics of Pesticide Poisoning among Mexican Farm Workers." *Latin American Perspectives* 13: 26–59.

Chapter 15:
The Dumping of Toxic Waste in African Countries:
A Case of Poverty and Racism
by Mutombo Mpanya

Agunbiade, B. 1989. "Rationalizing Jurisdiction for Industrial Pollution Control and Impact Management in Nigeria." *Journal of Environmental Management* 28: 11–24.

Centre Europe—Tiers Monde. 1989. Nos Dechets Toxiques L'Afrique a faim: Vila nos Poubelles. CETIM, Mars.

Editorial. 1989. "Uncle Sam's Toxic Folly." *US News and World Report*, March 27.

Greenpeace. 1989. "Greenpeace Analysis of the Basel Convention." *Greenpeace Waste Trade Update* 2(3): 3.

Handley, F. J. 1987. "Hazardous Waste Exports: A Leak in the System of International Legal Controls." *Environmental Law Reporter* 13: 4–89.

Maes, D. 1987. "Transboundary Waste Dumping: The United States and Mexico Take a Stand." *Natural Resources Journal* 27: 11–8.

Olokesusi, F. 1988. "An Overview of Pollution in Nigeria and the Impact of Legislated Standards on Its Abatement." *The Environmentalist* 8: 31–8.

United Church of Christ Commission for Racial Justice. 1987. *Toxic Wastes and Race in the United States: A National Report on the Racial and Socio-Economic Characteristics of Communities Surrounding Hazardous Waste Sites.* New York: United Church of Christ.

Uva, M. D. and J. Bloom. 1989. "Exporting Pollution: The International Waste Trade." *Environment* 31: 4-5.

Vallette, J. 1989. *The International Trade in Wastes: A Greenpeace Inventory, 4th Edition.* Washington, DC: Greenpeace.

Vir, A. K. 1988. "Africa Says No to Toxic Dumping Schemes." *Environmental Action* (Nov-Dec): 26–8.

Viswanathan, P. N. and V. Misra. 1989. "Occupational and Environmental Toxicological Problems of Developing Countries." *Journal of Environmental Management* 28: 381–86.

Chapter 16:
Summary
by Bunyan Bryant and Paul Mohai

Freudenberg, N. 1984. "Citizen Action for Environmental Health: Report on a Survey of Community Organizations." *American Public Health Journal* 74: 444-48.